JOURNALISM AND PRESS

Journalism and Press

(For PG Diploma & Degree Courses in Journalism & Mass Media)

Shahzad Ahmad

ANMOL PUBLICATIONS PVT. LTD.

NEW DELHI - 110 002 (INDIA)

ANMOL PUBLICATIONS PVT. LTD.
4374/4B, Ansari Road, Daryaganj
New Delhi - 110 002
Ph.: 23261597, 23278000
Visit us at: www.anmolpublications.com

Journalism and Press

First Published, 2005

ISBN 81-261-2344-3

PRINTED IN INDIA

Published by J.L. Kumar for Anmol Publications Pvt. Ltd., New Delhi - 110 002 and Printed at Mehra Offset Press, Delhi.

Contents

Preface

In Modern world, Journalism is one discipline, which attracts people like any thing, but, it is equally challenging and drastic in cases. Particularly, under the new world order and in current global scenario, its value has increased manifold.

Apart from being a glorious profession, Journalism, today is a full-fledged subject, mastery of which leads one to a successful career and an all powerful status in society.

As a discipline, Journalism requires proper training and a comprehensive course, if possible. Although, there is no defined qualification for appointment as a journalist, in any capacity, in any media organisation, yet it is always better to be properly qualified and well-equipped with all essential knowledge.

Of course, there are books on Journalism but not in a great number. And, if one goes selective, then only a few books would rest in hand, as there is still a dearth for exclusive and exhaustive books on several streams of Journalism.

This series of books on Journalism is an effort to fill the abovesaid vaccum only. Here are books on all subjects and topics, related to Journalism. The undersigned is confident enough that this humble endeavour would prove to be worthy on the basis of its merits and receive a warm acceptance by students of journalism, scholars and the working journalists, as well.

— **Editor**

1

Introduction

What changes are going to be made in the processes used for printing and how will the papermaker need to change his product to meet them? Unlike Alice, the papermaker does mind which way he goes because to make paper economically it must generally be produced on machines involving an immense capital outlay. Changes are likewise exceedingly costly. In planning for the future, then, some aestimate must be made of the customer's changing requirements.

Unfortunately it is not easy to find out what changes printing processes are likely to undergo so we must start with a number of generalisations. The capital investment in paper and print obviates the possibility of any sudden or drastic changes. From past developments we can reasonably extrapolate a few years into the future and at the same time see whether predicted requirements conveniently marry with possible demands from novel printing techniques now under consideration. We can safely anticipate that improved quality with increased economy will be required. Quality, however, relates to the individual consumer's viewpoint and is irrespective of how the results are achieved and may even differ from what is currently assumed to be desirable in paper.

Increased printing speeds are obviously going to be required, particularly as improved mechanical design of presses and better control of the main printing processes increase flexibility, reduce preparation time and justify these high speeds for shorter runs. Desire for greater speeds also applies to papermaking but increases the problems of machine dynamics and speed of response if variations in paper are also not to increase. For the printer, paper variations must actually be decreased if speeds are to be increased. These variations include not only those from point to point but also those throughout the full quantity being used for the particular job which could cause unnecessary breaks and loss of registration as well as variations in the general print quality.

Speed increases imply other changes. Continuous web-fed presses offer better prospects than sheet-fed machines except for special applications. The emphasis on paper requirements will consequently alter. Many complaints now arise from the use of multiple reel cutters and poor cutting-accuracy. Cutting subsequent to printing will eliminate this but will increase the demand for reel quality.

Paper strength, particularly for light-weight sheets, will become more important and here strength means not only average ultimate tensile strength but also consideration of full stress-strain performance under dynamic conditions, with due regard to statistical distribution of properties throughout the web. It has been found, for example, that if the average strength and stretch of newsprint are investigated they often show poor correlation with running performance even after due allowance has been made for obvious faults and reel damage. Normal running stresses imposed by a printing machine, however, are usually well below average paper strength. If the spread in paper properties is considered, and the probability of finding a weak spot corresponding to the actual running stress is estimated, then the reason for the failure of apparently strong papers is often found. In other words, if the average strength occurred in all areas no breaks would occur.

The most commonly observed variation in paper is its formation. This may influence printability and give print mottle due to variations in both sheet compressibility and roughness, leading to uneven ink transfer and to ink absorption differences. In lightweight sheets the influence on show-through and strike through should also be noted. Even if average opacity is the same for two sheets and strike-in effects can be ignored, the sheet having greater opacity variations on a few millimetres to millimetre scale will give greater apparent show-through. This follows from the eye's ability to detect small differences considerably better than absolute levels, and the brain's ability to recognise intruding matter when only a small fraction of the complete outline is presented to it.

If average opacity is the same for two papers then the one having the poorer formation is not making the most efficient use of available optical properties, nor for that matter of other fibre properties, since it is easy to show from Kabelka-Munk theory that use of the same scattering and absorption coefficients in a uniform sheet would result in greater average opacity. In practice the visual effects with poor formation are even more confused because of the variable ink transfer which also occurs with it.

Finally in considering sheet variations it is worth noting that variations, both small and large scale, in ink transfer are likely to become more important for newsprint and magazine work as the volume of colour printing increases. Despite current doubts about the economics and practicability of colour in newspapers it is difficult to see how use of colour will be avoided if the necessary advertising is to be retained, particularly when colour television is available in this country. Ink transfer variations with a black ink only give slight density variations, which are hardly spread. The problem is most acute for litho papers, where gradual accumulation of material on the blanket results in loss of quality and unduly frequent wash-ups, and for newsprint where halftone plate blockage and turner-bar build-up result in loss of quality and running efficiency.

There are several approaches to the problem. First, improved cleaning techniques can ensure that slitter or other dust does not find its way back on to the paper surface, general additives or surface sizing treatments may improve surface strength and water resistance or, in the case of coated papers, improved coating formulations can help. Basically, however, the problem can be more satisfactorily tackled by eliminating variations. Fluffing and dusting do not occur uniformly over the surface, and if they did the paper could not be run. Discrete fibre particles break away in a more or less random fashion and in many instances the average surface strength of papers is adequate for their purpose. Only when weak links in the chain have been eliminated and average strength is inadequate should additives, which must increase costs, be considered if further improvement in quality must be achieved.

This argument becomes even more cogent when litho developments are-considered as it would appear that high speed web-offset has a big future if cheaper papers can be utilised. Improved damping and elimination of separate damping and inking systems, coupled with lower tack inks and improved soft surface composite blankets, will enable the litho process to use cheaper papers and to make demands on the paper which are not significantly harder to achieve, at a noticed by the man in the street, but with colour printing the colour balance is likely to be lost, with disastrous effect on quality.

Apart from strength, many quality improvements required in reeled paper will result of minimising variations both on the small and on the large scale. More uniform substance allied with current developments in drying techniques should improve moisture content control and reel uniformity. On the other hand, problems of curl and dimensional stability in so far as they affect printing will tend to be less serious for reeled paper since electronic controls will cope with registration variations.

It is not surprising then, that in the future the papermaker will be increasingly concerned with the very difficult task of minimising sheet variations. Consequently there is considerable research activity into improved stock control and papermaking techniques which will allow optimum formation papers to be produced at the necessarily high speeds. The variation known as two-sidedness is also receiving its share of attention both in modifications to Fourdrinier machines and elimination of the normally asymmetric properties of machines.

The requirement of increased strength with speed applies not only to strength in the plane of the paper but also in the thickness direction if problems of fluffing, dusting and splitting are to be avoided. Unless lower track inks can be run, surface picking forces increase with given price, then demands made by other printing processes. For limited runs standard newsprint is already being printed by litho techniques. Standard newsprint, however, is already produced in some hundreds of forms (not counting the wide range of reel widths) all originally intended for letterpress presses and printers. Newsprints more suitable for litho printing are now being considered and improvement is sought in properties of major importance, such as uniformity of surface strength and elimination of dust, by methods that will not increase costs, but may, perhaps, sacrifice some of the fibres and prevents fluffing. Most sizing is fairly satisfactory although there is still a lot to be done to improve the technique. Fortunately research has this in its programme. The offset printer should find the bright, white finish most helpful: it brightens the highlights and gives more vigour and contrast to a process which can sometimes appear flat. Unlike letterpress where the film of offset does not seem to give rise to much dazzle in the type matter. As a rule a white paper can be used in offset with confidence.

All that has been said has been conditioned by my own experience, I have no doubt that others with different experience will have other ideas. I have attempted to indicate that the selection of paper is something to which thought should be given. It is important that the paper chosen should meet the double needs of sound manufacturing practice and pleasant, acceptable appearance.

The selection of paper is, of course, just part of the day's work. There are numerous wants and endless variety and I have only attempted to cover part of the ground. Virtually all jobbing printing is 'custom-made' and every job requires its manufacturing plan. As a rule in all manufacture the design that satisfies is the simple one and this is particularly true in printing. It is worth going for the simple specification; the finished work is likely to be 'unfussy' and good value for money.

The need for efficient conditioning is widely accepted, but so often even those who have installed efficient paper conditioning machinery merely pass the sheets through the machine and take no further precautions to maintain the paper in the ideal state throughout the sequence and register operations.

It is the aim of this chapter to pinpoint the fundamental factors that it is the purpose of paper conditioning to control, and to discuss the physical effect of these factors so that the requirements of the paper may be more readily understood, and the changes, particularly in physical dimensions, predicted and where necessary eliminated.

The term 'paper conditioning' appears to have such a wide range of interpretations that it would seem necessary to make the following definition as far as present considerations are concerned: Paper conditioning is the process of balancing the moisture content of paper into appropriate equilibrium with a specific atmosphere condition, usually being that prevailing in the pressroom, as defined by the relative humidity and temperature at the time when the printing and other register operations take place.

The two fundamental facts which have to be so firmly grasped by the printer that he is never in doubt as to his terms of reference are:

(1) That the physical size of a sheet of paper will expand and contract according to its moisture content. The higher the moisture content the larger will be the sheet, the smaller the moisture content the smaller the sheet.

(2) That in so far as a sheet of paper is out of balance with the relative humidity of its surroundings, it will take in or give out moisture until the balance is reached, regardless of temperature.

From these two basic facts, all other considerations are deduced. The first fact is so commonly recognised and accepted that it needs no further explanation. The second fact, however, is not so apparent, and the need for complete understanding cannot be stressed too highly since it involves consideration of the variable factor, namely atmospheric relative humidity, to which the sheets will be exposed.

Relative humidity (RH) may be considered as being the amount of water held in solution in the air at a particular temperature compared to the total amount of water that the air is capable of holding in solution at the temperature. The 100 per cent RH (saturation line) is plotted as being the maximum weight of water that one pound of dry air will hold in solution at varying temperatures without fog being formed. All the other lines are merely derived as being the appropriate percentages of this 100 per cent figure taken at the same temperatures. Thus, for example, at 60 degree Fahrenheit 100 per cent RH figure is .0 112, and the So per cent figure at the same temperature is exactly half of that, namely, .0056. Thus the RH may be considered as being the degree of wetness of air compared to the maximum wetness which can be held within Solution in the air at any given temperature. If the relative humidity remains fixed, the moisture content and hence sheet size will remain fixed.

As the moisture content of paper will vary according to the relative humidity of the air to which it is exposed, it also follows that at a certain moisture content it will be in balance and neither lose nor gain moisture from air of a given relative humidity, and will remain so until the relative humidity of the surrounding air is changed.

There can be little doubt that many readers will at this stage be thinking that the only conclusion to be drawn from the foregoing is that every pressroom should be completely air-conditioned and should only use properly conditioned paper. Whilst no one can deny that in theory complete air conditioning, together with efficient paper conditioning, is the only ideal answer, in practice we have proved that a thorough appreciation of the effect of changes in humidity can lead to an energetic battle to minimise these effects and emulate the advantages of air as it effects the paper. This battle can be waged and won at the merest fraction of the cost of complete air conditioning.

This may, perhaps, be better understood as being an acceptance of the fact that there are variations in relative humidity, understanding the effects of such variations and taking positive action to minimise them. This involves careful consideration of the circumstances under which the sheets of paper are free to interchange moisture with their surroundings, and also the degree of variation likely to be experienced in the average unconditioned pressroom.

Considering variations in pressroom humidity first of all, it should be realised that the outside conditions bear little or no relation to the conditions obtaining inside the factory. Most factories maintain a fairly even temperature, at least from day to day if not from summer to winter, and have a fairly uniform number of human bodies and other sources of moisture such as sinks, etc., so that the evaporation from these remains fairly constant. The evaporation rate, being determined by the temperature and relative humidity, serves to form its own humidity control and whilst this is nothing like as close a control as complete air conditioning will give, there is far less variation than is the case in the open air.

One of the greatest variations, however, can be from day to night, assume that the day time condition is 65 degree F and 60 per cent relative humidity (namely, point A on the graph) and that at night time the temperature drops to say 55 degree F, then as there will be in that time little addition or subtraction of the moisture from the air, the weight of water per pound of dry air will remain substantially constant, and the new condition will be point B on the chart. It will immediately be seen that the relative humidity has increased to nearly 90 per cent RH and remember that relative humidity is the factor that changes the moisture content of the sheets.

During this time the sheets will all be stacked since they are not being processed, and apart from the fact that the stack itself will decrease in temperature, only the edges of the sheets will experience changes in the relative humidity. Thus the effect of this rise in relative humidity overnight will be to induce Moisture into the sheet edges causing waviness. This will occur with equal effect on part printed work as on the unprinted stock.

To avoid the danger, it may seem sufficient to cover the stacks with moisture impervious material, such as polythene, thereby insulating the materials from the change in atmospheric condition. Unfortunately, this is not so since it will not prevent the stack of material from reducing its temperature, so that when worked in normal daytime temperature conditions, the same dangers will apply as become apparent when a new stack of paper is used straight from a cold storeroom without first having reached temperature equalisation.

It will therefore be appreciated that it is most desirable that the factory temperature should be maintained at a constant level day and night. However, even with temperature stabilisation there will still be a humidity variation between the day and the night, if only due to the absence at night time of the human bodies present during the day, and also the reduction of evaporation from non-usage of sinks, etc. The use of moisture impervious covers will eliminate the effect of this variation on the stacks of materials.

Paper storerooms are usually maintained at a much lower temperature than the pressrooms, and unless the paper remains in the stack in the pressroom protected by unbroken wrappers, or moisture impervious covers, until temperature equalisation has been achieved, wavy edged sheets will be formed.

A cold body-such as our stack of paper-standing in a warm room, will chill the belt of air immediately surrounding it. As the absolute weight of water per pound of air will not be altered, the belt of cold air will rise rapidly in relative humidity in exactly the same way as was shown when discussing the need for maintaining a constant factory temperature during the night-time as prevails in the day.

In precisely the same way, this belt of air intimately surrounding the stack of paper, will infuse its excess moisture into the sheet edges, and convection currents will ensure that fresh warm air is constantly being brought into contact with the stack, and chilled, so maintaining the supply of high humidity air around the stack. Thus, until temperature equalisation of the stack with the pressroom has been achieved, water will continually be induced into those parts of the sheet exposed i.e. mainly at the edge, causing them to stretch and become waved.

Learning from our wives washday experiences, sheets of paper will also be brought much more rapidly into equilibrium with their surroundings if the surrounding air is blown across the entire surfaces of each individual sheet.

The swift range of paper and board conditioning machinery, manufactured by the author's company, was fully described in the article published in July 1957. Let it be sufficient to say here that the largest standard machines made will fully condition up to 40 reams of paper, .003 inch thick, per hour, using a floor space measuring 31 feet X 8 feet 6 inches, and with a manpower of two.

The alternative to conditioning the paper in an efficient conditioning machine may appear to be to purchase it mill conditioned. However, with the best mill in the world the paper manufacturers cannot possibly supply paper to the printer in a condition that ideally suit his pressroom, and furthermore, our experience of mill conditioned paper has shown that whilst in a given consignment the average moisture content may be close to that specified, the variation from sheet to sheet and across individual sheet surfaces was such that trouble free printing would not have been obtained. If trouble is to be avoided, it is absolutely vital that each individual sheet of paper must be conditioned by the printer in his pressroom, or some other suitably equipped room having carefully controlled atmospheric conditions.

It has been the aim of this chapter to make printers more aware of the circumstances under which paper will change its physical dimensions during printing so that they will be able to apply this knowledge necessary for normal sized stacks of paper to reach equilibrium temperature with their surroundings for various temperature differences, and it is essential that the stacks remain in the pressroom, or at least in air at pressroom temperature, for this length of time before the wrappers are broken, or the moisture impervious covers are removed.

It will by now be fully appreciated that before printing commences it is essential that the paper has a moisture content that is in balance with the pressroom humidity whether or not this is controlled, and to achieve this, efficient paper conditioning is essential.

The most common form of paper conditioning, in which the sheets are hung either in fixed racks or on conveyors and left in the still air of the Pressroom for upwards of twenty-four hours, cannot achieve the desired effect unless the pressroom be fully air conditioned with respect to temperature and humidity throughout the twenty-four hours of a day. Anything short of this will result in the paper trying to adjust itself to the varying degrees of humidity, at least experienced between night and day, and no insulation of the sheets is possible while suspended.

It is obvious, therefore, that some means of accelerating this process is essential so that conditioning can be achieved in an hour or so, during which time there will be no change in the atmosphere humidity of the pressroom.

We all know that housewives, when drying their washing, achieve much faster results on a windy day than in still air, and although they probably don't realise it, all that they are doing is bringing their garments into moisture equilibrium in laying down practices to suit their own factory conditions. Each individual factory will have its own detailed characteristics to be taken into account, and it is for this reason that an appreciation of the basic principles and requirements of paper must be understood.

As a general guide, however, the following steps should be aimed at:

(1) Paper must be delivered to the printer efficiently wrapped, preferably in moisture impervious wrappers. In this respect bitumenised kraft, although by no means perfect, is in practice usually satisfactory.

(2) Care should be taken in unloading and storage to ensure the wrappers are kept entirely intact. Unpalletised stacks should not be more than 2 or 3 feet high to avoid risk of permanent distortions due to deformation of the paper fibre, a condition which cannot be corrected by paper conditioning.

(3) Before printing, the material to be printed should be brought into the pressroom or some other adjoining room at pressroom temperature and, still with the wrappers intact, allowed to stand there until the entire stack has reached the same temperature as the surroundings.

(4) When temperature equalisation has been achieved, the sheets should be removed from their wrappers and immediately fed into an efficient paper conditioning machine.

(5) Each stack of material, after conditioning, should be red by a moisture-impervious cover made from a material as polythene.

(6) This first printing operation should be commenced ask after conditioning as possible, and the work programmed to minimise the total time from paper conditioning to delivery of the finished products.

(7) In between all register process the stacks of material should be covered by moisture-impervious covers.

(8) The pressroom temperature should be maintained at a constant level throughout the day and night.

What is the object of the sample? Clearly it is one form of the communication of advertising, and as such it should be part of a marketing plan; to be good advertising it should give information. Does a blank sample not give as much information about the product as the bulk of printed samples in which everyone vies to produce a prettier picture? The gimmicks and the pin-lips rain out of the printing publications, all emphasising that the printed sample has developed to a point where, with one or two notable exceptions, the illustration and its choosing have become all important.

Sales managers and boards of directors too—every one of them either understands art or condescendingly makes a merit of not understanding it but 'knowing what he likes'! What advertising manager dares to express his views on the Balance Sheet, but what accountant would hesitate to say what he thinks should be the art for samples.

There are those in advertising, and a powerful lot they are, who preach that the product is not its own best advertisement. 'Do not', they say, 'sell the joint-sell the crackle and the smell!'

Do not sell the car but the beach at the end of the run (if you can get there!). The best advertisement for dehydrated soup is not necessarily a free sample if the reasons for buying are not there too. There may be ease of buying, of storage and use at a moment's notice-the little woman's triumph when the boss comes to dinner without any notice! Flavour, you may have discovered, is becoming the least important part of eating.

The soup sample without the information on why it should be bought and how to use it may be useless. This may be true, too, of the paper sample. The idea that there could exist any printer ignorant of the nature and behaviour of paper other than its performance on the machine is something that the paper trade has not yet fully comprehended. (It is only fair to pose the converse in the form of a polite enquiry: 'What does the paper trade know about printing?').

When you handle a sample of paper, can you pronounce an ink absorption?

What are its qualities in terms of stretch, shrink and curl? What is its capacity?

The question is in two parts: should there be samples? If so, what information should they give? My answer to the first part is 'Yes!' and as the most appropriate form of sampling is direct mail it seems equally appropriate to use the actual quality of paper that is being promoted

But I plead that now the time has come to stop the Christmas Card school of design. What do the bulk of these printings tell you, other than that the sample has been printed-well, or not so well-according to the standards of the sampler? How simple it is to produce a short, slow run of four-colour letterpress with an illustration that in itself is so attractive that it may become accepted for its own sake rather than as technical evidence. How much work of this sort will be produced by the printer, to whom the sample goes? If he is interested in long, fast runs of leaflets for plastic dustbins, he is more likely to be concerned with consistent performance from ream to ream and reliable freedom from fluffing and stretch.

Printing alone is not enough. The question is, 'What information do you want?' When you handle a sample of paper, can you pronounce on ink absorption or pick resistance? What are its qualities in terms of stretch, shrink and curl? What is its opacity rating? Are you concerned with pH value or chemical residues? Would it not help you to see samples of solids and tints related to their oxidation and evaporation? Will the paper varnish and fold?

I suggest that the time has come for printers to be positive about the information they want from samples and if, as an industry, they cannot be positive enough, papermakers should do this for them. It is not enough to know that a job was run on such-and-such a machine using someone-or-other's inks, the whole object of the co-operation probably starting from an original desire to cut down cost.

Considerable information has been published on 'What the printer ought to know about paper', but this is not the same as what the printer should be told. Printing has developed from a craft to a precision industry, but the least precise of the materials in use remains the most important paper! There is need for a much greater awareness, in a technical sense, of the end use of paper which, in this context, is for printing.

Unfortunately, there is such a conspicuous absence of co-ordination for this purpose throughout the paper trade, that it may need one far-sighted papermaker to make a pro-forma approach to the production of samples with full technical information. To do this he will present himself with two problems: the first, that of finding out what information should be given; the second, matching his products to this information. When someone does this successfully it may be found that the actual sample, printed or plain, is not as necessary as we have come to think. Adequate information could be dispensed in similar form to the excellent Patra folders: Buying Letterpress Papers and Boards and buying Lithographic Papers and Boards.

Is it fanciful to suppose that the collaboration of print and papermaking technologists could result in the first sight of the paper being on the machine? Imagine how it could work. Every machine enveloped within a standard, controlled temperature and humidity. The paper matured to this standard and delivered in containers that maintained the machine climate, having been ordered by a proforma specification, of what is demanded by the precise variation of the printing process.

Happily relieved of any responsibility for 'hard' selling, the sample could then be used for that part of advertising communication which most suited the sampler: PR pin-ups, for example, or as an opportunity for the chairman's relatives to exercise their artistic talents. It will still have to be paid for. This might lead some sales manager to think that he preferred salesmen to samples.

2

Salient Features

A printing unit is the part and parcel of print media and journalism. Normally most of the journal editors inherit a printer, unless the journal is a new one. Book editors looking for a publisher are influenced to some extent by the quality of printing and production of the publisher's other books; that is, by the typeface, quality of illustrations, layout-whether the pages looked cramped or spacious, easy or difficult to read-and strength and quality of the binding. Most publishers use several printers and can influence many of these variables according to an editor's requirements, though only within the limits of the printer's capabilities and the publisher's own financial constraints.

Finding or changing printers is not a step to take in a huffy. Any editor faced with this task should visit several printers and ask them to set some material to show the range and quality of their work. It is important to know what facilities the printer can offer (copy-marketing, proof-reading, binding in-house, distribution to subscribers, invoicing), proof-reading, binding in-house, distribution to subscribers, invoicing), what form quality control takes, and how large the printing team is. Other points to note are the error rate in proofs (ask to see some proofs) and whether the agreement includes penalty clauses for errors or for late delivery. Most publishers of any size will employ experts to deal with these matters but will expect editors to take an interest and become involved in the production processes.

Here, we deal first with the general question of design, mainly as it applies to journals, and then with the specification and style sheet that the editor and copy editor should agree with the printer, either directly or via the publisher. And since editors need at least a theoretical knowledge of the main procedures, ancient or modern, that go towards the making of books and journals, the rest of the chapter discusses typesetting, printing, artwork, proofing, paper and binding, with a final note on offprints and reprints.

The Format

New editors often feel they should change the design and format of the journals or book series they have taken on, and scientist-editors sometimes think they now more about the design of scientific publications than any professional boo k designer. As consumers they are sometimes right: but major changes in design raise complicated issues and the arguments for and against a new look should be carefully weighed. A distinctly obsolete appearance, for example may seem to be a disadvantage, yet it may turn out to be a selling-point for a journal because it emphasizes that the journal is long-established. The important issue is whether the format or design impedes legibility or comprehension. If necessary, the editor or publisher should call in a designer, whether free-lance or employed by the publisher or printer, and explain what problems need to be solved.

Cover Design

The cover design of a journals is one candidate for change. Here the designer must take into account both the essential and the desirable items for the cover. The editor should provide at the outset as much information as possible about what is wanted, so that the designer does not have to produce innumerable mock-ups of possible covers.

A change in a journal's page size is rarely popular with librarians and should never be made in the middle of a volume. An increased page size may, however, allow tables or figures to be printed where readers most want to see them—on or opposite the pages where they are discussed, If the increase in size entails a change from single to double-column layout, the editors should make sure that the new layout is appropriate for the journal: where there are many complex equations or large tables a single column is preferable.

Page Size : The designer and the printer can advise the editor which standard page size (economically available in the type of paper required) would best suit the needs of the journal. The printer should at the same time advise the editor whether a new mailing wrapper or envelope can be provided easily and economically.

In the text itself, the editor will want headings and abstracts to stand out boldly. Typefaces should be chosen to marry happily (and economically) with the type used in the text, and here a typographer's help is particularly valuable. In principle many typefaces are available but not every printer carries every fount. Some founts are more suitable than others for particular kinds of work, for example mathematics. The typographer can suggest which typefaces should be used, after making sure what the printer has to offer.

If type size is reduced, more words can be printed on a page, saving paper and mailing costs. The 10-point type still used in some scientific publications can with advantage be reduced to 9-point, but any further reduction in type size would be bad for readers' eyesight. (A 'point' as used by British and American printers is about 1/72 of an inch, or 0.3515 nun; a point in the Didot system, widely used in Europe, measures 0.376 nun.) The 10/12 setting (i.e. 10-point characters on a 12-point body, giving a 2-point space between the lines), formerly widely used, is now often replaced by 9/11 or 9/10. Subsidiary matter such as acknowledgements, footnotes, appendixes and references can be reduced to 8/10. To save space, some journals reduce the type size for references to 6/8; this is the lowest permissible limit, even for material that is not read continuously but only referred to. Computer typesetting can provide many gradations in point size, giving 9.2 on 10.5 and so on. This flexibility is useful if there are short or long pages.

In spite of the general need to save space, wide inner margins, i.e. those forming the 'gutter' of a double-page spread, should be specified so that the reader can make satisfactory photocopies from the bound book or journal volume. Publishers may resists this (because they wish to discourage photo-copying); so my designers (because they will say that the double-page spread falls apart visually); and so may printers (who will think it is untraditional). They should all be overruled: photo-copying of single items for individual users is legitimate and desirable for the progress of science, and this is what counts.

A well-designed book or journal has a unified appearance throughout, with all the chapters or articles styled in the same way, and with the cover, prelims and indexes fitting in with that style. If, for example, all chapter or article titles, legends, headings and sub-headings in the text are printed flush with the left-hand margin (which saves typing and typesetting time and is therefore more economical than having them all centred), the jacket or cover looks best if it matches this style. The tables and illustrations should then in theory also be set to the left instead of being centred, although to many eyes this looks peculiar. In this style, if there are more than three levels of subheading which should not often be necessary a variety of type sizes and typefaces will be called for if the reader is to understand the structure immediately. "The flush-left style then presents its own impediments to the achievements of a unified appearance. One solution is to centre all main headings as well as all tables and illustrates but otherwise keep to the flush-left style, making sure that third-order headings are clearly subordinated to second-order headings. The important principle is that aesthetic considerations, important though they are, must be secondary to the reader's rapid grasp of structure.

Layout is in the printer's domain, but some printers are over-fond of the notion that each page or double-page spread should look balanced, with (for example) two illustrations always placed at diagonally opposite corners of a page or spread. This idea should be forgotten: Illustrations must be printed as close to the relevant text as possible, and if the balanced look conflicts with this principle it will have to be abandoned it is not a work of art that is being created but a carrier for a piece of scientific information.

Manuscripts with a high ratio of illustrations to text present other, layout problems. Editors can help to minimize these problems by asking authors to supply clear and simple illustrations that can be reduced as far as is consistent with legibility; or pairs or triplets of illustrations can be combined; or photographs can be cropped so that only the strictly relevant parts are shown-at full magnification but taking up only as much room as is strictly necessary.

Copy and Style

The designer and the printer's typographer will be concerned not only with overall design but also with the detailed printing specification. This should be agreed between the editor, copy editor and publisher or printer at an early stage. A well-thought-out specification is a powerful time saver for the editorial office. It may take weeks or months to get it right but the effort is worth it. The editor (or publisher) should be guided, but not bullied, by the printer in discussions of the specification. The printer knows what is routine in the printing plant, what is easily arranged, and what will lead to difficulties and mistakes. On the other hand, if the publication has special requirements that the printer cannot meet, another printer will have to be found.

The specification will include some or all the following:

(a) size of page and size, quality and weight of paper;

(b) type of binding;

(c) approximate number of pages in the book or in each issue of a journal;

(d) type founts for all parts of the publication, including prelims, indexes, running heads, headings, references, legends, tables and footnotes (if any) for the text;

(e) type size and body for the different parts;

(f) type areas or imposition size; that is, the length of the lines and the number of lines on each page—or, put the other way round, the size of margins;

(g) style or arrangements of legends, table titles and columns headings;

(h) use of horizontal lines and their relative weights in tables, and use of vertical lines, if allowed (these should be used rarely, if at all: they are expensive to set);

(i) symbols for linking footnotes to tables (Superscript letters, Superscript numbers, or other symbols, such as ?)

(j) typeface, size and placement of acknowledgements

(k) style for reference lists;

(l) method of identifying mathematical symbols or Cyrillic or Greek letters in the margins of typescripts (either spelt out, e.g. 'Gk mu' or by means of a code referring to the type found, e.g. 'Gk no. 34');

(m) spacing above and below illustrations and on the title page of chapters and articles;

(n) placement of page numbers;

(o) typeface, size and number of indexes.

Once the specification has been agreed, specimen pages showing chapter openings, sub-headings and so on are usually prepared and shown to the editor. When the details have been approved, a style sheet can be prepared for printer's copy-maker, showing what has to be done in marking up typescripts. The editor and printer (or publisher) also discuss whether typescripts will be fully copy-edited, partially copy-edited, or perhaps no copy-edited at all. It is important for both the editorial office and the printer to know how much marking should be down, and by whom: there is, for example, no point in copy editors marking every Greek mu in a paper full of measurements in micrometers. With a well-prepared style sheet which lists the relevant points from the specification, copy marking becomes almost automatic; with modern typesetting methods it can even be partly computerized.

This brings us to the basic process of 'printing,' which in fact consists of several processes, the two main ones being composition (type-setting or key-boarding), and the actual printing (presswork, machining) during which recognizable patterns appear on the paper. For information about these two processes I have relied heavily on Jennett, Varley, Dessauer and Seybold. Plate-making, which takes place between the main two processes is not described here.

The Composition

Three are four main methods of composition:

(1) hot-metal or hot-lead composition on Linotype, Monotype or similar machines;

(2) handsetting, which is used as little as possible;

(3) typewriter (strike-on) composition, including IBM Composer composition; and

(4) filmsetting and photo-composition, usually computer-assisted.

Typewriter composition and photo-composition are also known as 'cold composition'. Editors who want to mark and arrange typescripts intelligently, with the smallest probability of causing misunderstanding and costly mistakes, should visit their printers and see the processes in action.

With Linotype composition whole list of type are cast from a reservoir of molten metal after the compositor has keyboarded the copy. Monotype casters produce single characters from a similar hot metal alloy. The keyboards on Linotype and Monotype composing machines look like large typewriter keyboards, except that on the Linotype machine the characters are arranged in a different order.

The Monotype compositor has seven alphabets, Plus numbers and extra characters, to choose from. For book work (including journals) the alphabets might be upper-and lower-case roman, italics and bold face, and small capitals. The monotype machine produces a punched paper tape which is used to drive a separate casting machine. Some Linotype machines are type-driven too, but they have a built-in caster.

Compositors using either Monotype or Linotype machines must judge, when they get near the end of a line, how many more characters can be fitted in, since books and journals are conventionally justified (aligned) on the right as well as on the left. The compositor may decide that word should be split at the end of a line, according to well-defined hyphenating rules, or that the spacing between words already on the line should be increased in order to extend the line to the full measure. On the Monotype machine a measuring device shows how much space is left and the compositor presses justifying keys which punch spacing instructions in the tape at the end of each line. Since the tape is fed into the casting machine backwards from the end of the last line of the piece of copy being set, the spacing instructions reach the machine first and spaces of the correct width are set in each line.

The Monotype casting machine holds an exchangeable Matrix case containing 255 characters in one type found and size. The punched tape instructs the casting machine to centre the required character in the matrix case over a mould, Molten metal is pumped into the mould, the character is stamped out and the resulting piece of rectangular type is quickly cooled and ejected. The character on the piece of type is reversed left-right so that it comes out the right way round when printed on the page. The size, or body, or the rectangular piece of metal in relation to the size of the character determines the width between lines of text (e.g. a 9-point letter on an 11-point body).

As the type comes out a Linotype machine or monotype caster, the metal slugs (Linotype) or separate pieces of type (Monotype) slide into long metal trays called galleys. When enough galleys are fully, the type is inked and proofs are pulled of checking by the printer's reader. Who marks obvious errors on these pages. Corrections are made almost immediately. With Monotype setting, in correct letters can be picked out with a pair of tweezers-, the correct letter is then substituted from a tray of ready-cast spares and the line re-justified. With Linotype machines, the whole slug has to be reset on the machine if a line contains a single mistake. With either Linotype or Monotype setting, a damaged or dirty matrix will produce a defective letter every time that matrix is used. This is why sections of proof are sometimes found in which almost every 't', for example, seems to be broken. The printer's proof-reader usually sees this and replaces the 'broken' letters.

The speed of the Monotype caster is limited to about 11000 characters an hour by the stop-start mechanism and the time the metal takes to cool. Another limitation is that a matrix case contains only one typeface in one size of type, so the matrix has to be replaced each time a different typeface or size is needed; alternatively, sections of the copy may be set separately on different machines. Linotype composition can be a little faster than Monotype and it was, for a long time, the machine used for setting newspapers. However, its slugs of type make it less flexible for book or journal work than Monotype and it has not been used so often for these purposes in Europe as it has in the USA.

Both Monotype and Linotype are labour-intensive-and they are both rapidly being superseded by cold composition. But where hot metal composition is still available, it may for various reasons cost less than photo-composition, and some printers may be using it for many years to come. The vocabulary of printing is largely based on this method.

The Setting

Handsetting may still be used for display work in which unusual type sizes are needed, for lettering that runs diagonally or vertically, and for complex tables, mathematical equations or chemical formulae. With this method ready-cast Monotype characters are inserted by hand between blanks (for spaces) in a pattern as close as possible to the author's or designer's requirements. The process is, of course, expensive. This is why editors should instruct authors to translate terms such as a/b, which usually has to be handset, into a/b, which can be set mechanically. Authors (or editors) should also transform exponential functions with superscripts and super-superscripts into logarithmic functions, and simplify the construction of tables as much as possible-for example so that column headings can be set straight, not sideways, and so that vertical lines are not necessary.

The cost of conventional printing can be cut drastically if perfectly typed material is provided which is suitable either for photographing and printing by offset lithography or for feeding though a scanner which produces a drive tape for a photocomposer (see next section). Typescripts ready to be photographed ('camera-ready copy') may be supplied by the author or prepared by the editorial office, the publisher's staff, specialist outside firms or the printing firm itself (Printing unions often object to the first three of these, and editors thinking of changing to this system should enquire first about the local attitude.) The copy mug-fit within stated limits and special typing paper with limiting rectangles and lines printed in blue is sometimes provided by publishers or required by printers who use this method. The luxury of justified typing is usually abandoned in favour of the more economical (and possibly more legible) ragged right-hand edge. Although justifying typewriters exist, most people consider that the slightly improved appearance does not warrant the expense. Typewriter composition may be done on anything from an ordinary typewriter with a fresh ribbon, or an electric typewriter with a one time carbon or plastic ribbon, to an IBM Composer or a word processor. The IBM and other typewriters that offer a choice of typefaces an sets of symbols on exchangeable 'golf ball' heads can produce results which on the printed page compare well with the appearance obtained with hot-metal systems.

With typewriter setting, authors know exactly how the finished pages will look and can insert diagrams and figures just where they want them. They see their work in print quickly too, since the production process is fast and proof-reading for typesetting errors is not necessary. The editor will, however, have to do some checking of proofs for other kinds of mechanical faults. Publishers may agree to publish material produced in this way even when they expect sales to be small, because their production costs are much lower than usual (although marketing costs are unchanged).

The disadvantages of the method are that typed characters take up more space than typeset characters, so that more pages are needed for the same amount of material, and that some readers (and authors) dislike the look of the product, although this prejudice is disappearing as typewriter setting becomes more widespread and techniques improve.

Film and Plates

Mechanical filmsetting led composition out of the age of hot metal towards the era of electronics. The Monophoto filmsetter, for example, is based on the Monotype caster but uses a case of photographic images instead of a metal matrix case. The filmsetter contains a lamp, lenses, prisms, mirrors and a drum of film and is driven by punched paper tape produced on a slightly modified Monotype keyboard. The punched tape causes the required characters to be projected in turn by the lamp through the system of lenses, Prisms and angled mirrors onto the film. The mirrors move as each line is being set. Reflecting the characters to their place on the film. At the end of each line the film moves on, ready for the next line. A major advance over hot-metal systems is that different sizes of 'type' can be produced from one matrix by adjusting the lenses and prisms. Mechanized filmsetters are still in use but they work at only about the same speed as the hot metal caster around 11000 characters an hour.

Electromechanical photo-composing machines work 20 to 30 times faster than film-setters, although they operate on a similar principle. Photo-matrix (transparent) characters are held on a spinning disc, a drum or a grid, and the machine operates with a light source and a system of lenses and mirrors or prisms. The light source, often a xenon flash, projects each character onto a photosensitive medium (film or paper) in response to instructions from a punched paper or magnetic tape, or direct from a keyboard operator. Many type sizes and founts are available on these machines, and changes from one size or found to another can be made automatically.

Cathode-ray tube (CRT) photo-composers operate even faster than the 'second-generation' electromechanical machines, producing up to a million characters an hour. In CRT photo-composers, characters stored either on a photographic master or in digital form are generated on the CRT by an electron beam and then photographed. Photo-composers are highly flexible devices which can be instructed not only to change the type size and fount but to expander condense letters horizontally, change them from roman to italic or bold, and compose complete pages, dealing with line-end hyphenation and justification and all the other problems of page make-up.

The paper or magnetic tapes, cassettes or floppy disks that drive second-and third-generation photo-composers are usually produced by computer-linked keyboards. Some keyboards produce a paper copy ('hard copy') as well as computer-input tape; others are linked to a video display which shows the operator what has just been keyed, and the tape can be corrected immediately, if necessary; a third kind of keyboard produces only tape or, disks, though many machines of this kind now display the last 16 or 32 characters keyed by the operator. The keyboarding step may be eliminated if the original manuscript' was typed, with or without coded printed instructions, in an optical character recognition (OCR)-readable typeface. Perry, Courier-12, OCR-A and OCR-B typefaces can be 'read' by a scanning machine such as the Compusan Alpha. Scanners produced paper or magnetic type for driving a photo-composer or they may be linked directly to a photo-composer.

Direct-entry photo-composers: are now available which are technologically somewhere between the first-and second-generation machines and are much cheaper than the more advanced photo-composers. They have small memories and set one line at a time. They produce good quality work and are easy to use-as the name implies, the copy is entered directly from a typewriter-like keyboard that has extra type-setting commands to control founds held on film or on a glass disk.

With all kinds of photo-composition, the images captured on film or photo-sensitive paper are transferred to metal, plastic or rubber plates for the printing process described in the next section. Once the film has been made corrections are often expensive, as pieces of corrected film may have to be stripped in carefully by hand. Authors should therefore be encouraged more strongly than ever to avoid making trivial changes in proof.

The main advantages of photo-composition over other methods are speed, flexibility of type size and form, and the degree of automation which can be achieved with the help of computers. Not all photo-composers now in use are linked to computers, but future developments will undoubtedly depend on such links.

In spite of the great speeding-up of this part of book or journal production, photo-composed text is at present still being printed by the mainly mechanical processes described next.

Printing

The three printing processes in widest use until now have been letter press, offset lithography and photogravure. Printing is done either direct from metal type (letter-press) or from plates (all three methods). Only letter-press and lithography are mentioned here, as photogravure is rarely used for books or journals.

Letter-press, used mainly in conjunction with bot-metal composition, is the long-established method in which sheets of paper are pressed directly against the inked surface of type held on a flat bed press, or in which sheets or rolls (webs) of paper are pressed against inked plates. The printing plates are moulded from the metal type and they may be flat or curved, and made of metal, plastic or rubber. Curved plates are made for rotary presses, which work much faster than flatbed presses. 'Perfecter' presses are rotary presses which print both sides of the paper in one pass through, the machine. Another development is the Belt Press, in which the printing plates for one or more books fit on a continuous belt, which prints in sequence on a web of paper. The machine also slits, folds and collates the pages ready for binding, and may bind them too, which greatly speeds up the production processes.

In offset lithography the film produced by the composition process is photographically reproduced on printing plates. Each plate is wrapped round a cylinder on the printing press and then moistened and inked. A chemical process allows image areas to accept ink but not water, while the non-image areas accept water but not ink. When the cylinder rotates, the image is transferred-that is, offset-onto a rubber blanket on another cylinder, and from that blanket onto the paper.

The only difference in quality between good offset printing and letter-press is that letter-press may give a slightly sharper effect. Illustrations (see the section on Artwork below) are easier and cheaper to print by lithography, and cheaper paper can often be used than for letter-press. Offset lithography is therefore likely to be the method of choice until new methods are discovered and developed.

For printing by letter press, line drawings are first photographed and then transferred to a plate from which the non-printing areas are etched or hand-tooled away, leaving a raised surface to be inked. For offset plates the image is transferred to the plate surface photographically, as for the text.

For half-tone illustrations, the original prints are photographed through a screen of two sets of fine lines crossing each other at right angles, each set being regularly spaced at (usually) 100, 133, 150 or even 200 lines to the inch. The finer the detail required, the more lines to the inch are needed, i.e. the finer the screen. For a photograph of a piece of equipment, the print might use a 100-

mesh screen; for a light micrograph. 150-mesh with offset printing; and for an electron micrograph, possibly 200-mesh will be used. The finer the screen, the more care has to be used to prevent the ink from smudging, and the better the quality of paper needed. In letter-press printing, 200-mesh is about the finest screen that can satisfactorily be used, even on coated paper and with careful engraving; when screens finer than 200-mesh are used there is a loss of contrast. With offset lithography, screens of 133 or 150 lines to the inch are quite common.

The principle of the half-tone process is that light reflected from the photograph through each square in the mesh impinges on the photo-sensitive plate, and the greater the degree of blackness in the original print, the smaller the area Within that minute square that is affected. A white area on the original print will produce a series of discrete exposed ('black') squares on the plate. For letter press printing the plate is then dipped in an etching fluid which dissolves away the 'black' areas, leaving the unexposed areas-corresponding to black in the original—raised above the exposed ones. When the plate is inked these areas will print black. Grey areas in the original give rise to exposed squares of varying size according to the depth of grey. The purpose of these hundreds of tiny squares is to break the picture into dots, with areas of white between the inked areas. The printed picture then looks as if it had various shades of grey.

In letter-press printing the half-tone process, with its metal plats mounted on wooden or metal blocks, is expensive and authors are usually asked to keep the number of illustrations to a minimum. The original photographs must be of the best possible quality, since some quality is lost in even the best reproductions. If the high quality paper needed for 200-mesh reproductions is too expensive for a journal, the editor should warn authors and settle for medium quality semi-gloss paper and 1000-mesh screens.

To reduce costs without sacrificing the scientific evidence, the editor may select portions of photographs supplies by the author and reproduce them at full magnification rather than reduce whole photographs. Authors' photographs should never be cult instead they should be cropped or masked. That is, the margins of the photograph are marked to show which part is to be reproduced; or a rectangle of the appropriate size is marked on an overlay fixed to one edge of the print. In letter-press printing the process known as 'routing out, can be used to remove any small blemishes from a plate, and this is cheaper than having a new photo-engraving made. Nothing can be added to, or altered in the engraving at this stage, which explains why photographs must be sent to the printer in the best possible condition, having been well protected throughout the editorial process. Paperclips must never be used on photographs and only the softest pencil should be used to identify them on the back. A completely flat surface, to be pressed against the screen, is essential, though slight bending or rolling is not armful. Several small photographs may be mounted together on white card if this is carefully done but, in general, authors should be asked not to mount individual photographs; some glues produce a bumpy surface, and if each photograph is mounted, mailing costs soar. A piece of thin cardboard on either side of each set of photographs protects them adequately during mailing and the editorial process.

The editor, or printer, may chose to reduce costs by grouping several photographs together to make a large plate, which is latter cut up as necessary. It is not a good idea to combine photographs and line drawings if an engraving is being made, first because it is twice as expensive as an ordinary block, and secondly because the screen needed for the half-tones will maker the line drawing look grey.

Most illustrations are reduced in size during printing. The editor may have to decide which illustrations can be reduced to one-column width and which should run right across the page or occupy a full page, turned sideways if necessary. The larger the page size, the greater the choice in this regard. The degree of reduction can be stated simply as 'Reduce width to 50 nun', or expressed as percentage: (desired width of the illustration) divided by (actual width of the original) x 100%.

Colour reproduction costs too much for most scientific journals and books. If colour is wanted, the editor will either have to persuade the publisher that colour is essential for scientific or commercial reasons or ask the author to cover the extra costs-which are amazingly high.

The principles of 'process' colour printing are the same as for black and white, except that four different plates are usually made for each photograph. Three plates are made by photographing the original through coloured filters (red, blue and green, for printing in blue, yellow and red respectively); the fourth plate is made for printing in black, to give richer shading and contrast. The final reproduction is made by printing from each of the four plates in turn. The skill and expense lie in getting the four plates exactly aligned, or 'in register.'

Two-colour printing (for line drawings, diagrams, etc.) is less expensive than four-colour, process printing. It can be by prior separation of the colours, that is by getting an artist to prepare two separate versions of the picture, each showing where one of the colours is to go.

An inexpensive alternative to two-colour printing for book-jackets or journal covers is the use of screens of different mesh sizes to produce shades of colour with a single ink.

Strictly speaking, galley proofs are produced only in letter-press printing, where metal type is collected in long trays (galleys) as described earlier. But the term is widely used for the first set of proofs, which usually go to authors as well as to the editor for correction. The first proofs may be 'page on galley', already measured into numbered or unnumbered pages on the long galley sheets, or they may be actual page proofs.

The paste-up process varies with each printer's practice. In the most orderly, and leisurely, procedure it goes as follows for hot-metal composition. Galley proofs are pulled by hand from the type standing in galleys. When corrected galley proofs are received, corrections are made in the type accordingly. Another proof is made, and this is cut up and pasted onto pages ruled to the size of the book or journal. Illustrations are placed appropriately, and the paste-up artist deals with problems like headings that land at the very bottom of page, or single word lines ('widows') that land at the top of one. The paste-up person does this usually by instructing the printer to adjust the amount of space between lines or around headings, sometimes by directing that the type on several lines should be squeezed closer together or that a tightly set line should be opened up to make an extra line. This set of planning may have to take several pages into consideration.

When the paste-up is satisfactory the type is moved from the galleys and arranged, together with the blocks for the illustrations, in page 'formes' (metal frames) in accordance with the paste-up. Page numbers and running heads are added before the forms are locked tip ready for carrying to the press. These forms hold 16, 32 or other multiples of four pages, and the pages are so arranged that they will come out in the right order (and the right way up) when the printed press sheet is eventually folded into signatures (a portion of a publication containing however many pages are printed on each sheet).

To speed up publication, the total process has been streamlined by modern printers. Paste-up may be done while the authors are correcting proofs. Then, when authors' corrections result in an increase or decrease in the number of lines ' of text, the paste-up has to be adjusted before the type is placed in forms. Some printers do not only the paste up but also the page make-up before sending out the first proofs. For either of these procedures it is evidently highly disruptive if the author makes changes in proof which alter the number of lines, or the number or sequence of illustrations, and this is why such changes are so strongly discouraged. Sometimes the editor or other proof-reader can make a judicious further change that shortens or lengthens a sentence slightly and brings it back to its original length without changing its meaning.

Direct photography of typescript and photo-composition are easier for the printer to work with than hot metal, as there is no heavy type to be moved around in the late stages, with the attendant risks of small pieces of type being lost or getting out of alignment. On the other hand adjustment of vertical or horizontal spacing by cutting and stripping in small pieces of film is difficult to do well. Re-setting a whole page by computer may be done in a moment, but it can be an expensive moment. Alterations in any system are troublesome; that is why it is important first to find a printer who makes few typesetting errors and then to provide well-prepared thoroughly edited copy.

Final page proofs usually go to the editor only, unless an author insists on receiving a set too. Corrections must be kept to the absolute minimum at this stage. When final ad ustments-for example inserting page numbers in the contents list or index—have been made, the book or journal is ready for printing by one of the methods already described.

Quality of Paper

The editor should ask the printer's or publisher's advice before specifying a particular quality of paper for a book or journal. Printers can work more economically with some papers than others, depending on the machines they use and other factors. Economy usually has to be balanced against the quality desired. For textual material, near-opaqueness, lightness of weight and a matt surface giving good contrast without glare are the desirable properties. If the book or journal has many illustrations calling for first-rate reproduction (e.g. electron micrographs), a glossy paper may have to be used throughout. Where there are only a few photographs in one or two places, the heavier paper can be inserted in four-page sections but this makes printing and binding much more expensive than usual. Articles with electron micrographs, or the electron micrographs alone, are sometimes grouped on glossy paper at the end of a journal so that cheaper paper can be used for the rest of the issue. Another method is to have single sheets of glossy paper tipped in or 'hooked in' glued to the following page or 'wrapped round'-wrapped round the first and last page of a section. With all these method machinery has to be stopped for manual processes, at exorbitant expense, so that if superb reproduction is essential it is sometimes cheaper to use glossy paper throughout. Because of the manual work involved, fold-out pages are expensive too.

Paper may be either 'free sheet' (wood free) or groundwork stock. 'Free' means that the wood pulp has been chemically treated to remove the impurities and reduce the acidity of ground wood. Woodfree paper is the kind mainly used for scientific books and journals, though coated groundwood stocks with a reasonably long life are now available.

The weight of a paper is quoted in grams per square metre (g/m, sometimes written as 'gsm') or as pounds per ream (500 sheets). Papers weighing 75-100 g/m are commonly used for books and journals. Papers of the same weight may differing bulk (measured in pages per centimetre or inch), depending on how much air has been whipped into the pulp during milling, on how much fibre content there is, and on the method of milling. Except in North America (for the present), paper is usually supplied in 'A' sizes or the book sizes (Demy, Royal, Crown) and a press sheet may hold 16, 24, 32, 48, 64 or more printed pages, depending on the size of the press and the size of the book being printed.

The opacity and finish of appear are important. It is distracting to read a page if the text from the next page shows through clearly. Substances such as titanium oxide are added to increase opacity. The 'finish' refers to the final treatment in the manufacturing process, when a paper may be coated with china clay, to give it a glossy appearance, or 'super calendred'-pressed between metal rollers to make it very smooth. 'Machine-finished' papers are the kind most commonly used when a glossy finish is not needed.

The colour of the paper ('white' is not a precise term), and whether it has a high or a low glare, are other important qualities to take into consideration. Some coated papers now have a low glare, which makes for easier reading.

Good Binding

Binding may be done either in the printing plant or in a separate bindery. Journals and paper-back books are usually bound in the printing plant, and binding may follow printing without any interruption. The processes involved are folding, gathering, sewing and/or gluing, trimming and attaching a cover. A book may be given a dustjacket, and books and journals may also be protectively wrapped for mailing, all in one series of mechanized processes.

The printed sheets that come off the press are folded into signatures, each signature representing one press sheet. The uncut signatures are gathered or collated to make up complete books or journal issues, and they are then saddle-wired (stapled at the back, for publications of up to 64 pages), side-wired (stronger than saddle-wiring and taking more pages), sewn (with the pages in each signature swwn together and sewn to the next signature), 'or glued direct to the spine without any stitching (so-called 'perfect' binding). Perfect binding is probably the most widely used method for binding both journals and paper-back books.

For books that are to have hard covers, 'endpapers' are attached at the beginning and end before the paper is trimmed, and the backs ands, (spines) are ten rounded. Reinforced gauze ('crash') and 'headbands' and Tootbands' are attached to the spines and these are glued to accept the covers ('cases'). Cases usually consists of 'boards' of various materials to which cloth, plastic or certain kinds of treated papers have been glued. Covers are usually prepared in advance, with wording and design as agreed in the specification. The title and other lettering are stamped on the front cover or spine, or both, with ink or through coloured foil. The books are then either pressed between heavy boards until the glue has died and the characteristic crease along the spine has taken shape, or they are seasoned to this stage in a few seconds in 'building-in' machines. Dustjackets, if used, go on last of all.

Finally, binding practices for journal volumes should be mentioned. In the USA, UK and some other countries-though not in Scandinavia, it seem-binders customarily remove advertisements and other 'extraneous matter', as well as covers and contents pages, from journal issues before volumes are bound. Where pages are removed in this way the editor should arrange to have at least one copy of each volume bound exactly as the issues were published, complete with covers, and stored in the editorial office. Queries of various kinds including legal problems, may arise in later years and a reference copy is essential.

Here I need only mention the methods the printer uses to produce extra copies of chapters or journal articles. Authors are often given 25, 50, or sometimes more, free copies of their chapters in a book, and sometimes of articles in journals, in partial recompense for writing the chapter or article. They can usually order further copies at a price slightly higher than the cost of producing them. The printer makes the extra copies either by printing more sheets than are needed for the print run of the book or journal issue, or by reprinting copies by photo-offset from the finished book or journal issue in accordance with the numbers of copies ordered. The offprint or run-on method provides authors with their copies as soon as, if not before, the book or journal is published (which authors like); however, orders can be accepted only until the time that the relevant signatures go on the press. The second, or reprint, method, is more flexible in that reprints can be made at any time, however late the order is received; and no paper is wasted since only the required pages (and not unwanted ones in the same signature) are printed.

The relative costs of the two methods depend on many factors, including the variability in size of reprint orders for different articles the size of the printing plant, and the way it is organized. The editor's main object when negotiating reprint or offprint arrangements with the printer should be to ensure that the copies, especially of journal articles, are reliable available within a few weeks of publication.

3

Production Stages

Making the many diverse and independent functions inside the newspaper plant fit together like the intricate parts of facing executives. But there is no substitute for a harmonious blending of these production factors into a unified effort, and nothing else contributes more to the profitable and satisfying rewaards to be found in newspaper publishing.

In the same way that a fine automobile spins along on four well-balanced wheels, newspaper production depends on four carefully aligned factors: flow of work, saving of time, capacity standards and expense regulation.

Main Tasks

Publishing a newspaper requires a ready flow of ingenuity, work, copy, films, and metal. To keep that flow evenly paced and uninterrupted requires clear organization, constant supervision and direction, and the most careful and earnest cooperation.

Editorial : From the start of the publication period until press time, the news department must keep newsworthy information flowing into the office and the composing room. As any good reporter knows, there is nothing so stale as old news. At times a reporter may think the editors or publishers are hard taskmasters, but actually they are compelled by tradition and by the practical copy flowing steadily. That's newspapering.

Covering, writing, and editing stories; picture taking; and other newsgathering responsibilities are no different on a weekly than on a daily. They are merely done by fewer persons; and even though the production interval is a full week, a steady flow of copy must be maintained once work on the weeks issue is begun. An alert and efficient editor will do the following

1. Plan ahead. Once an issue is out. Work must begin on the next. In fact, much of the work must be planned days before the date of issue.
2. Keep a date or futures book to reveal what subject matter is to be covered immediately and what news stories are in prospect. This serves a twofold purpose; the paper is not so likely to missimportant stories and assignments can be made according to an organized plan.
3. Use judgement in making assignment. The editor knows which reporters are best equipped by temperament, knowledge, and experience to handle specific types of stories.
4. Plan for early completion of stories to go on inside pages. Which are made up first. Interesting copy must be available at all times for quick makeup.
5. See that department editors plan and complete features and stories well in advance. Some publishers measure the worth of department editors as much by how well they plan ahead as by the quality of the copy produced by their staffs.
6. Clear the news wire machines regularly, sort copy in an orderly fashion, and edit it rapidly. For the daily newspaper the wire machines roll out endless sheets of news from all parts of the world. The problem lies in what stories to select and when to send them to the copydesk or into the computer. Only experience will develop the kind of foresighted judgement needed for the job.

7. Keep a backlog of time copy handy-features and other material that may be used to fill in on days when general news is light.
8. Edit copy carefully to avoid revisions in proofs, which may cause delays near press time.
9. Write headlines plainly and transmit them with copy to the composing room. Late headlines cause delay and often are placed incorrectly in makeup.
10. Read proofs promptly. A dilatory and inefficient proofreader may wipe out all the speed put into copy preparation by the news staff.

"We made a general outline of the type of material to be used in the Small explains. "Then we proceeded to assign specific stories to reporters, and the fact that we told them that they should have one in every three or four days seemed to increase their interest. Naturally we had to have close cooperation and a great many staff meetings."

For a fiftieth-anniversary edition, the publisher of a small daily began formulating plans a year ahead and began actual work on the edition six months before it was to be distributed. The publisher first drew up a general plan, deciding that edition should have ten sections, each dealing with a particular phase of the community's development in which the newspaper had an important part. Next, each section was planned, with a list of the local advertisers who should be represented and the phases of community development to be covered in news and feature stories. Each prospective story was carefully outlined so that the reporter, upon receiving the assignment, had a clear understanding of what facts should be included. A deadline was set for each section. Pictures were taken, copy was prepared and printing of the section took place within a month after work was begun on the edition.

Work then started on the next section, which was to be written, edited and printed within two weeks. That two-week schedule continued until the ten section were completed. Each section was stuffed inside those previously printed, and the constantly developing edition was stored in a protected corner of the pressroom.

The work on the anniversary edition extended over a long period, but by careful planning it was done by the regular staff during some welcomed overtime ours without interfering with work on daily issues.

Business : Work should proceed steadily and evenly in every section of the business department. Records in the office must be as up to the minute as the news that appears in the day's issue if the newspaper is to meet the standards of a going concern. This can be realized only by :

1. Giving definite instructions to office help.
2. Having proper forms for tabulating required information.
3. Issuing statements and making collections promptly.
4. Avoiding delay in answering correspondence.
5. Acknowledging all advertising and subscription orders immediately.
6. Paying bills promptly and taking advantage of discounts.
7. Maintaining adequate personnel and equipment.

A publisher encourages efficiency, accuracy, and promptness in the business office by requiring up-to-date facts about the business. Forward-looking business managers are making dramatic use of computers for keeping an almost instantaneous check on minute details of the business operation.

Advertising : Keeping ahead in preparing and selling advertising and feeding copy to the composing room in a way that will keep the machines busy is the advertising department's job. To accomplish this, most newspapers have deadlines for advertising copy.

The Bloomington, III., Pantagraph has an advertisements of such perishables as fruit and meat. On those the deadline is 5 P.M. the day before publication.

Table. Advertising headline requirements

Size of ad	*Days Preceding publication*
Double page	5 days
Single page	4 days
Half page	3 days
Quarter page	2 days
Smaller ads	1 days

The composing room refuses copy that does not conform to this deadline schedule. Such a schedule puts the advertising department on its toes and counteracts excuses from the composing room.

When putting out a special edition, the steady flow of advertising copy to the composing room for many weeks prior to publication is a important as a steady flow of editorial copy. The Atlantic city, N.J press stimulated its advertising force in a unique way for a special edition. To provide competition and thus create a steady copy flow, members of the staff were selected by team captains of the "Write Sox" and "Purple Hose". A "nine-inning game" started with last week in December and continued until mid-February. Each page of advertising counted as a run. Each week counted as an inning. The keenness of the competition reflected in the final score; Purple Hose, 51; White Sox, 50.

Other techniques used to maintain a more even volume of advertising are:

1. A special rate to merchants who carry a minimum amount of daily or weekly advertising.
2. Bonuses and commissions for extra volume produced by salespeople during slack periods.
3. Definite linage goals established with suitable rewards for the staff when the goals are reached.
4. Last year's linage figures kept constantly before the staff.
5. Special pages of cooperative advertising produced for otherwise dull periods.

Some newspaper have found it advantageous, as far as stimulating the flow of advertising copy is concerned, to offer discounts to merchants who deliver their copy "camera-ready" to the newspaper. This practice obviously eliminates the work of the advertising representative in obtaining the copy from merchants, and relieves the newspaper of typesetting, composition, proofing, and delivering finished ad proofs for approval by the client.

Circulation : No department of a newspaper runs more risk of getting off balance in its work flow the circulation department Papers. Papers must be delivered to homes at regular hours each day or week, and they must be in good order or subscribers are dissatisfied. Circulation totals must rise continually at least remain stabilized at a profitable level.

A carefully planned adaptation of a semi-automatic book keeping machine-the National Cash Register book keeping machine, Model 3100, with a 26-inch carriage has eliminated much paperwork by district personnel in the circulation department of the Santa Rosa, Calif, Press Democrat. Formerly, the district staff posted their "stops" and "starts", then totaled their new draw for each route or dealer and turned in the completed figures to the book keeper. Under the new draw for each route or dealer and turned in the completed figures to the bookkeeper . Under the new system, the stops and start for each route or dealer go at once to the book keeper who posts them on the daily draw sheets, arriving at the days draw as well as at the cumulative total for the month. When the total draws at the last day of the month are compiled, figures are immediately available for posting the monthly billings, without the necessity of balancing the month's work.

Rapid circulation growth led the Toronto, Ont., star to modernize its mailing room to speed the movement of papers from the presses to trucks and other carriers. To supplement the equipment it already had in the mailing room, the star publishers had their research-engineering department design a machine to feed bundles directly from a Cutler-Hammer paper conveyor, end on the roller-slat conveyor, and then directly through a company-designed automatic self-feeling, wire-tying machine. This specially designed bundle feeder is know as the Starstarter.

To the casual spectator, the mailrooms of modern metropolitan dailies are marvels of mechanical ingenuity, where the pace of activity can become quite feverish as the pressroom hits full production. Conveyor systems are customized to speed freshly printed sections of the newspaper in sometimes bewildering configuration-horizontally, vertically, around curves, and through machines that automatically insert stack count tie in bundles, address, or perform other specialized duties.

The Memphis publishing Company has added a computer-directed system that determines automatically the distribution of bundles through chutes to waiting trucks four floors below. Some of the specially designed equipment for faster and more efficient mailroom operations can give this part of the newspaper plant an exciting appearance.

A perennial problem facing circulation managers is that of carrier turnover. Some newspaper deposit to a carrier's credit half the value of a U.S. Savings Bond when he has been on the route three months. To collect the bond, the carrier must stay on his route nine more consecutive months and do good work.

Mechanical Jobs : Management once looked upon the composing room more as a necessary evil than as a profitable operating department, but this attitude has been changed by time studies, cost systems, and analyses.

An unusually detailed presentation of desirable trends in newspaper makeup was provided in comments by the judges of the 1979 Typoraphy and Design Contest of the Inland Daily press Association, as reported in Editor & Publisher magazine. The judges were Hayward Blake, Evanston.IIL, graphic designer; and two educators from the Medill School of Journalism at Northwestern University: Assistant Dean Dave Nelson and Professor Jack Sissors.

Here are some of their observations:

1. The better newspaper use functional rather than formula makeup. Traditional newspaper have a sameness that makes them look designed by formula, whereas the best tend to use makeup that fits the news.

2. Wider columns appear most functional and attractive.
3. Newspapers do not waste white space but are careful to distribute it throughout any given page.
4. Column rules are disappearing.
5. Newspapers tent to use type family throughout the paper.
6. Varying the graphic treatment of special sections tends to create interest.

Here were some of their criticisms:

1. Too many nameplates are too large too ugly.
2. Bad standing heads suggest that many newspaper managements should buy the service of a graphic designer.
3. Too many newspapers use italics too much instead of saving it for use as a contrast face.
4. The use of the same kind of rule borders for boxed stories and advertisement should be avoided.
5. Too few subheads are use to break up body type.

Subheads should be boldface and of a typeface that represents a change.

Firm policies on typographical usage and makeup variations will contribute much to the flow of work in the mechanical department.

Economy of Time

Newspapers today buy time as well as talent. The rate of pay to most newspaper employes is as much on the basis of time as ability. The tendency among labour leaders is to have work measured by the time spent rather than by its productive power. Employes work a specified number of hours each week, and a half. When manufacturers are buying time of his sort, they want as little of it as possible.

Time clocks used in some newspaper plants not only calculate the hours put in by employes but also make them conscious of their responsibility to make time count and to give full measure.

There is some question, however, about the advisability of time clocks since they may have an undesirable psychological effect on employes. This some publishers have learned, is true for the editorial, news, and clerical department. However, there usually is some from of checking in and checking out where a large number are employed.

Non-productive work time includes such time-consuming operations as repairing machinery, plate removal and storage, cleaning up the composing room, and losses due to machinery breakdown. Daily coffee breaks and vacation periods represent many non-productive hours for which the newspaper willingly pays the same as for productive hours.

In some plants there has been a tendency to abuse the privilege of coffee breaks by staying out longer than the time agree upon between employer and employes. To avoid this, a number of newspaper serve coffee in the plant.

Vacation policies are established mainly on the length of time a person a person has been on the company payroll. On some newspapers the employe works for the company for year before a paid vacation is earned. In addition to the prescribed vacations, six holidays are generally granted during the year: New Year's Day. Memorial Day, Fourth of July, Labour Day, Thanksgiving, and Christmas. Many newspaper make a birthday. With smaller newspapers, vacations and holidays may be on a less formal schedule.

Editorial-News Department : Speed in making assignments, preparing copy, and editing is important in the newsroom. To accelerate work there.

1. Help the reporter off to a quick start by clearly outlining the assignment and explaining its importance.
2. Have sufficient telephones in the newsroom to avoid any bottleneck in phone calls.
3. Organise routine telephone calling, such as that for the society page.
4. Have plenty of copy paper on hand, conveniently placed.

5. Have enough typewriters or editing terminals so that reporters need not wait to write their stories.
6. Keep average sentence length reasonably short.
7. Hold copy reading marks to a minimum.
8. See that reporters as well as copy processors understand copy editing standards and proofreading symbols.
9. Devise simple deadline schedules.
10. Provide chutes, elevators, pneumatic tubes, or other types of carrier systems to convey copy quickly to composing room.

For covering special events and correcting situations within the editorial-news office, special timesaving arrangements sometimes are necessary.

To achieve quick coverage of the home football games of the University Miami, the Miami, Fla., Herald has a wire machine installed in the press box, and the operator punches out the story on a direct wire to a phototypesetting machine in the composing room. Thus the type is set direct.

Visitors to the editorial-news office to report happenings, to discuss editorial policies, or to complain about how certain items were handled often consume much of the editor's time. To cut down this wasted time, the Winston-Salem, N.C. Journal and Sentinel carried in its columns a series of "Talks with Readers". One carried an informal photograph of the publishers sitting on his desk, glasses in hand, explaining that newspaper publishers have the tremendously difficult job of managing an operation that is both a business and a public service. Other pictures explained the duties and trials of the editorial director and staff; and copy indicate why certain stories appear in the paper even though the staff, if it could have its way, would prefer not to use them and explained the impossibility of "suppressing" any news story. Discussing one newspaper towns, the publisher side: "The Journal and Sentinel are only of moderate size, yet last year it cost something like three million dollars to publish these papers.

Publishing costs explain why nine out ten towns are served by only one publisher".

Working Office

In a fast-moving newspaper organization it is imperative that accounting methods keep pace with other operations. Modern accounting equipment saves many expensive hours of manual labour.

As part of a general modernization programme in the accounting department, the Cleveland, Ohio, press installed a Remington Rand accounting machine. Which handled the accounts payable record work in less than half the time required under the newspaper's previous of the work, the daily time ran to an average of seven and one-half hours. Using the new accounting machine, a single operator handled the same work in an average of slightly less than three hours a day.

Leslie Moeller, former director of the School of Journalism of the University of Iowa, cites other ways to save time and reduce costs in the newspaper business office.

Writing letters cost money and a printed memorandum sheet take the place of a letter. It is less expensive to print and quicker to type, and you do not have any extended addressing of salutation. The fact that the space is smaller helps to cut sown on the long-windedness which often seems to go automatically with the full-size letterhead.

Another step cost cutting is to shift to a postcard. You can carry your letterhead on the reverse side, and if you wish you can make a satisfactory carbon from such a postcard. If you use ten of these cards a day in place of standard letters your overall saving will be at least $150 a year if you take into account postage, printing, cost stock, secretarial time and of the other factors.

Modern dictating equipment will save you much time and money. Many publishers who type their own letters can save real money with this equipment. If your plant is small and you do not use a full-time secretary, you will find it easy to hire a stenographer who would like to work a few hours a day. The equipment is not complicated; you will be able to use it in a few minutes, and any competent typist can learn to transcribe in a little while.

Saving time in the advertising department is a matter of carefully planning copywriting and sales work, giving special consideration to the wants and needs of readers and prospective advertisers and providing proper training for personnel. Some tested timesavers are:

1. Printed layout sheets, for preparing any size ad up to a full page, save many minutes that otherwise would be spent measuring space and ruling borders.
2. Flat-topped filling cabinets permit advertising services to be arranged in order for quick reference and to be opened immediately without going to a table or a desk.
3. A file where advertising ideas for special days each month, anniversaries, special weeks, and the like are compiled.
4. Standard forms for writing classified advertisements and for soliciting want ads by mail enable the ad taker to prepare the ad as it is received and help the mail advertiser to arrange facts systematically and estimate the cost easily.
5. Tilt-top, broad-surfaced copywriting tables raise moral of the advertising department, encourage neat layouts, and speed production.
6. A timetable should be provided for sales personnel to make regular calls on prospects without duplication of effort. Each salesperson should be given a specific list of prospects or a definite territory to over.
7. A sticker on proof to be delivered to the advertiser indicates when proof was delivered and the time proof must be returned to the office to have corrections or changes made.

In many newspaper plants much time is lost in handling general advertising copy in the composing room, due to careless preparation of order and instructions by the advertising department. To improve this situation in its plant, the Green Bay, Wis., press-Gazette instituted a system whereby ad material was field by date rather than by product. After that there were few missed insertions, repeat ads were handle almost automatically, and old printing material was eliminated.

Careless handling of layouts is expensive. The copy should be clear, readable, and understandable for the compositor. Much copy prepared by merchants and submitted to newspapers should be redesigned and retyped before it goes to the printers.

Advertising sales personnel for the Chicago, III,. Tribune are trained to sell more than an advertisement- they sell a campaign. The idea is use by telephone solicitors in the classified department. They are trained to tell a caller "I'll start your ad today for seven days," which often converts a potential one-time ad into a multiple insertion order. It takes no longer to sell a seven-time ad than it does to sell a one-time ad, or to sell a series of 13 display ads than to sell a single ad.

All advertisers are billed at the open rate by the Carroll, Iowa, Times-Herald and if the account is paid by the tenth of the following month, contract advertisers receive discounts ranging from 16 percent to 28 percent depending on the space used. If a customer uses less space than previously and thus reduces the allowed discount, a call is made to suggest ways of qualifying for a larger one. Discount are listed on the rate card, but the contract states that they are given "for a consistent and adequate advertising programme." Since the discount also is based on prompt payment, it serves to keep collections in good order and to eliminate otherwise necessary work by collectors, according to James W. Wilson, publisher.

With the impending conversion to the metric system facing it, the Iowa City, Iowa, press-citizen was one of the first newspaper in the nation to begin computing all its advertising measurements and contracts in centimeters rather than in column inches. Adjusting early to the new system has already begun to produce savings in time required to educate advertisers and readers to the change. Other pioneers in the transition to metrics include the Bangor, Maine, Daily News, the Columbia, Mo., Missourian, and the Ypsllanti, Mich., press.

Questions to consider in the circulation department are:

1. How may we lessen time consumed in stuffing when the newspaper is printed in several sections?
2. How may we speed transit of the paper from the press to delivery trucks?
3. Could we reach outlying points of our circulation area by some better delivery methods?
4. Are any of our carriers to begin and complete deliveries more promptly?

Stuffing papers by hand is a long and troublesome task. Tying bundles and getting them ready for delivery may also be time consuming. The Des Moines, Iowa, Register and Tribune has made a number of changes in its system of transporting papers from the press to the delivery trucks.

"The overhead conveyor system, once used for moving papers around our mailroom, has been removed," says J. R. Hudson, circulation manager, and stockers have been installed on the press conveyors. Tying machines now in operation use a plastic tape fastened with a metal clip. The old Pollard Ailing machine has been replaced by new Magnacraft equipment and the mail list has been transferred to the computer. We no longer use the Wallastar tying machine. The bottom wrapper on out bundles is now put on automatically with equipment built by our own machine shop people."

In a major redesigning of its mailroom, the Grand Rapids, Mich., press installed high-speed feeder tables and roller conveyors to link inserters, tyers, and loading dock in a timesaving operation.

The importance of getting papers to readers rapidly is never overlooked by an alert circulation manager. At one time, the Salina, Kans,. Journal served 16 town in 3 counties with daily delivery by airplane. A licensed pilot flew 180 air miles and delivered 1,000 papers per day, 5 days a week.

Another pilot flew 275 air miles to deliver 2,000 paper per day. The papers were wrapped in round bundles and each was dropped from 20 to 50 feet into field at the edge of the town where papers were to be delivered by car; but bad weather prevented airplane delivery only a few days in the year. For four week one winter, skis were used on the plane for safe landings at Salina on return trips forced landing was made in two years, and that was caused by the collapse of an oil strainer. Circulation in the area doubled in the two years of airplane delivery.

Circulation distribution is a continuing problem for all newspapers. They can improve distribution by applying these timesaving methods:

1. By going to press at regular times. Late runs upset the entire delivery system.
2. By providing mailers with good equipment and teaching them now to use it. A mailing machine that operates poorly in stamping addresses on newspapers or wrappers can easily cause late mailings. The same is true regarding a mailer who does not understand the machine operation.
3. By tracking papers to carriers who deliver in outlying districts, thereby enabling them to start promptly.
4. By using motorcycles for delivery in suburban and rural areas, where homes are far apart and routes are long.
5. By rewarding carriers who complete their delivery routes within reasonable time and with no complaints.

The composing room is one of the most expensive departments of the newspaper organization, and there is consequently a tremendous loss involved in any careless management or waste of time. If materials are scattered, it is hard to concentrate employes operations. Loss also occurs when employes do not have enough material when needed or when they must wait to use a piece of equipment.

To reduce production bottlenecks, the Cleveland Ohio, press installed a Haploid FotoFlo photocopying camera in its composing room. This equipment produced an advertiser's layout full-page size in seven or eight minutes per photocopy so that everybody concerned could start work simultaneously. In addition, time was saved in the engraving department by furnishing photocopy type proofs in reverse, such as black on white and type with screened backgrounds, for the general run of advertisements.

With an week Positive Printmaker, the Lexington, Mass., Minuteman a weekly newspaper with a circulation of 9,5000, reports a saving in time of 48 hours per week in production, plus many hours formerly required for editorial layout work. The Itek 1113, made by the Itek Graphic Products company, requires one minute to make positive prints from original photographs and eliminates tedious "stripping". An additional benefit is that errors are almost totally eliminated.

Time reduction in the mailroom was achieved by the San Antonio, Tex., Express and News when it installed a new Sheridan on-line inserter. A twin-delivery arrangement per minutes a top speed of 36,000 fully inserted copies per hour.

At the New York N.Y. Wall Street Journal satellite plant in Orlando. Fla., fantastic strides have been made in remote control economy of operation.

The six unit Gross Metro offset press is run by a computer console that provides instant, response in the supply of ink, water, or registration adjustments. The management has reported what may be record times for edition start-ups and also believes that losses from newsprint waste have been reduced to the lowest experienced by any newspaper.

The highly automated Gannett newspaper have found that productivity per person has improved by 9 percent since converting to modern electronic production in the mechanical department. Also the Spilled newspapers have noted that fewer people are turning out greater results with improved equipment so that the average of hours worked of hours worked has declined 3 percent despite an increase in number of pages and volume of advertising produced.

The Raleigh, N.C., News and Observer and Times has trimmed its composing room force from 101 to 57 since conversion from letterpress to often, with electronic data processing equipment added.

Another remarkable achievement in timesaving is that of the Minneapolis, Minn., Star and Tribune. According to Paul Brainerd, assistant to the operations director, the newspaper is showing up to 30 percent in overall timesaving; 85 percent in markup; 50 percent in pasteup; and lesser reductions in proofreading, keyboarding, making corrections, and the like.

Detailed as some of these time whittling steps may seem to be, they to be they all add up to increased efficiency and higher profits.

Basic Factors

Another basic factor of production is department-by-department capacity. The desire to increase production always exists, and it is the responsibility of management changes wherever practicable and advisable.

Adequate lighting, ventilation, and safety condition must prevail in all departments before production can reach a satisfactory peak. The reporter becomes drowsy and sluggish if forced to prepare copy under a dim light. Advertising personnel who have difficulty pulling mats from cabinets in shadowy corners lose time that should be spent in copy preparation and selling. Compositors need the benefit of good lighting. Accidents in the pressroom are less likely when there is proper illumination.

Newspaper publishing in many instances is an around-the-clock operation. Consequently, the lighting system must be adequate and independent of natural light is effective only within a few feet of the windows and varies greatly depending' on the weather. Illumination must be adequate not only in quantity but also in quality. The correct combination provides high visibility of detail and overall seeing comfort.

According to William H. Kahler, lighting engineer for the westinghouse Electric Corporation, Cleveland, Ohio, the composing room should have general illumination of 20 to 30 foot-candles provided by low brightness luminaires such as semi-indirect fluorescent equipment, and each machine should be equipped with a supplementary luminaire to furnish at least 50 foot-candle on the copy.

Lighting plays an important role in the pressroom where operators must maintain precise control of modern high- speed machinery. Fluorescent luminaires of the enclosed, vapour-tight type are recommended. Each luminaire contains two 40-watt fluorescent lamps and consists of a steel housing, inner white-enameled reflector, and a hinged dust-tight cover. Illumination along the sides of the press is about 40 foot-candles. The light inside the press is considerable less, but here again quality is more important than quality. The direction and diffusion of light from the continuous rows of fluorescent luminaires provides excellent visibility on the press cylinders and permits quick plate changes.

Every newspaper plant presents an individual lighting problem. A combination of careful planning, reliable lighting equipment, and regular maintenance will contribute to high production standards, efficient plant operation, and better morale among the workers.

The physical comfort of employe's has a strong bearing on their capacity to produce. Maintaining an even temperature within the newspaper plant the year around eliminates many problems that otherwise would arise. Air- conditioning is expensive, but it contributes greatly to the speed and composure of those responsible for producing a newspaper efficiently and promptly. Temperature has its effect on machinery as well as personnel. An every temperature and humidity should be kept in the pressroom for the proper operation of the presses—state electricity develops easily under adverse conditions of hest and moisture. Some provision must be made for removing surplus heat or fumes that might be produced by a piece of equipment. Efficient ventilation is the obvious answer for all departments where stuffy or odor-laden conditions of air prevail.

Publishers, as well as other manufacturers, are bound by their own responsibility and to a certain extent by law to provide safe working conditions for employes. But machinery around a printing plant presents hazards even under the most extensive protective provisions.

Lack of uniform safety measures for printing plants is the cause of many accidents. A worker transferring from one plant to another usually finds different machinery and different safeguards. A great variety of signaling methods is used in printing plants throughout the country to indicate staring of a machine—bells, horns, whistles, flashing lights. Another cause of server and sometimes fatal accidents is the location of the power control button, which is in almost as many different positions as there are machine. This makes it extremely difficult for workers to shut off the power in an emergency if they are not familiar with the machine or if they are on one side and the button is on the other. However, several devices have been created to shut off power automatically when anything happens to prevent smooth operation, and these should be considered in developing plant safety.

Preliminary steps have taken by the American Standards Association to develop a safety code for signaling devices and control for graphic arts equipment. In addition, strict regulation codified and enforced by federal and state and governments under the general supervision of the Occupational Safety and Health Administration keep the publisher informed of detailed requirements for the elimination of plant hazards.

Fire hazards develop easily in a newspaper plant if the situation is not watched carefully. An analysis made by the National Fire Protection Association of 1,053 fires in the printing industry reveals these general cause; common hazards, 52 percent; Special hazards, 27 percent; unknown causes, 21 percent. These special hazards are further broken down into the following types; paper ignited by gas dryer or static neutralizer flame, 35 percent; type-metal melting, 17 percent; ignition of paper shreds by friction sparks from processing units, 21 percent; ignition of gasoline, naphtha, alcohol, and kerosene used in cleaning, 11 percent; ignition of benzol and other ink thinners, 9 percent; overheating of the glue pot, 2.5 percent; ignition of collodion deposits, 2.2 percent; ignition of varnish vapours, 2.5 percent; overheating of wax, 1.8 percent; miscellaneous, 4 percent.

In the news department it is difficult to say how much copy a good reporter should produce in a day. That depends to a great extent upon the type of beat to be covered or the kind of copy requested. Some reporters will turn in enough in a day to fill five columns. On some of the large city newspapers the management will be satisfied if its best reporter will turn in one good news story each day or fill one good assignment. The requirement standards on some newspapers are higher than on other, depending on how exacting the editorial-news department is regarding the style and accuracy of copy.

The reporter, as well as the executive, can easily estimate the cost per story or per column of the copy submitted. Employers sometimes remark that a beginner "writes the perfect story, but has yet to learn the tempo of the newspaper. The stories cost too much".

News department production standards may be raised by an alert editor who keeps in close touch with readers and knows how to explain their attitudes to staff members.

The publisher of the Washington, Iowa, Journal, in a unique survey questionnaire, asked readers: "If you were the Journal editor, how would you change the paper?" The questionnaire was a full newspaper-page size. The questions touched every department, feature, advertising idea, comic, panel, occasionally, regular column, editorial, and so forth that appeared in the Journal. Readers were asked to check readership as "always," "occasionally", "seldom", or "never" and to comment on whether the feature or department was liked "very much" "just so-so", or "not at all". The reverse side of the page had space for additional comments and the name and address of the newspaper, with postage prepaid so that the form could be folded and returned by this means the publisher used reader reaction to point out to staff members the standard of interest created by their work in the news and advertising department.

The state editor and the public officials of the South Bend. Ind., Tribune made personal visits to public officials of small communities in the circulation area. In each community they called upon the mayor or president of the city council and the superintendent of schools, asking their cooperation in obtaining news events in their communities. Reception of the idea was excellent. Officials were gratified by this evidence of the Tribune's interest and became good community reporters.

The interest of staff members in better reporting may be stimulated also by:

1. Providing regular and conscientious criticism of stories and methods.
2. Posting samples of excellent reporting and feature writing from other papers.
3. Holding staff meeting to discuss methods that should be used in following important leads and covering outstanding events.
4. Offering rewards to staff members for good story tips.

Valuable suggestions for improving methods in the business office may be obtained from employes. A suggestion box prominently placed and labeled with an appeal for entries and an announcement their own performance and cooperate in improvements.

Bert Stolpe, while director of promotion and public relations for the Des Moines Register and Tribune, concluded, on the basis of a survey, that American and Canadian newspapers are not getting maximum value from the tens of thousands of minds assembled in their plants. In the great mass employe mind lies the future of newspaper industry, he contends, for things don't just happen-somebody makes them happen. In this tight era of mounting costs, revenue-producing and cost-cutting ideas are of paramount importance. Other industries are making hay with suggestion programmes. Why not newspapers?"

Other helps toward maintaining a high degree of efficiency in the business office are:

1. Give employes the best equipment the business can afford. A machine that can increase the productive capacity of an employe builds enthusiasm and morale.
2. Recognize accuracy as well as speed. In the accounting department it is better to have statements issued correctly

a day late than to have them rushed into the mails without a careful final checking.

3. Pay more for efficiency and less for overtime. In other words, employ efficient help to do a full day's work well rather than low-pay help that will carry you into many hours of overtime.
4. Urge your book-keepers and clerks to complete the work laid out for the day and carry none over for the next day. Each day then has a fresh beginning.
5. Create a congenial but business like atmosphere in the office.

In normal good times the advertising department is expected to produce to the limit. There may be a time, however, when it is necessary to curtail production because of newsprint shortages or mechanical restriction within the plant. Ordinarily it is more difficult for an advertising manager to curtail production than it is to increase it. No advertising manager likes to draw the disfavour of an advertiser by announcing that only so much space is available and no more. The merchant is bound to feel that the newspaper is favouring another advertiser, probably a competitor.

Many types of accounts are handled in the advertising department. There are users of much space; those who run small but consistent day-by-day ads; and those who use an extremely small but amount of copy, probably an inch a week in a business directory, under a special heading, or on the classified page. The salesperson who handles copy for the large-space user naturally produce more revenue than the one who works on very small ads, but at the same time both are important to the newspaper. Small advertisers, if properly handled, may someday be the newspaper's greatest buyers of advertising space.

Incentive plans will raise the capacity standards of any advertising department. To keep its sales force constantly trying to increase the volume of advertising of advertising linage over the preceding year, the Mexico, Mo., Ledger paid each person, every month of the preceding year.

The Wooster Ohio, Record increased its sales of classified display advertising auctioneers and farmers through suggested copy mailed to the "colonels" of that area. "Public sale season will soon be here; have you contacted an auctioneer?" read one of the suggested ads. "If you are planning a spring sale, book it now for a choice of date." Another provided space for the auctioneer's picture under the heading, "More Dollars, No Worries! Auction sales Are My Business." This not only brought advertising from the auctioneers but it also recalled the Record to farmers when it came time for them to advertise their auction sales.

Production standards in the advertising department may be raised by:

1. Establishing goals to be reached within a limited time.
2. Planning special advertising campaigns for single firms on a communitywide basis.
3. Encouraging repeat selling.
4. Requiring sales personnel to submit reports showing the number of firms served, the number of calls made, and the volume of advertising obtained.
5. Checking other newspapers for ideas.
6. Helping sales personnel to become better acquainted with their community and the possibilities for developing new accounts.
7. Stepping up newspaper promotion.

The circulation department has different classes of clientele to deal with which require varied approaches in presenting the newspaper's merits. More time per prospect is necessary for selling subscriptions in rural areas than for those in densely populated urban sections. Soliciting is more successful in the fall than in the spring. People di more reading in the winter, when they are indoors, than in the summer, when they are busy with outdoor work and pleasure. The amount of promotion behind a salesperson also helps to determine the number of subscribers added.

The number of new subscriptions that can be obtained on a route does not depend altogether on the personality and sales ability of the carrier. It is also determined by the time available to devote to selling and by the inducements offered by the circulation department. If obtaining a certain number of subscriptions will qualify for a college scholarship, the carrier may give greater thought to that than to the extra revenue the additional subscription will bring.

The accomplishments of the circulation department depend greatly upon the energy, far-sightedness, and ingenuity of the manager. Ed Roberts, former circulation manager of the Denver, Colo., post, decided that circulation could be increased by efficient carrier service and route management as well as by direct solicitation by carriers and special salespeople. To test the theory, he evolved the following simple plan:

1. A monthly point contest within each district based on the success with which a carrier handled the route and produced orders.
2. A suitably engraved award to the carrier in the entire city who was outstanding for each quarter, presented with the pomp and ceremony appropriate to the importance of such recognition.
3. Insignia indicative of outstanding records established over several months or years.
4. Some form of scholarship to reward outstanding carriers on a annual basis.

Circulation sales personnel will do twice as well in obtaining new subscribers in a given area if they are sent there as part of a well-organized campaign with special incentives and rewards for honest effort and with plenty of promotion behind them.

In a summer campaign to increase rural circulation, one newspaper sent a reporter into the country with a member of the sales staff. Before the salesperson began to talk about the merits of the newspaper, the reporter drew news from practically every family visited about the children, poultry, livestock, or crops. On some weekly newspapers, a man and his wife make up the reporter-sales combination.

The superintendent of the mechanical department knows how much copy a composing machine operator should handle in a day. The way the work is laid out, the encouragement given by the supervisor, and the condition of the plant are important, too. The business manager should have a clear understanding of production possibilities and should confer with the superintendent about conditions in the mechanical department and their effect on production. The abilities of the compositors, press operators, and other employes should be discussed freely with the superintendent; and the poor performers should be worked with to improve their capacities, or they should be weeded out.

The speed with which an advertisement is set depends to a great extent upon its nature and the condition of the copy. If the copy is poorly laid out and instructions are not well outlined of the copy. If the layout calls for unusual arrangement of cuts and type, or if it contains much solid matter and few display lines, more time will required than for a conventional arrangement of type and cuts with much white space. Any simplifications in setting ads will raise capacity standards. Accuracy as well as speed must be sought in composition because careless work means excessive corrections, and that cuts production capacity.

Proper care of presses and paper stock will step up pressroom efficiency. For example:

1. Cleaning the press regularly and oiling it at proper intervals will help to prevent costly stops.
2. Care in adjusting forms on the press increases capacity by permitting top running speed. Even more important, such care prevents accident.
3. A sufficient supply of newsprint for the run, placed conveniently before starting, will prevent capacity-cutting interruptions.
4. Careful handling of newspaper will prevent web breaks on presses using rolls and will prevent stoppages and waste on presses using flat sheets.
5. Good-quality inks will permit capacity speeds and produce clean impressions.

Controlled Budget

The necessity for watching expenses and regulating them so that they comply with income has a definite effect on production. When expenses are rising, it is not always possible to keep income within the same range of increase. Management then is compelled to guard expenses with an austere eye and to handle operations with a firm hand.

In the light of these mounting costs, it is important that the newspaper manager analyze the amount and character of all phases of work in the newspaper office and plant. By so doing, standards can be set that will aid in determining hourly pay rates, size of staff needed for operation of a given plant unit, kind of employes wanted, and standard time required for each operation.

Editorial-news Department : Expenses mount easily in the editorial-news department, where the best efforts should go into producing copy that will give readers what they want and make the newspaper a credit to its community. Publishers have been interested more in improving personnel than in increasing it. Less help of greater efficiency is better than more help of low caliber.

Reporters and others in the news department should understand the publisher's desire to produce a good newspaper as well as the problem of doing so when expenses are bouncing against the ceiling. Persons in other departments of the newspaper organization and even residents of the community, with the proper approach, may be induced to give assistance that will help to hold down production expenses.

Employes in the advertising and circulation departments should be encouraged to be alert for news tips as they go about their regular duties. Residents of the community who really have a "nose for news" often become helpful part-time reporters and are willing to serve at little expense. The agricultural committee of the National Association once suggested that newspaper that could not afford to pay the wages offered college-trained reporters could develop good farm reporters in their home communities, and such home-trained reporters could write successfully for farmers who were looking for better ways to increase their farm incomes-incomes that were to be spent at hometown retail stores.

Other ways of curtailing expenses in the news department are:

1. Challenge each member of the reporting staff to produce a feature story a week. Most reporters are busy, yet they will gladly tackle a special assignment. One summer when a member of the staff was absent most of the time, the managing editor of a small newspaper asked each of those remaining on the job to turn in an additional feature story each week. This proved to be a sort of contest to see which could produce the best feature story, with the result that plenty of local material was produced without employing extra help.
2. Have reporters carry cameras. Many newspaper publishers when hiring journalism school graduates as reporters ask for those who know how to use cameras. A combination reporter- photographer is a valuable staff member because the pictures enliven the stories and this saves the publisher the expense of employing a photographer. Almost any reporter, if supplied a camera, can be trained to use it. There is always the possibility, however, that for a time at least interest in picture taking will be so great that more photos will be taken than the newspaper can use. Photographers and photographer-reporters should learn to select their pictorial matter with care because the camera is valuable when used for pictures of unusual interest but expensive when used for routine shots.
3. Engage district reporters on a pay-per-item basis. Select a news-conscious person in each of the four or five main sections of your city and agree to pay so much for each item written that is termed newsworthy by the city editor. This brings in news at minimum cost from sources not usually touched by regular reporters.
4. Invite persons interested in community history to write articles. Facts of extraordinary community interest never

before revealed may find their way into the columns of your newspaper by this means.

5. Have some member of the staff devote a certain period each day to other newspapers in search of local interest articles. Newspapers from which such articles are taken are complemented when you consider their copy worthy of your columns and they readily grant permission.

The care and attention given to cost studies, receipts, and general expenses by those in the business office help greatly to regulate expenses in other departments. A good way to control costs is to set up a budget. Also, use these economy measures for buying materials, supplies, and services:

1. Centralize the buying authority in one person.
2. Wherever practical get prices from two or more suppliers.
3. Be sure you have "minimums" for each item so that repurchases automatically come up well in advance of the "out-of-supply" date. This avoids rush shipments and permits ample time for proper cost-saving buying.
4. Watch your costs for office forms. Many can be produced on a duplicating machine at nominal cost. The copying machine may cost less than 41,000.
5. Keep purchasing records showing names of suppliers furnishing services or supplies, date and cost of the last order, and annual requirements.

The business office must watch expenses and effect economies in other departments as well as in its own. It knows that contemplated expenditures must be consistent with the newspaper's financial ability. Administrative department conferences may result in a change in the newspaper's page width and column sizes, in elimination of the optical scanner step in computerized composition, or in the sale of company-owned trucks to be replaced rented delivery cars.

Not many advertising departments give serious , consideration to production costs; their main goal is volume, and often it is volume at any cost Expense regulation, however, should be applied in this department as in all other. Consideration might well be given to the cost of producing every ad, from the two-line local to full-page display.

Some small advertising accounts require so much time and attention that they cost more than they bring in. Some of that cost is unnecessary. Salespeople who have been handling accounts on a personal basis may be do just as well by telephone.

The classified advertising department's success at selling by telephone should represent a challenge to those who sell display advertising. The manager of a small daily newspaper selected one of the best phone saleswomen in the classified advertising department to use the telephone a few weeks before Christmas to see how many small display Christmas greetings ads she could sell. She made a list of prospects, then clipped from the ad service all the Christmas greetings material she could find. She laid out hundreds of small ads, mostly 2 columns by 3 inches, using her own judgment as to what each prospect might be willing to buy. With the copy before her she called each prospect, read the copy planned, gave the cost, and in nine cases out of ten landed the order. She was paid a commission of 10 percent above her regular salary. For two weeks she more than doubled her income and at the same time sold more display advertising at less cost than many of the regular sales staff.

Other means of reducing expenses in the advertising department:

1. Eliminate some of the free service given to general advertisers in promoting advertised products. This is a service feature of the advertising department that, in connection with most accounts, may be abridged or expanded without seriously affecting results.
2. Insist on customers having their copy ready when the advertising representative calls. Many valuable moments, for which the publisher pays well, are lost when the representative is required to cool his heels while the merchant makes up his mind about copy to be used.

3. Insofar as possible have merchants prepare their own advertising copy. Many newspaper advertising departments have increased department expenses and spoiled advertisers by preparing all copy for them.
4. Urge advertising copywriters to avoid use of fancy composition that requires extra time in setting.
5. Set monthly linage goals for advertising sales staff and pay bonuses to those who exceed. This speeds up selling and increases volume.

Newspaper delivery operations sometime may be combined to provide more satisfactory service and at the same time reduce delivery costs. The Janesville, Wis., Gazette delivers papers to farmer subscribers from trucks that take papers to carriers in country towns. It delivers 2,000 papers to rural residents, while covering 900 miles a day at a cost of 15 cents a mile. Considering the fact that so many farmers receive delivery from a truck used to convey bundles to dealers and distant carriers, a fair portion of the cost is chargeable to delivering to farmers.

At one time the Independence, to Examiner had an arrangement with carriers of the Kansas City, Star whereby they delivered the Examiner while delivering the Star. This was done at far less expense for the Examiner than if the paper maintained its own trucks, and it provided additional revenue for Star carriers.

The efficiency of a circulation department may be increased and expenses may be reduced also:

1. By inducing rural correspondents to sell subscriptions. Many weekly and small daily papers pay a commission to correspondents for subscription collections in their area. One newspaper puts on an annual subscription contest with its correspondents, offering prizes or boriqaes to those obtaining the greatest number of subscriptions. This is in addition to the regular commission paid on subscription collections. Newspapers have found this to be an effective and economical way of building circulation at a reasonable cost.

2. By employing a man and wife as a manager team for the circulation department. With the man as manager and his wife a assistant manager, a unified salary more than takes care of family expenses. Furthermore, the manager is free for house-to-house solicitation, knowing that his wife will take care of details in the office. This arrangement work out well for the Columbia, Mo., Missourian, where Mr. and Mrs. Jack Carr were in charge of the circulation department, and at the Willows, Calif, Daily Journal where Mr. and Mrs. Oscar F. DeSoto directed circulation.
3. By using a simplified from of bookkeeping for the circulation department. The more details to be watched the more opportunities there are for errors.
4. By watching all accounts and seeing that payments are made promptly overdue accounts are hard to collect and often are never collected.
5. By closely watching the pressrun each day and the number of paper sold and delivered. Newsprint is costly and may be wasted by overruns.

The mechanical department superintendent often has opportunities to reduce expenses by more careful distribution of work and by observing the way employes perform at the machines, at the makeup tables, or in the pressroom. Attention to minor details sometimes results in savings.

The production manager of the Gannet newspapers says that considerable extra cost in a great many pressroom is due to the fact that papers changing in size so rapidly. The trouble begins in the advertising department. Too often the people there do not seem to realize that by adding two pages they increase the number of employes needs in the pressroom by two or three, who a great many times are working at over times rates. Sometimes it even increases the number in the mailroom.

For many years the Ottawa, Ont., Citizen relied on outside help for all its electrical work, care of machinery, and minor repairs; and costs ran high. Finally when a new building was erected and a new press installed, a full-time position was given to the electrician who installed wiring for the new building. Since the electrician also had some knowledge of welding and machine shop practice, the publishing company set up a modest machine shop with a drill press, are welding set, grinder, and other small power tools. The savings on minor repair jobs more than covered the expenses of this full-time operation.

Overhead Expenses

Overhead expenses in the mechanical departments of newspapers may be cut down in other ways:

1. By having a superintendent who knows enough about the machinery to make minor repairs.
2. By making negatives or plates for other newspapers and business firms. The rental cost of an offset camera of a platemaker is sometimes divided between several newspapers receiving material from the same machine.
3. By hiring a helper in the composing room to do the office janitor work, thereby combining two jobs in one.
4. By having compositors double as press operators. This is a satisfactory arrangement in the plants of small dailies but could not be worked out in large unionized shops.
5. By arranging working hours in 35-hour or 40-hour shifts to avoid overtime hours.

Many other factors-postage; width of newsprint roll; cost and availability of paper, ink, film, and other materials; general economic conditions; unpredictable personnel problem-will have a bearing on production. Among the constant factors today, it may be said that the degree of modernization of technology will probably have a more direct effect on flow of work, saving of valuable time, capacity potentials, and regulation of expenses than any other single influence over which management may have control.

4

Book Production

When we hold a book in our hands we seldom think of the process, or processes, it has been through before coining into our hands. Whether it is a text book, novel, a legal book, a newspaper or magazine, a letterhead or business card, product literature or a circular, or any of a thousand different kinds of printed matter, they all go through some or the entire process of printing. As recently as the last century, the making of a book was a laborious process which could last several months.

With the advances in technology in this century as well as the increase in literacy, the number of publications has increased phenomenally. In India alone there are more than 25,000 different publications and which figure puts India in fifth place. India also has more than 100,000 printing presses.

Origin and History

We do not know when man first began to write. One can imagine that messages were scratched into the soil or blazes were made on rocks or trees, tens of thousands of years ago. In the beginning of recorded history, the Phoenicians and the Sumerians, used a sharp instrument to make impressions in a soft clay tablet, which was then baked hard. The Egyptians and, later the Romans and the Greeks, chiseled characters into stone tablets. The oldest papyrus rolls date from about 3500 B.C. and are the first form of paper as we know it today. Writing on papyrus was done using reed pens. Red ink was derived from iron oxide and the black from lamp black. Paper was actually invented in China in the second century AD. It took almost a thousand years to migrate to Europe and the paper mill was built in Italy in 1270 AD.

Books began to take the place of parchment rolls around the fourth century AD. They had to be laboriously written out by hand. The centers of learning were concentrated in the various monasteries and with the Royal houses in Europe and the monks had to write or copy out the books manually with pen and ink. Copies of a book were few and far between.

The first reproductions made by man were from images carved on flat stone. These were intaglio, i.e. indented, representations. An inky substance was deposited in the indentations and then transferred onto paper.

Around the ninth century AD, raised impressions on wooden blocks was used in China. In this period metal plates were engraved and used for reproduction as well. The engravers at this time were goldsmiths. As the demand for books grew, it became obvious that a better method of printing was required.

First Printing Press : It was the invention of movable type which made such printing possible. In the middle of the fifteenth century, Johann Gutenberg invented individual type which was used for many centuries after and is still used today for the hand setting of composed material. Gutenberg cast individual characters in a brass or copper mould, in which a character of the alphabet had been punched. The punch was created manually by drawing a character in reverse on the face of a hard steel block and carving out the area around the character. The resulting cast of an individual alphabet came to be known as type. These castings were made for the entire alphabet and in different sizes as well. He then placed the characters together to form words and a complete line of text, clamped the type together in a metal frame, applied ink to the raised surface of the characters and fixed the frame to a wooden wine press. A wine press consists of a wooden screw with a handle on top and a flat plate at the bottom, within a frame fixed over a flat bed. When it was pressed down onto a sheet of paper, the ink left an impression much like a common office rubber stamp. In this way, he could set an entire page at a time and make several copies in less time than it would take to write out one page. This process came to be known as the setting of type or, in other words, typesetting. Over the next four centuries, the role of the publisher switched from churches, governments, royal families and universities to the Printer. The printer did his own type casting, his own typesetting and printed and bound his own books. The Press, as it was usually called, acted as the publisher and distributor. Minor improvements were made to this basic process the press was mechanized using the steam engine and later electric motors. This kind of press was known as the Letterpress.

The typesetting and printing functions remained with the publisher, and under his control, as is still the case today with certain newspapers, for example. However, there developed a separation between the writer and the printer, the type designer and foundry and the typesetter.

Typewriter : Sometime in the eighteenth century, a machine was invented which provided a method of writing more legible than the pen-the typewriter. Soon thereafter, the use of carbon paper as well as stencils and duplicating machines made it possible for small offices to take over their own internal publishing requirements. Mark Twain was among the first to purchase a typewriter. The keyboard was arranged as logically as possible, not based on the efficiency from the standpoint of the operator, but from the viewpoint of the mechanics of the machine, which kept jamming frequently due to collision of the keys. The most commonly used "QWERTY" keyboard is, in fact, very inefficient from the operator's standpoint.

Typesetting Machines : From the time of Gutenberg till Mergenthaler's Linotype or Lanston's Monotype linecasting machines, there was no practical way to set type by machine. The Linotype (line of Type), introduced in 1880, had a keyboard and the operator typed the text on the keyboard which put together a series of moulds of the characters typed, called matrices, and a molten alloy of lead was poured into the mould forming a complete line of text. This single unit was delivered to the galley all ready to go into the form. The complete line as a single unit was less likely to get jumbled up.

At about the same time another invention was getting developed photography, which was to have a big impact on typesetting. The printing presses were also being improved with automatic sheet feeding of the paper. Drawings and photographs could now be printed by making a block.

Offset Printing : By the mid twentieth century, a shift had already occurred from Letterpress to Offset printing, at least in Europe and North America. Letterpress requires printing to be done on a flat bed causing it to be much slower than offset, which uses a rotary drum. While Letterpress requires printing from raised type, the offset process requires exposure of the plate from a photographic negative or positive, and therefore, the use of raised type for typesetting became a liability.

To make an offset plate, the process was, and is, to place a photo negative on a sheet of metal which had been sensitized with a light sensitive chemical and exposed to light. The metal sheet was then washed with a mild acid and the unexposed area got etched, leaving the dark areas of the photograph slightly raised. When ink was applied with a roller, only the raised portions received the ink, which could then be transferred onto the paper.

Phototypesetting Machines : The need for a photocomposition device became readily apparent. In the 40's, another process was developed to expose type directly onto a roll of film. The First Generation Phototypesetters used the same mechanical principles as was used in the Hot metal linecasting machines. Instead of the moulds for the hot metal, the phototypesetter used a negative film of the characters. Using a lens, a beam of light was passed through the negative and onto Silver Bromide-photographic paper. The Second Generation Phototypesetters switched from a film negative matrix to a disk, which was essentially a photographic negative of the characters of the alphabet arranged in a circular form. The film was then moved laterally by the space of one character and the disk was spun to align the next character and the light was beamed through to the paper. This was repeated until the entire page or column was exposed. The exposed film was then processed in a dark room and resulted in the positive, which could then be used to make a plate for printing.

Digital Typesetter : The First Generation Photo typesetters were adapted from hot metal models and worked as nearly as possible on the basis of the same principles. A Second Generation machine was one which was especially conceived and designed to set type by photo-mechanical means. Both machines were Typesetters, i.e., both generation machines set type and were not capable of graphics. A Third Generation Typesetter is one which does not expose type directly from photographic masters but reproduces them electronically on the face of a CRT, a Cathode Ray Tube. The images thus created are in turn photographed (either the same size or enlarged or reduced by using lenses) directly from the screen. Each page was reduced to a number of pixels (picture elements) and the resultant resolution was indicated as Dots Per Inch (DPI). The resolution of these first of the Third Generation Typesetters ranged from 300 to 900 DPI and the prices were upwards of US$ 200,000. However, there were some significant advantages of these digital typesetters-(a) the image on the screen can be manipulated electronically in a number of interesting ways; (b) the setting speed was much faster; (c) there were fewer mechanical parts which present maintenance and reliability problems and (d) one was not restricted to setting images of alphabets only; the CRT was capable of setting graphics.

The Laser : The Laser was invented in the sixties and has also been applied to Typesetting technology. The laser is capable of generating a very fine and intense beam of light. It is possible to interrupt this source so that the light emissions can be pulsed; it is also possible to deflect this beam of light from a mirror surface. These Fourth Generation Photo typesetters used laser technology to expose film or paper and worked in a raster scan mode. In Raster Image Processing, instead of individual characters being laid down, a horizontal slice of an entire page is exposed at a time. Using a process similar to photocopiers, laser printers, which could print directly on plain paper, were built but at a very high cost of over US$ 150,000.

The principle of the Laser printer is explained here. The laser printer consists of a photosensitive drum which is sensitive to light. The drum is given a positive charge at one point. As the drum rotates, the laser beam "writes" the black portions onto the drum at another point negating the positive charge. As the drum rotates further, it passes positively charged toner particles which are attracted to the negatively charged parts of the drum at a third point. The plain paper/film is given a negative charge, which attracts the toner off the drum, and adheres to the paper at still another point. The paper and toner are processed finally by passing through a fusor, which applies heat (at 200° C) and pressure to the toner and fuses it to the paper.

The Computers : Computers had made an impact on the world soon after the Second World War, but it was not until the seventies that computer technology was brought within the grasp of the common man. Several companies had started manufacturing Personal Computers in the mid seventies including Commodore, Tandy and Apple. Even IBM, the mainframe manufacturer, launched its PC in 1981. As prices dropped over the years, the use of PC's grew till, today, there are an estimated 80 million installed worldwide. With the advent of the PC, software companies began to write composition software on PC's.

Video Terminals : The video terminal represents the single most important development in the field of computerized page composition. Earlier, the process of composition was "blind" the operator of a hot metal typesetter could not immediately see what he had typeset. The video terminal gave us our first window into this process. More importantly, we now have the opportunity to review and change and also to see the effect of that change. Most terminals have been designed for text processing but since 1984, with the launch of the Macintosh, the graphic arts industry had a terminal which could be used not only for text processing but for all kinds of art as well. WYSIWYG, What You See Is What You Get, was the next step. One could see on the screen the exact layout including graphics, before giving the command to get a hard copy. Video terminals came to be 'Known as front end terminals.

Composition Software

The main categories of composition software have to do with the following:

Justification : which is a broad term for arranging text horizontally across a page.

Hyphenation : which is a sub-set of justification, concerned exclusively with how words should be divided (split), when necessary, in order to achieve better justification.

Pagination : a method of composing text both horizontally and vertically, so that text is properly spaced out to fill a page and appropriately divided into pages.

Editing and Corrections : directed to the elimination of input errors or to resolve problems created during the pagination/ layout process or to introduce changes by the author.

Graphics : a very broad term for the input, creation and subsequent editing of non-textual matter, like drawings, photographs, charts, etc.

Networking & Communications : required especially where more than one terminal is used or where terminals of different types are used or when the terminals are installed at different geographical locations.

Operating and File Management Systems : Vital supporting programs

The above categories may or may not be incorporated into one software program. As video terminal systems become more common and more useful and because the editing and correction work may take place at various stages of the composition process, it makes sense to seggregate the applications into separate modules rather than to have one large unmanageable program.

Modern Devices

With Terminals becoming more and more common, there had to be a way of communicating between a number of terminals connected to the same typesetter. Different users, the author, editor, artist or illustrator and the composer, needed to exchange files without having to take a hard copy or exchange floppy disks. The solution was to "network" the terminals so that files could be transferred over wires electronically, a Local Area Network (LAN). Also, with Wide Area Network, the author need not be in the same location nor in the same city, even. Files of text or graphics could be communicated over ordinary telephone lines to remote locations for editing, proofing or composing. Different kinds of terminals also had to communicate with each other. Files formatted under one system had to be "understood" by another system.

Latest Trends

The publishing industry is coming of age. With electronics progress in the last decade, publishing has come a long way from what it was a century ago. It has, however come full circle in the sense that during Gutenberg's time, the functions of the typesetter, printer and publisher were all under one roof. Later, these functions separated and today are coming together again. By 1983, Tom Hagan, president of CAMEX reported: "In the 1950's and 60's the thrust of development in pre-press systems was to 'get the Lead out'. In the 80's it will be to 'get the Silver out'. We are now striving to eliminate the mechanicals and paste-ups as part of the printing and publishing process... I cannot imagine a more exciting time to be involved in this industry." Publishing systems, today, could be summarized as requiring some or all of the following components:

Front End Terminal

A compact personal computer

Standard keyboard layout

Built-in mouse or other entry system

Output Device

Plain paper output

Fast output of both text & graphics

Storage Media

Large capacity

Scanner

To input graphics or text

Black & white or colour

Suitable Software

"A document printed on a laser printer is acceptable as camera-ready-copy, a printing term meaning that printing plates can be made from photographs of laser printed pages ... using a laser printer to produce camera-ready copy eliminates the long and laborious steps of typing and formatting your document on a photo typesetting machine, proofing it and making corrections, composing it into pages, and proofing it again before printing plates are made. Using the copy produced on the laser printer, the printer need only create printing plates of the copy, and print as many copies of the publication as needed."

Film Paper Processor : In a traditional setter, the image is set on a sensitized medium, such as paper or film. After which the exposed film is passed through a film paper processor. "Film processing machines are designed to carry the exposed film through a series of baths in which the film is developed, stopped, fixed, washed and dried in controlled conditions."

Typesetter Comparison

	Photo-Mech	*CRT*	*Lasersetters*	*Apple Laser Photo Type setters*
Font Setting	On film	Floppy Resident	Floppy/ Resident	Floppy
Style Type	Mechanical	Electronic	Electronic	Electronic
Optical System	Flash Tube/ Lens/Mirror	CRT/Lens/ Optic Fibre	Laser/Mirror	Laser/Mirror
Exposure by	Light Non-coherent	Light Non-coherent	Light coherent	Light coherent
On	Permanent Sensitised coating	Permanent Sensitised coating	Permanent Sensitised coating	Renewable Photo Sensitised coating
Imaging	Internal	Internal	Internal	Internal
Fixing	External Wet Chemical Process Removal of Resin	External Wet Chemical Process Removal of Resin	External Wet Chemical Process Removal of Resin	Integral Dry Thermo Process Deposition of Resin
Output	Positives on Paper/ Film	Positives on Paper/ Film	Positives on Paper/ Film	Positives on Paper/ Film
Master	Film Negative	Film Negative	Positive	Positive
Photo ready			Negative	Negative

In plain paper laser setters, the film paper processor is built in. Since these setters use a dry process of depositing toner on plain paper, the processing consists of the application of pressure and heat to fuse the toner to the paper. The result is a fast output of the finished master without requiring the exposed film to go through the time consuming process described above.

5

Offset Printing System

Among the metals used for offset plates, zinc is a bluish white metal, heavier than aluminium, extracted from natural ores, chiefly zinc blende and carbonate calamine, melts at 800° F (301° C) and is soluble in hydrochloric, nitric and sulphuric acids. Zinc plates are melted down, cast into suitable sizes, passed between heavy rolls and transformed into sheets.

With specific gravity of 7. 18 when rolled and tensile strength of 10 tons per square inch parallel to grain and 3 tons per square inch across grain, zinc stands about 13 foldings crosswise and 6 foldings in the direction of rolling and stretches more than aluminium. When etched with muriatic acid, it becomes water repellant. In damp atmosphere, it becomes coated with basic carbonate.

Zinc is more grease receptive which makes it easier to add work with tuche emulsified ink with pen or brush but difficult to correct without leaving a tint.

Aluminium occurs combined with oxygen and associated with iron oxide in mineral bauxite. In its extraction by electricity, bauxite is decomposed by previously mixing it with cryolite, into oxygen and aluminium. It is a white metal capable of being polished, malleable and ductile with great tensile strength, high thermal and electrical conductivity, softer when rolled, of 2.6 specific gravity and melts at 1252° F (675° C).

Various Plates

Aluminium plates of 80% aluminium and 20% iron for denting are used in offset plate making. Rolled plate has yield strength of 2 tons per square inch and ultimate tensile strength of 2½ tons per square inch. Offset plates are made in rolling mill, hardened and reduced to required thickness by cold rolling. Crystal structure of aluminium is closer and finer, gives fine grain surface with better hold for water, but shorter in life than zinc. Aluminium takes slightly sharper and deeper grain than zinc and due to relative hardness, is capable of giving longer impressions.

Aluminium plate weighs less than half as zinc and less cumbersome to handle but must be handled carefully to prevent kinking which cannot flatten. Aluminium being whiter and brighter makes the image areas visible. But its surface is quickly covered by oxide film on exposure to air.

While nitric acid has no effect, sulphuric and hydrochloric acids dissolve aluminium, slowly, and rapidly when hot. Aluminium dissolves rapidly in caustic soda and caustic potash solutions with the evolution of hydrogen and formation of alkali-aluminate.

Zinc Plate : Thickness of zinc and aluminium plates for surface and deep-etch process varies with the press size from 0.009 to 0. 12 inch for demy to 0.25 inch for 46 x 72 inches size machine. Plates should be of required gauge as mentioned in operation manuals of offset machines, tolerance, at least one side free from scale, scratches and dent. If plate is buckled, it will not lie flat on vacuum frame or on press cylinder and registration in colour work will be affected. Gauge tolerance for smaller size plate is + or 0.0005 inch and for larger size plate or 0.001 inch. Plates should have good resistance to abrasive and dimensionally stable.

Zinc		*Aluminium*		
	Annealed sheets	*Lithographic plates*	*Annealed sheets*	*Lithographic plates*
Tensile strength (lbs per sq. in.)	Below 10000	22000	13000	22000
Elongation %	0	12-15	30-33	3-4
Number of 90° bends to break	—	20-30	—	5-7

Composition of litho/offset plates: Zinc 99%, lead cadmium, iron 1%. Aluminium 99%, silicon, manganese and iron 1%.

Mechanical properties of zinc and aluminium are:

Image areas of offset plates are olephilic or grease attracted and non-image areas hydrophilic or water loving. Metal forming the image area is selected for its ability to accept ink while metal forming non-image areas is selected for ease in moistening and its ability to be desensitized to ink.

Copper Plate : Copper in combination with oxygen and sulphur is found in copper pyrites or chalcopyrite and malachites or cupric carbonate. It is a lustrous metal with pinkish brown colour, malleable and tough and is a good conductor of heat and electricity. It has 8.95 specific gravity, melts at 1976° F (1080° C), slowly tarnished in air acquiring dull reddish colour but due to moisture becomes coated with green deposit called verdigris. Copper is readily dissolved by nitric acid but slowly affected by hydrochloric or sulphuric acids. Ammonia dissolves copper in the presence of air. It is softened by heating to dull red heat.

Multimetal plates when compared to zinc have advantages like saving of graining time, uniform plate quality, lesser stoppages on printing machines, etc. They have smooth surface to obtain better reproduction of tonal values and point sharpness. Compared to zinc, bi-metal foil has enhanced number of tonal values to 16. Damping is 1/4 that of grained zinc plate due to separation of water and ink carrying metals.

With proper care, it is possible to print 10 to 20 lakhs impressions. However, bi-metal plates are not economical for short and medium run but suitable for newspapers in multicolours. Bi-metal plate consists of two metals one having preferential affinity for ink, the other for water.

Bi-metal Plate : In bi-metal plates copper is common for image areas. Aluminium, stainless steel and chromium are chosen for non-image areas because these accept water in preference to greasy ink. When copper and chromium are used together they are usually electroplated on zinc and steel plates, called polymetal plates. Bi-metal plates with zinc, iron or aluminium base are electroplated on one side first with copper and then with chromium, layers being thin, copper being 0.0000 1 to 0.00 1 inch thick and chromium being 0.00005 inch thick. Chromium layer has a dull, matte appearance to retain moisture while printing. Electro-chemical voltage series of metals are decisive for their selection. Ink carrying metal acts positive to hydrogen electrode.

In voltage series, it stands to the right of hydrogen whereas water carrying component of plate consists of a metal standing to the left of hydrogen and acting negatively to hydrogen electrode. Ink carrying metal remaining copper, by electroplating, chromium coat acting as water carrying constituent is applied to copper layer. Other water carriers may be aluminium, nickel or steel.

Bi-metal plates may be grained or ungrained. To make grained bi-metal plates, base plates are first grained and electroplated with copper and chromium. Electrolysis is adopted to coat layers of copper and chromium, an oxide layer on aluminium plate surface called anodising and electrolytic graining.

Anodising is a means of electrolytically producing film of

aluminium oxide of controlled thickness on surface which is highly water receptive and resistant to chemical action and abrasion on the press. Anodised plates, though used mainly for deep-etch process, are also used on wipe-on and pre-sensitised plates, resisting corrosion and oxidation.

Images and Non-image Metal : Possible types of bi-metal plates are electroplate, an image metal on a plate of non-image metal forming an acid resistant positive image on the layer of image metal, etch away the image metal from all areas except image areas and remove acid resist from the image area, and electroplate a non-image metal on a plate of an image metal or on a plate which carries surface layer of image metal, forming a stencil or negative image by acid resistant coating on the layer on non-image metal, etch away non-image metal to lay bare the image metal in positive image areas removing protective stencil from non-image areas.

Base	*Non-image metal*	*Image metal*
Stainless steel	Stainless steel	Copper
Aluminium	Aluminium	Copper
Plastic	Aluminium	Copper
Mild steel	Lead	Copper
Mild steel	Chromium	Copper
Aluminium	Chromium	Copper

Bi-metal foil is supplied gummed and packed in cardboard roll, on opening they are checked for creases and ruptures, cut to required sizes, gum washed in water basin before use.

Two metals may be carried on a third to make tri-metal plate. Besides affinity for grease or water other considerations that have a bearing on choice of metals include suitability of metal to form top layer for electro-deposition on lower layer. Top metal should allow suitable processing technique to be used and it should be possible to dissolve top metal without affecting lower one.

Tri-metal or polymetal plates are made from base plate of zinc, iron or aluminium; an electroplated layer of copper on base plate; electroplated layer of chromium, i.e. non-image metal over copper, only layers of copper and chromium being affected by plate making and in printing.

Machines for Reuse

It came to pass that many dealers of used graphic arts equipment practised their skills, spreading joy and goodness in the oversized pages of the most widely-read and most well-respected paper for graphic arts readers.

And so many of them spoke of their minds and their hearts to the classified ad manager of this publication, and they told him secrets of their experiences in dealings of the heavy iron; and he listened.

And in the fourth month of the ninth year of the ninth decade of the twentieth century of the modem era, there was produced a very wonderful issue of this most-revered paper, and it was called the "Used Equipment Roundup".

Thus it was that the classified ad manager gathered to himself their notes and records of such secrets as he had collected over time from these wise and seasoned veterans of the trade.

And he shifted through them, and pored over them and digested them, and drank much of the bitter fruits in order to understand them the better, and meditated upon these pearls of wisdom at length.

And when he could stand no more, he distilled them into words, and his head swam with the richness of it, and he began for all who would read of it.

1. No rule on buying used equipment is more important than this one.

If you haven't had business dealings with the seller personally, ask for references. Any reputable dealer will be happy to supply you with a list of satisfied customers.

If you buy through a private sale, you may think you're getting a really "hot deal". On the other hand, you may just get burned.

Any used equipment dealer will tell you: his reputation is his most important asset. Take advantage of this fact and get the goods on your man before the goods go on your van.

2. The worst thing you can do is to buy equipment that is just sufficient to handle your present needs (unless you have no plans to grow).

If in six months you find your sales have outgrown your machinery, you'll be faced with taking a cash loss on the disposal of your present equipment and a loss in production time when you set up its replacement.

Plan carefully for the short term and the long term. Be sure the equipment you're getting today will be compatible with whatever you intend to add down the road.

3. Be prepared to travel, if necessary, to see equipment in operation. This, of course, goes in spades for major piece.

   Don't take the seller's word for it that the machine runs perfectly" or "just like new".

If you don't feel you have adequate knowledge with regard to the purchase, take along an expert to check the machine's performance. If you have to, pay a qualified independent serviceman or experienced operator-mechanic to go along with you when you make your inspection.

Whatever you do, don't rely on a "friend who used to be in the business" or a brother-in-law who once worked for a printer, or the like.

4. This is a perfectly obvious, straight-forward rule-and one that is overlooked almost every day.

   Before you buy, ask yourself: will this machine fit through my door? Up the stairs? Down the stairs?

If your shop is on the second floor, will you have to hoist it up the side of the building to get it in? Then what?

If you're in the basement, can you get it down there without having to dig a special tunnel for it?

Will the floor hold it safely?

Will you have to completely disassemble it? Who's going to pay for the expense of moving it if it turns out it won't go in?

If you don't manage to get it in, will there be enough room left to run it without continually hitting or falling over something?

Think ahead. It may save you a barrel of aggravation.

5. Make sure your available power source is compatible with the machine you're buying.

Many paper cutters and larger presses require 550 volt or 220 volt three-phase power. If you don't have three-phase hydro in your building, you may have a problem. It may be very expensive to install it; it may even be impossible.

If your building does have three-phase hydro, you will still have to install a small transformer. This however, should not present a major difficulty.

Whatever you do, don't confuse 220 volts one-phase (domestic hydro) with 220 volts three-phase (industrial hydro).

6. Remember that "reconditioned", "refurbished" and "rebuilt" are sometimes used interchangeably.

Find out exactly what has been done to the machine, and by whom. Ask a lot of questions. If the answers aren't forthcoming, or seem vague or noncommittal, pass on the deal. Too often "reconditioned" machines are sold with nothing more elaborate than a fresh paint job.

Inspect your potential purchase inside and out before you make a commitment.

7. Every machine, no matter how well it runs when you first get it, is destined to need service and/or replacement parts sooner or later.

When it does, will you be able to find a reliable technician to work on it? If you do, will he be able to get the parts he needs without waiting weeks or months for them? If it is an obsolete model, parts may not be available at all.

Bargains can sometimes be had on machines with unfamiliar names-but beware if you need service.

If, like most people, you can't afford lengthy down time, stick to equipment made by manufacturers with established networks of service and parts suppliers. When it breaks down in the middle of your busiest time, you'll be glad you did.

8. If delivery and installation is not included in the price, you will have to pay movers, carpenters, electricians, etc., out of your pocket. Have you figured this into your calculations?

In addition, if the equipment you are buying is unfamiliar and/or complicated, is the seller going to provide any kind of training?

If not, you may find the true cost of the equipment is a great deal more than you anticipated after you add the extra time it will take for an operator to learn by himself how to run it properly and the productivity you lose in the process.

9. "The best laid plans of mice and men", as they say, can go awry.

What if, after all your careful consideration, the machine doesn't perform up to your expectations, or your needs change faster than you expected? Will the seller take back the machine? If so, on what terms?

This is an important point to establish. In the case of a private sale, you will have to dispose of the equipment yourself. Some dealers, however, offer "trade up" or "trade-back" programs with varying terms and conditions.

10. Whatever "guarantees" or "warranties" are included by the dealer, make sure you have them in writing.

    There's nothing worse than going back sometime later with "I thought you said..."

At the same time, you should satisfy yourself that the seller is in a position to give up to his promise.

6

Screen Printing

It is perhaps seldom realized that the twentieth century is not so much the 'atomic' age as the age of mass communication better, faster, more efficient international communication; an age of which the atomic race is only one aspect.

'Visual communication', a term coined only recently, embraces the graphic and typographic arts.

Since the second world war the output and standard of printing have grown to an extent no one could have possibly anticipated.

This tremendous upsurge has affected even remote and obscure processes of printing and graphic reproduction. Fifteen years ago screen printing was not a major printing process; it has now emerged from comparative absurdity to acceptance as the fourth basic method of printing stencilling. From a handicraft first introduced at the turn of this century, screen process printing has developed into a mechanized industry.

The concept of a crude process used only for short runs is giving way to an appreciation of the special characteristics, effects and advantages of screen printing; new and unexpected applications in contemporary printing and graphic technology are being researched and applied almost daily.

Specialized industrial applications of the process, as for example in textile, ceramics and wallpaper, are being intensively developed in many fields hitherto unfamiliar to the letterpress, lithographic and intaglio printer.

Screen printing is essentially stencilling, through a sieve consisting of a tightly stretched fabric. A stencil is defined by the Concise Oxford Dictionary as a 'thin plate of metal etc. in which pattern (interrupted when necessary by a thin bar of the material left to prevent pieces from falling out); is cut out.' 'Stencilling, the COD goes on to say, is to produce (pattern) on surface; ornament (surface) with patterns; by brushing paint etc. over stencil plate laid on the surface. Hence stenciller .... (etomceler sparkle, cover with stars)'.

This is an excellent summing up of the most obvious and important characteristic of screen printing, with the emphasis on shape, ornament, brightness, sparkle and paint quality. Screen printing can be defined in exact terms as: selectively blocking out a sieve-like screen fabric, silk, metal or synthetic, and forcing a viscous ink through the mesh openings by means of a squeegee rubber on to a flat, curved or irregular surface of paper, metal, glass etc. which has been placed in register on a base board, table or special device.

The term silk screen printing is therefore inadequate and inaccurate; in addition to silk bolting cloth, other materials such as stainless steel, nylon and terylene are in constant use today. In Western Europe the term serigraphy is current, derived from drawing on silk (Latin-sericus, Greek-graphein) on the analogy of lithography.

As it is often difficult to distinguish a screen from a lithographic print, it is important to consider the special characteristics of screen printing. It is essential for the printer, print buyer and designer to know and recognise these particular qualities in order to realise their full potential.

The stencilled character of screen printing is the decisive factor throughout as it results in a relatively thick ink film, with depth of hue, and variable covering power, depending on the type of ink; screen prints have a certain graphic solidity. Screen printed half-tones are usually limited to between 45-65 screen; on examination they reveal a characteristic heaviness in the shadow areas and rather forced highlights, with a narrow range of middle tones. Type-matter down to eight point can be printed satisfactorily even during long runs, provided a letter design suitable for reproduction by screen printing is chosen and that the printer knows his job.

The Equipment

The basic printing equipment consists of a frame carrying a screen and stencil. This gives the printer maximum freedom with flexibility in stencilling without limitations on size, surface, rigidity or section of the material. It allows the regulation of the ink film thickness and the use of a very wide range of inks from mat to glossy, transparent and opaque; colour changes are quickly made, an attribute which, for instance, has helped to establish the process in textile printing.

The printing frame, a relatively simple and cheap item of equipment, can be easily made to a specific size. This simplicity of equipment and the easily acquired basic operation of squeegeeing have led to the mushrooming of many backroom printers; as a fast turnover is essential for their survival, quality, performance and prestige of the process have consequently suffered. But it has also enabled graphic artists to express themselves more freely, and directly than is possible with traditional autographic processes and as a result screen printing design has been greatly enriched. The preparation of stencils is faster and simpler than litho plate or letter press engraving and the materials are cheaper.

Setting up for manual or machine printing is not elaborate; thus giving the screen printed job a fast start. Printing speeds are slow compared with other process, especially slow with manual printing; hand production ranging from 100-400 iph according to the type and size of the job. Nevertheless, runs of 10,000 are not uncommon. The mechanization of screen printing has resulted in a considerable speeding up with top speeds in the region of 3,500 iph while average speeds of 1,000 iph have helped in maintaining consistent quality.

Because of the special formulation and the thickness of the ink layer, screen process prints cannot be stacked immediately after printing. Ink drying therefore is a major factor in slowing down production and causing bottlenecks. Even the most expensive and elaborate drying equipment has not yet succeeded in solving this problem.

Due to the relatively brittle nature of stencil materials they are more likely to break down during long runs than metal blocks or plates; register depends on a number of factors such as humidity, which are difficult to control. These are limitations to be carefully considered. A less important but often mentioned aspect is the 'mess' and smell associated with screen process printing. The former limitation can be avoided by organization and craftsmanship, the latter by improvements in ink formulation and the introduction of proper ventillation and air conditioning.

The Printing

The earliest examples of these are signs and fabrics. Today there are few aspects of modern living, in home, street or factory, which are not affected by new developments of the process. By its versatility, screen printing has lent itself increasingly to advances in graphic and industrial technology; it has played an important role in the growth of the plastic and electronic industries. Marking processes, i.e. container and bottle printing, transfers, dials, etc., would be inconceivable without screen printing.

Metal, glass and plastic signs in flat, or three-dimensional units, plastic packaging pre-filled or vacuum formed are invariably screen printed. The rapid growth of television advertising has given a great boost to the printing and production of display and point-of-sale materials. The demand for bright, patterned textiles and wallpapers has extended the use of screen printing into these two highly specialized and competitive fields. Thus more conventional uses have been outstripped by specialized industrial applications.

Screen printed half-tones for posters, in size ranging up from increasing quantities. Photo-mechanical techniques, such as posterization, with a quality close to gravure and collotype, have affected design, and are leading to novel new uses.

Financial Aspects

When is screen printing more economical than any other printing process? This question, asked quite often, is difficult to answer while allowing for any and every eventuality.

As can be seen from the general characteristics of the process, screen printing might often be thought in fact to be the more expensive process. Nevertheless it is still used because of the special graphic effects sought by the designer.

Many different factors decide the use of any printing process; the size and character of the design, the number of workings, the quantity required, the material selected or specified, the competitive cost. But there is no denying that where rich graphic colourful results are sought, screen process has a quality not easily matched by other printing processes.

A further aspect needs some clarification. It is true to say that a screen printing business can be set up with very little capital. It is equally true that, unless the printer has experience, a thorough knowledge of the process and excellent business connections, he will quickly run into trouble in the highly competitive field of printing.

Various Tools

The screen printer's equipment is, by tradition, crude and simple. Even now, the simplest and cheapest equipment can be found side by side with expensive precision machinery in up-to-date establishments. Is such expensive equipment necessary? The flow of new machinery, printing aids, and equipment seems to indicate real and pressing needs. For example, fast machines could not be built without new and efficient drying equipment. The growth of screen printing would be retarded; the expansion into new fields could not take place.

The screen printer's basic equipment consists of a frame, hinged to a base, the squeegee, a piece of flexible rubber mounted in a handle, and some sort of drying rack. Frames are mostly made from timber, even some machines have wooden frames or insert bars to hold the silk. Aluminium frames have been introduced since 1948 on account of their greater rigidity, lightness and freedom from distortion. The screen fabric has to be stretched tightly over wooden frames by means of battens, glue or tacks; some of the latest aluminium frames include stretching devices, which allow quick and even tensioning of the fabric, with easy adjustment of parts. The screen fabric must be drawn tight for stencil adhesion, register and sharp printing by the use of special stretching devices, ranging from simple floating bar frames to expensive and complex stretching tables. The squeegee consists of a rubber or synthetic blade fitted into a wooden or aluminium handle. Special squeegee sharpeners are used, as blades have to be kept even and ground to a variety of profiles according to the needs of the designer. The printing table must be rigid and of a convenient height for feeding in stock and printing. Hardboard, aluminium or plastic bases are best. Register marks made from card, gummed paper, plastic or metal are placed on the surface.

Vacuum base tables are a great improvement. They consist of a plastic or aluminium base with small perforations connected to a vacuum pump. The air is exhausted as the frame is lowered and the vacuum released when raised. This prevents the stock from adhering to the screen fabric after printing because of the highly viscous screen printing inks. The stock is held firmly, tight to the base, making faster printing possible. The one arm squeegee (a further improvement introduced about ten years ago) travels along a shaft mounted on the table opposite to the printer, enabling him to pull the squeegee along without effort, thus making it possible for one operator to print even 60 in. x 40 in. posters. These tables have micro-register adjustments.

The German SPS tables have an automatically moving hinge bar, which transform them into semi-automatic machines. Stainless steel fabrics stretched by a pneumatic device and squeegees holding a blade on an identical principle are designed for aids to high precision printing. There are a number of specially constructed precision printers on the market; they are essential for the exacting demands of electronic circuitry, dial printing and marking.

Mesh Fabrics : It is difficult to find a parallel in the orthodox printing processes for the sieve-like fabrics used in screen printing. It is perhaps nearest, by analogy, to the printing plate, as the sieve carries a negative image of the design to be printed.

Choosing the right screen fabric influences the quality of the screen printing. It is important therefore to understand the structure and behaviour of these fabrics, to correctly assess screen printing technique. Improvements in existing fabrics and the recent introduction of synthetic materials such as nylon and terylene have opened up new fields to the screen printer.

The original fabric used by screen printers was identical with the flour miller's sieve the silk 'bolting' cloth-hence 'silk' screen printing. Silk has a number of advantages, such as relative cheapness and wide range of width and qualities. It is hygroscopic and coarser in weave than metal or synthetic fabrics. Quality and register can be seriously affected by the cloth tightening with heat and slackening with dampness. Silk bolting cloth is produced in two basic weaves; interlock and plain weave. The interlock type weave consists of full-gauze, where all warp and waft threads are interlocked at their intersections, and of half gauze, in finer weaves, where only every other thread is interlocked, with alternative threads passing over and under each other. Plain weave silk cloth consists entirely of such threads. Therefore though it is less rigid than interlock, the mesh openings are larger and more regular. This results in a thicker ink film and better definition, as the mesh opening is unaffected by knots or twists.

Synthetic Fibres : Nylon and Terylene are used increasingly now a days. Synthetic fibres consist of a single smooth filament. Plain weave construction, a greater ratio of mesh opening to thread, fineness, imperviousness to humidity and certain acids, are their main advantages over silk fabrics. Disadvantages are: the price, and difficulties with stencil adhesion unless the fibres are roughened up. An additional drawback is caused by lack of elasticity. When the stretched fabric slackens it is impossible to tighten it any further.

Phosphor Bronze Fabrics : These can be conveniently grouped together. A fine, monofilament thread with large regular mesh openings, and plain weave structure is characteristic of these fabrics. They are costly; accidental dents render the damaged area useless; the thread needs very thorough degreasing for the adhesion of dischromated gelatine stencil materials. Mainly for these reasons metal fabrics are usually employed by transfer and industrial printers, who require long wear, a fabric unaffected by heat or humidity, and fineness of definition with a heavy ink deposit.

Where special inks are needed for ceramics, plastics, fluorescence and phosphorescence, resists and adhesives, screen printing is the in-ideal process as these inks depend on the thickness of the ink layer for their maximum effect and perfect bonding to the surface. There is no other process capable of printing to vacuum formed plastics; the same applies to the printing of luminescent dials and certain ceramic applications. Fluorescent screen printing inks have been found more lasting and stronger, as the strength of colour depends on the thickness of the ink film. Resists printed on copper-plastic or copper-paper laminates also depend on the same factor. Pinholes in the resist will render the circuit useless.

Special Inks : The latest developments are intended to help printers in individual ways by providing inks which work best under certain drying conditions in relation to certain surfaces; thus tackling the problem of drying at its source-the formulation of the ink. It is claimed for instance that vinyl inks, developed in the United States, dry in ten seconds on twin jet dryers and in twenty seconds on a jet dryer; but drying time is increased to over ten minutes if left to dry on drying racks. This new approach to ink formulation is of the greatest importance for the process. With increasing mechanisation and faster printing speeds the printer has now a wider choice of inks; with new drying and printing equipment, faster drying is now practicable.

In the early days of 'silk' screen printing, about fifty years ago, only a few stencil materials were used; these were prepared by screen printers. The classic book of Hiett and Middletone, written and compiled at that time, carries a wealth of information on how to prepare pigment paper, how to shellac paper, and so on. Today screen printers are in much better position. There are numerous excellent supply houses at their disposal; they can choose from many new and improved materials brought regularly on to the market.

Stencils can be grouped conveniently under three headings; hand drawn, knife cut and photographic. Hand drawn stencils are worked on the screen surface itself with various filters. White lines are obtained by blocking out with glue, shellac or paint; black lines and textures by drawing with lithographic ink or crayon. The latter technique, 'serigraphy' popular in the United States among artists, has led to acceptance of the process for autographic print making. In this country a full appreciation of the potentialities of this technique for prints is unfortunately still lacking.

Knife cut stencil materials are most commonly used by screen printers. The earliest stencil material, paper, is still in use today for large letters, backgrounds and when heavy ink deposits are required. Paper is too fragile for long runs, any detail of small letters must be kept in position by connecting ties, showing typical stencil effects. To overcome this paper was shellacked and then ironed on to the screen after the printing areas were cut out.

Further improvements resulted in the well-known profilm and bluefilm, paper laminates; the former coated with shellac, the latter with fish glue. Bluefilm was introduced when it was found that cellulose inks destroy the shellac coating of profilm stencils.

These heat-adhesive materials are being slowly replaced by solvent-adhesive knife-cut stencils. Developed during the last ten years in the United States, adhesion to the screen fabric is affected (as the name implies) with a special solvent. The stencils are made in a more expensive plastic material, but are easier to see through; quite small detail can be cut sharply, and the ink layer can be regulated. Available in a wide range of colours, any coloured original can be worked from without difficulty.

Further research has resulted in a new plastic-base water adhesive cutting film. It can be used with any ink, does not require special solvents for adhesion and is easily removed with water. Other plastic films are removed with cleaners, Profilm is soaked off with methylated spirit, Bluefilm washes off with water.

Photographic Stencils : The introduction and perfection of photographic stencils has been an important factor in the steady advance made by screen printing. These stencils now make it satisfactorily possible to print type down to eight point even during long runs, to keep accurate register, to render fine detail and clear halftone subjects. Duplicate stencils can be produced quickly and accurately from the same original and identical stencils for subsequent reprints. Photographic stencil materials are long lasting, relatively cheap and most are easily removed from the screen. A positive transparency is required for their production, but photography as such is not always required as it is possible to produce these transparencies with hand methods also. The quality of the transparency is of the greatest importance. Transparent parts must be clear and opaque areas impervious to light with sharp, dense edges. Only stable plastic base materials and process plates or films should be used.

Photographic stencil techniques are based on the tanning of colloids by light. A stencil is produced by preventing the rays of light from reaching parts of the gelatine and then washing off those soluble areas. Even illumination from a light source rich in the blue special range is needed. Unless stencils are required continuously no bulky and expensive equipment or dark room is required.

Use of Fabrics

All screen fabrics irrespective of material are numbered to denote the fineness of their weave. Silk bolting cloth numbers end at 25, the equivalent of approximately 250 threads per lined inch. Numbers 10-12 are used by most screen printers for the average job, but meshes from 14 onwards are needed for halftone printing. The 'quality' or thickness of the thread is expressed by X. The most commonly used quality is XX. Nylon and metal meshes carry on in fineness where silk leaves off. There is no international coding system for fabrics and their grade can only be ascertained therefore by consulting charts supplied by each manufacturer.

Different Inks : Screen printing inks have specific characteristics, totally different from orthodox printing inks. They must pass through small openings without clogging, and dry fast on the printed stock. There is no ink on the market as yet which can completely satisfy all these requirements.

As we have already noted screen printing started as a branch of sign writing. It is not surprising therefore to find that the first inks were decorators' oil paints suitably altered for the process. These inks are still with us today, but adjusted to drying faster, with thinner ink film. The characteristics of opacity, a heavy ink deposit and slow drying (mainly by oxidation), have remained. There are mat or gloss inks; if a transparent base is added they can be used for transparent over-printing.

Natrocellulose inks adapted from aircraft finishes were introduced after the second world war. A thin film ink was obtained with an egg shell litho-like finish. Faster drying was achieved by evaporation; the thinner film made the printing of halftones and of fine detail possible. These inks are self-dissolving, screens can thus be left without the danger of stencils getting hopelessly clogged; they do not require thinning and do not skin up. The main disadvantages are, translucency, expense, special solvents and a strong unpleasant smell. Some of the cleaners have a low flash-point and therefore these inks come under the regulations of the Cellulose Act. The clear base mixed with metallic powders makes an excellent metallic ink and a range of trichromatic colours is available for halftone printing.

Great efforts have been made by ink manufacturers during the past ten years to perfect screen printing inks, developing an ink with the advantages of both oil base and cellulose. The 'synthetic' inks were the result; these dry by evaporation with a thin film, but are more opaque than cellulose inks. The solvent is white spirit, but they do not skin up and are self-dissolving as cellulose inks. The unpleasant smell has been eliminated. There are now a number of these inks on the market, suitable for a variety of surfaces, drying mat, semi-mat or glossy.

Photo Stencil : In the modern age of mechanisation and automation, it is comforting to know that craftsmanship still reigns supreme in the field of silk screen printing. Nevertheless, a wise silk screen artist endeavours to make best use of the facilities which photography has extended to this process. In the past, the silk screen artist also used to be endowed with drawing and designing ability but that is not so at present. Thanks to photography, any design can be photographed and most of them can be reproduced by silk screen. The versatility of the process is unquestionable since one can print on almost any surface-paper, board, fabric, glass, bakelite, wood etc. and it is not even necessary that the substrate receiving the ink should be plane and flat.

Before preparing a photostencil, one must have a sharp positive of the design or original to be reproduced. Most of the silk screen reproduction consists of line work though halftone work has also been attempted successfully.

The conventional method of making a photographic positive is by contacting a negative on a piece of process film. The negative is made on a process camera or any other camera suitable for copying work. The original design is placed on the copyboard of the camera and evenly illuminated by a suitable illuminant which may be carbon arc lamp or white light fluorescent tube or photoflood lamp to name a few. The camera lens must be a good anastigmat. An apochromat lens would be ideal but quite expensive at the same time. Having focussed the original to the desired size, a sheet of orthochromatic line film or ortho lith film is loaded in the camera and exposure is given to the original. The orthochromatic film is not sensitive to red region of the spectrum (600-700 millimicrons;). Hence the film can be processed in a dark room fitted with red safelight. Development is done in the developer recommended by the film manufacturer. If the recommended developer is not available, any one of the following developers may be used.

Caustic-Hydroquinone Developer

Solution A

Hydroquinone	25 gm
Potassium hydroxide	50 gm
Water to make	1000 c.c.

Solution B

Potassium hydroxide	50 gm
Water to make	1000 c.c.

For use, mix A and B in equal volume just before use. During development, the exposed areas of the film are affected and the silver halides present in these areas are converted into a form of black silver. Thus opacity is produced in the exposed areas. The developed film is then quickly washed in water in the following solution:

Sodium thiosulphate (hypo)	250 gm
Water to make	1000 c.c.

The above solution reacts chemically with the residual silver halides forming a water soluble complex so that when the negative is washed, the soluble complex is removed from the gelatin layer.

Hydroquinone-Carbonate Developer

Sodium Sulphite (anhydrous)	150 gm
Hydroquinone	20 gm
Sodium Carbonate (anhydrous)	50 gm
Potassium Bromide	10 gm
Water to make	2000 c.c.

The above is a single solution developer which must be used undiluted. Development time is five minutes at 20° C.

Whichever developer is used, if the negative is correctly made, the design will be obtained in a transparent form against an opaque background.

The Positive : A positive is now made from the above negative by contact printing. This operation is performed in a printing cabinet of the vacuum type. If such a cabinet is not available, a photographic contact printing frame may be used. If that too is not available, two thick glass plates may be used. The emulsion side of the film is placed in contact with the emution side of the negative. The combination is held together between the two glass plates. Exposure is given through the negative using a frosted glass filament lamp. Light will be transmitted through the transparent areas of the negative (which constitute the image of the design) and expose the film. There after the film is processed as in making the negative. The result is an opaque image against a transparent background.

Chemical Reversal : Instead of preparing negative, a positive can be directly prepared by chemical reversal. In this method, the copy is exposed and the film is developed in the recommended developer. The exposure must be somewhat greater than normal and has to be determined by trial and error. After development, the negative is well washed in water. Then the silver formed in the exposed areas is removed by 'bleaching' in the following solution:

Solution A

Cupsic nitrate	300 gm
Potassium bromide	10 gm
Acetic acid	150 c.c.
Water to make	1000 c.c.

Solution B

Hydrogen peroxide	2%

The working solution is prepared by mixing A and B in equal volumes. The solution dissolves the gelatin in the exposed areas. When 'bleaching' is complete, white light is switched on and the bleached negative is washed in water. The unexposed silver halides in the image areas are now exposed by the light. The film is then redeveloped, washed and fixed. The result is positive.

The original is a Flag in two colours-red and blue. A negative (ii) is made from the key drawing. The negative is retouched with photo-opaque leaving only the red areas open. A positive (iv) is made from this negative which will be used in making the red printing photostencil. The key negative is now washed and dried. It is again retouched (v) to stop out all areas except blue. Another positive (vi) is made from the negative which will yield the blue photostencil.

Halftone Reproduction : Although it is possible to prepare photo stencils for halftone reproduction, the result cannot be of a high quality. The limitations imposed by the process make it mandatory (i) to use a screen not finer than 33 lines per cm (85 lines per inch) and (ii) to avoid fine tonal gradation because it is neither possible to maintain fine isolated gelatin dots in the shadow nor force the ink through very fine openings in the highlight areas of the gelatin stencil. For best results, negatives (halftone) must be made on a process camera using lith films or coarse magenta contact screens. The negative is contact printed on high contrast film to obtain positive with dense and sharp dots.

Photo Stencils in Gelatin : The positive (line or halftone) so prepared is now used in obtaining a photostencil in gelatin. This can be done either by the direct method or by indirect method commonly known as transfer method.

In the direct process, a layer of gelatin of suitable thickness is deposited over the silk screen. A number of coating solutions have been recommended by different workers. The following is a typical formula which gives fairly good results:

Gelatin	90 gm
Sodium Carbonate	2 gm
Potassium bichromate	20 gm
Glycerine	7.5 c.c.
Water	1000 c.c.

Gelatin is the film forming colloid which is rendered light sensitive by potassium dichromate. Glycerine makes the stencil pliable so that it may not develop cracks. Sodium carbonate raises the pH of the solution by reducing its acidity, a dye such as methyl violet may also be added to impart colour and improve the visibility of the image in the stencil.

In preparing the solution, gelatin is first soaked in about 600 cc of water and then warmed to a temperature of about 45° C to obtain an emulsion. The dichromate and the carbonate are separately dissolved each in 200 cc of water. When the gelatin has dissolved, the carbonate and bichromate solutions are added taking care that the temperature is maintained at 45° C. The glycerine and the dye are added last. The emulsion is thoroughly stirred.

For coating, the emulsion is warmed to 45oC and applied to the screen by a wide camel's hair brush. Both sides of the screen are coated and care is taken to obtain a film of even thickness on the silk screen. Drying is effected by a fan. Both sides of the screen are then given a second coating. The coating and the drying operations must be carried out in yellow light otherwise the coating solution is likely to get fogged.

The sensitized screen is now printed under the positive. Actinic light should be used for exposure. Development is done in water at 45° C. Both sides of the stencil are developed until the unexposed gelatin has been washed away leaving a clear cut design in the stencil. Development is arrested by applying cold water. Linen sheets are then used to absorb as much moisture from the stencil as possible. Further drying of the stencil is done under a fan.

After printing, the gelatin stencil is soaked in twenty per cent solution of sodium or potassium hydroxide and then scrubbed under warm water until all traces of gelatin have been removed.

The transfer process though somewhat expensive is extremely popular these days since it is quick working and gives excellent results if the manufacturer's instructions are followed. A large variety of materials is obtainable based on transfer process of which two are being described below.

The first is a presensitized red pigmented gelatin coated on a transparent polyester base of good dimensional stability. The product is commercially available as 'Five Star' and is manufactured by Autotype International Limited, England. The film can be handled in yellow light. Stencil preparation is extremely. The film is first cut to the desired size. The positive is placed in contact with the non-gelatin side so that the stencil will be right reading when viewed from the gelatin side of 'Five Star'. While maintaining a firm contact, exposure is given through the positive using a source of actinic light such as a carbon arc lamp or mercury vapour lamp. Sunlight may also be used. The sensitivity of 'Five Star' lies mostly in the ultraviolet and blue region of the spectrum. Exposures vary a great deal since there are many variants. It is therefore best to find correct exposure by first making a trial exposure.

The next step after exposure is hardening of the exposed areas of gelatin. This is done by immersing the film in 1.2% solution of hydrogen peroxide at 20° C. The commercially available hydrogen peroxide has its strength expressed in 'Volumes'. Thus a 20 volume solution contains about 6% of hydrogen peroxide.

The gelatin film is then developed in a spray of warm water at 40-45° C until all the unexposed gelatin has been removed from the image area. The silk screen which has been previously cleaned is moistened with water and the stencil is applied to the underside of the frame carrying the screen. Moisture is removed by gently dabbing with clean newsprint which is placed inside the frame. Thereafter, the stencil is allowed to dry in gentle breeze of a fan. The base support is then peeled off.

In another indirect process, the film material is supplied unsensitized along with a liquid emulsion and a sensitizer. The emulsion and the sensitizer are first mixed and then coated on the unsensitized film through the silk screen. The coating is allowed to dry after which the backing material of the film is removed. Exposure through the positive is given as before so that the image will be right reading when viewed from the top side of the screen frame. Develaopment is done in plain water. Finally, cool water (20-21° C) spray is directed over the surface until the image areas are washed away. The stencil is then dried as before.

7

Film Process

The photographs can be almost as important as news releases. A good picture is worth any number of words for it can communicate a point quickly and succinctly, and in any language. Editors like pictures and many a mediocre press release has found a place because it was accompanied by an eye-catching or interesting picture.

However, adding photographs just for the sake of it is not a good idea. Photography is extremely expensive and should only be undertaken if it is necessary-which is not the same as being marginally useful or pleasant. There are, of course, occasions when photographs are taken to please the chief executive or for company records. This is all very well in its way, but do not make the mistake of thinking that the media will also be interested; unless the picture tells a real story they will not be.

The true value of a picture lies in its ability to illustrate a point or to act as an eye-catcher both to the editor and subsequently to the reader. If the same picture can achieve both purposes then so much the better. A PR executive faced with the task of showing the strength of steel-capped safety footwear hired a double-decker bus and had it photographed as it drove over the foot of a man wearing the boots. He certainly made his point. Another successful bus picture was taken by the sponsor of a fleet of painted buses from London, Birmingham and Manchester. The buses were offered to a leading charity to take deprived children on a trip to Woburn Safari Park. The buses were photographed with a few surprised giraffes looking in the windows. All the parties concerned gained publicity which they would probably not have achieved otherwise.

Sometimes, of course, the subject is either so technical or so complicated that a photograph of the laboratories or of a piece of machinery would not make the point and the use of drawings should be considered instead. Nevertheless there are few editors who do not like to use at least one or two photographs and the relevant drawings might be backed up with shots of the inventor or the experimental staff at work. It is sensible, however, to check with editors of really specialist publications whether or not they can use a good picture.

What you should photograph, depends entirely on editors' requirements. Study the publications on your specialist media lists and get to know what sort of pictures are likely to be used.

A very effective way to achieve publicity for a new factory opening, an exhibition, a fashion show, a lunch or a conference is to issue a photocall or general invitation to photographic agencies and to the picture editors of the daily press. Such an invitation should give an indication of what pictures could be taken or which parts of the event lend themselves to photographs. There may be innovative processes at the factory, new products on display at the exhibition and new designs at the fashion show. A lunch or conference may feature well-known personalities and speeches may be made which will be of interest to the media.

Once you have issued the invitation it is important to make sure that the photographers will be able to do their job. Space must be left so that they get an uninterrupted view, extra lighting may need to be laid on and someone must be on hand to make sure the photograph has an accurate caption. Some freelances have been known to leave without getting a full caption. You may also need to lay on a messenger service to deliver the film to the newspaper building while the photographer goes on to his or her next assignment.

You should also arrange to take your own photographs of this type of event, for they give you an opportunity to show off the newsworthy aspects of your organisation. You should arrange for both black and white and colour shots, but do make sure that you check the requirements of the specific publications before sending them out.

News of the day-to-day happenings within the organization can be communicated with much more interest by photography. Examples include the installation of new plant, moving an unusual load or shipping fridges to Iceland, the chief executive leaving on a trip to China, long-service presentations and involvement in local community activities.

The Production

This can be one of the trickiest areas of photography, for very often the product is not very different from many others on the market and what differences there are may be difficult to illustrate photographically. So before going ahead with photography of products stand back and assess whether editors will be able to use the picture you are planning.

If you do decide to go ahead, there are a number of ways in which the product might be photographed. It can be photographed on its own or in a likely setting. It can be photographed in its packaging if it has any, it can be photographed in use or it can be photographed in an unusual setting.

Depending on which publications you believe will be interested, you may need to photograph the product in two or three of these ways. The consumer press, for example, will not be interested in any kind of pack shot and brand and company names should be removed or kept very small indeed. There are some publications which simply will not use a picture if it has any brand identification whatsoever.

Shots of the product in use or in an unusual setting are the type to aim for in this area. But do not get too carried away with the idea of a gimmicky photograph. It may just make one of the down-market dailies and thus please the marketing director, but it is probably not going to sell very much of the product. Such a photograph is more likely to help sell the newspapers. On the other hand there may be publications on your media list which will be interested in showing the packaging, particularly if it has any unusual features or uses new techniques. Retail publications, too, are more likely to be interested in close-ups of the product itself or in the promotional and publicity material which will help them to sell it.

Photography for Features : For certain types of consumer product it can be very useful to have a selection of photographs to be placed with supporting feature material. Food products are an excellent example. Very often the packaging is too heavily branded to be able to use a straight pack shot and a picture of a plate of soup or a bowl of cornflakes is not going to stun the readership. However, if these items are made up into attractive dishes they can be photographed and used to good effect with features on 'Supper Dishes with Soup' or 'Crunchy Toppings'. Some of this work should be in black and white for use in some regional media, but the majority will need to be in colour.

For economic reasons many consumer magazines are increasing their use of outside photographs. Sometimes these are commissioned for specific features following an approach from the PRO. Others have been taken 'on spec' and placed with suitable magazines at a later date.

Beauty features highlight another problem which can arise if the parent company is based abroad. The parent company, perhaps in France or in the USA, will probably have taken a portfolio of beauty pictures when the products were initially launched in their home country. Very often they expect UK PROs to use the same photographs in their own press campaigns. This rarely works. The models look indefinably 'foreign' and unless the feature is on French or US fashion the pictures will not be accepted by the UK press. A new set of pictures will have to be shot.

Checklist for Photographs

1. Decide if a photograph is needed. Will it be able to tell the story better than the release?
2. Make a list of those media to which the picture will be relevant, showing black and white or colour requirements.
3. On the basis of this list decide what exactly should be photographed and how it should be presented.

Choosing Process : Photography is a highly specialized business and apart from the odd record shot it is not usually a good idea for the PRO to take his or her own photographs. For one thing there are usually very many other things at an event which need to be organized and directed by the PRO and a well-briefed photographer can take at least one burden off the PRO'S shoulders.

For product and feature work it is even more important to have a professional. Photographers are trained to get the best out of models and to arrange the lighting to the most dramatic effect, and they are usually very creative as well. Photographers' fees are, of course, quite high and there can also be a problem choosing photographers for events outside the area in which you normally operate. In these circumstances a PRO who has a good camera and who knows what he or she is doing may decide to take publicity shots of local events and newsworthy items such as new employees, new sports facilities or retirement presentations. Remember, though, that this is not the end of the story. The pictures have to be developed and printed to a suitable quality for the media and you will need enlargements, possibly in some quantity.

Some large companies employ their own photographers but often these people are expected to handle a lot of clerical work as well as take and process all the photography. Some of them are very good indeed but it is unlikely that they will have had the opportunity to develop skills in such highly specialized areas as industrial photography, beauty photography or still life.

Most PR executives will need to build up a repertoire of photographers skilled in the areas covered by the media relations programme. A good industrial photographer will not be particularly good at portrait work and a fashion photographer will probably not know how to handle food, so if all these areas are represented by the activities of your company or client organization you will need to find photographers in each field.

The number of photographers you work with in each field will depend upon the volume of work that you have and your personal relationships with the photographers concerned. It is sensible, however, to work with at least two and possibly three different photographers in any one field. This cuts down the risk of a photographer becoming stale and running out of ideas about how to present the material. It also means that if one photographer you know and like is booked up the other one may be free to work with you.

The Sources

Contact : This is a purely visual directory of photographers.

Smaller volumes on photographers specializing in fashion, cars and computers are also available.

Elfand Ltd, Unit 39, Bookham Industrial Park, Church Road,

Bookham, Surrey KT3 3EU.Tel: 01372 459559 Fax: 01372 459699

Creative Handbook : The directory lists a wide range of creative services including photographers and picture libraries.

Reed Information Services, Windsor Court, East Grinstead, West Sussex RH19 1XA. Tel: 01342 326972 Fax: 01342 335612

Hollis Annual : This lists a limited number of firms, some of which have branches in different parts of the country. Hollis Annual, Contact House, Lower Hampden Road, Sunbury-on-Thames TW16 5NG. Tel: 01932 784781 Fax: 01932 787844

Institute of Journalists Freelance Directory : Two Dock Offices, Surrey Quays Road, London SE16 2XU. Tel: 0171 252 1187 Fax: 01 71 232 2302

NUJ Freelance Directory : National Union of Journalists, 314 Gray's Inn Road, London WC1X8DP.Tel:0171 278 7916 Fax: 0171 837 8143

Other sources include the Yellow Rages and Thomson Directories or services such as Pirns Townlink Network and Two-Ten Photo Assignment. The problem with using these directories is that you have no way of knowing whether a particular photographer has the experience to carry out your work or even if he or she is competent. The agency photographers should be adequate but these facilities can be expensive and tied in to other services.

Perhaps a better idea is to try the news or picture desk of the local or regional newspaper. Most of these publications use freelance photographers as well as in-house staff and these people have the advantage of knowing what kind of picture their local paper will use.

Matter of Choice

Always arrange to see some sample work when choosing photographers for specialist work, and if possible have a talk with the photographers in person. You may also want to see the studio and check on any special facilities which might be needed, such as access for large items, a working kitchen or space to build room sets.

This kind of assessment may be difficult if you are looking for a photographer at the other end of the country. Here a telephone conversation will usually have to suffice. But do keep records. It may be very useful to know that there is a first-class industrial photographer in Tyne side or that such and such a photographer near the Exeter depot should not be used again. If the job is very important it may be worth the cost of sending someone whose work you know well to cover the assignment. This may cost more at the time but could save a lot of money in the long run.

The quality of the photographer's work is not the only factor which you may need to check on. It could be that one first-class photographer takes much longer on studio work than another or that another industrial photographer cannot work without bringing in extensive lighting systems. There will be occasions when a slight loss of quality, provided that it is not too great, will be offset by budget gains or less disruption on the production line. The only way to find out this sort of information, short of using the photographer once, is to talk to other people who have used him or her. If you see samples of the photographer's work you will be able to contact the clients who commissioned the work.

If you want to place a picture in the national press it is common practice to work with an experienced newspaper photographer who will advise you on the composition of the photograph. For example, one paper might like unusual angles to a shot whereas another will like to include people in the picture. The photographer will take the pictures with particular nationals in mind and then sell them in for you through his contacts on the picture desk. A fee will be charged for the photographic session with a further fee for selling the picture in.

Checklist for Choosing a Photographer

1. Does the photographer specialize in the area in which you need to commission photography?
2. Have you seen examples of his or her work?
3. Are you sure that the chosen photographer's working methods will be suitable for the job in hand?
4. Do you need to find an experienced photographer who can also sell-in the photograph?

Choosing Models and other Specialists

It is rarely sufficient to put the product on the table and expect the photographer to get on with photographing it. The photographer may have sensible suggestions for backdrops and for simple accessories, but very often rather more is required. It may be that the product would be shown off to best advantage in use. This means a decision must be taken on whether the in-use setting can be re-created in the studio or whether the photography should be done on location. It also involves the use of models.

The Models : With highly specialized products the models will probably be people who are already working with the product. Professional models do not always look very convincing in a factory or a highly technical laboratory.

If you are using 'real' people, make sure that they will be reasonably comfortable in front of the camera. Some people freeze up and look completely false. The only way to check is actually to point a camera at the people chosen before the main session. Try to keep the pictures looking as real as possible. Too many beautifully clean and pressed white coats, for example, can look staged, and best clothes are quite unbelievable at work.

More often the photographic session will be in the studio and it will be virtually impossible to work with people who are not professional models in these very artificial circumstances. Professional models are trained to look at ease and to be able to produce spontaneous-looking smiles and expressions to order.

Not all models are the curvaceous female variety and studio shots can be set up with less glamorous professional models where this is required. Models, like photographers, specialize in certain types of work and they usually have portfolios to show off how they look in a variety of poses. This specialization can be quite important; there are good reasons why a model specializes in hair fashion photography rather than hands or feet. Indeed pretty hands can be one of the most difficult things for a PRO working in beauty to find.

Most models work through photographic model agencies. Some of these also specialize in male models, children and so-called 'uglies', or the less glamorous type of model. There are also agencies for animal models. Check the telephone directory or *Hollis Annual* Yellow Pages or ask the photographer with whom you plan to work to recommend some agencies. The agency will send you either their complete portfolio or a suitable selection of models to fit your brief.

If at all possible interview all models with whom you have not previously worked. Some models can be a very disruptive influence in the studio, particularly if there is more than one model on the session. It also helps to brief the model in advance so that he or she is aware of what is involved and will bring the right selection of clothes or accessories. If you are using models frequently keep a model book with notes on how each one has been used before, what they look particularly well in and any other relevant notes.

One final point: always make sure that all models sign a release form or contract to ensure that they cannot suddenly demand repeat fees on a photograph which is widely used.

Other Specialists : For some types of shot models will do their own hair and make-up, but if you are acting for a manufacturer of hair preparations or beauty products you will probably need to use a hair stylist and a make-up artist. Remember that leading professionals in these fields must be credited in the captions. Do not try to save money by using unknown or inexperienced people in these areas-the results can be disastrous.

For certain types of photograph, particularly those for feature use, you will need to think about the accessories you will use in the photograph. This may simply mean adding a flower, an attractively draped scarf or a glass of wine to the products to be photographed, but it may also mean creating a complete atmosphere. One product may be used in a feature on Italian cookery while another may be the dominant part of the decor for an elegant drawing-room set and yet another may appear in a greenhouse. For all of these photographs a large number of accessories or props will be needed to create the desired effect.

Photographers who specialize in food or in room set photography will probably have a good selection of props. In addition manufacturers of household goods are willing to lend their products for use in photographs for non-competing items in return for suitable credits. Large shops and department stores will be equally helpful.

However, if you are trying to create a period shot or a specifically national look you may have to hire props. Sometimes the photographers will organize this for you, but if there are a large number of photographs to be taken then you should consider using a specialist photographic stylist whose job it is to provide a good selection of suitable props from which you and the photographer can choose on the spot.

This type of photography also calls for other specialists such as home economists to prepare and present the food in front of the camera, room set designers and model makers. All of these specialists must be chosen with care and with an eye to the particular skills required. Some home economists are excellent at cake decorations, for example, while others are better at all-round cookery or pastry work. If you have not worked in these fields before ask the advice of the photographers. They will have specialists with whom they like to work.

Setting up the Picture

Briefing : To take really good pictures photographers need to be properly briefed. They are not mind-readers and unless you explain, in some detail, what you are trying to achieve with a particular photograph they will not be able to do their best work. You might, for example, be photographing a tractor. A picture intended to show the pulling strength of the tractor will need to be quite different in composition from one designed to show the gradients which it is able to climb or the revolutionary design of a new gearbox.

Photographers also need to be informed of the printing process involved in the publications for which the picture is intended. Some processes do not reproduce pictures very well and the subject needs to be in bold relief without too much fussiness, whereas other processes are able to reproduce every detail. They also need to know the type of publication for which the picture is intended. The composition of a photograph for the *Truck Drivers Weekly* would be quite different from that for *Science Today* or for *Vogue Magazine.*

Location Photographs : For location work it is very helpful to the photographer to visit the site beforehand. A good photographer should, if necessary, be able to produce good pictures without a previous visit, but he or she will certainly produce better results if there has been sufficient time to look round and plan the most effective camera angles. Such a visit should involve talking to personnel to try and understand something of their jobs and to work out how best to tell the story in visual form. Any technical points should be discussed with the relevant experts to avoid any arguments about the pictures afterwards.

Obviously the plant or area manager should be alerted both to any pre-shooting visit and to the photographic session itself. He or she, too, needs to be briefed on the need for and the purpose of the photographs, for it is important to ensure cooperation. Disruption of normal activities should be kept to a minimum. This is important not only in the interests of keeping production flowing but also in obtaining the most natural pictures of the operatives and staff involved.

However thorough the briefing, the PRO still needs to go on the shoot. Once briefed, the photographer should be left to compose the pictures and if he or she says something will not make a good picture this judgement should be accepted. But as the PRO you can smooth the way. You can also check the final picture before it is taken.

Not all location photography is centred on plant, machinery or buildings. Quite a number of 'mug shots' or portraits will be needed as people join the company or move their positions within it. This can be a very tricky area as most people are self-conscious in front of the camera. It is the PRO's job to help relax the subject. You can also brief the photographer on any idiosyncrasies, on interests and on which parts of the person's job might lend themselves to photography. In this way it should be possible to obtain a more interesting picture. Show the transport manager with one of the lorries in the fleet or talking to a driver, the canteen manageress in the kitchen or the sales director at a briefing session.

Studio Work : In the studio the conditions are, of course, rather different. There is usually less urgency, though the time factor cannot be ignored since studio time costs money. The photographer will be in charge here but he or she will still need a detailed briefing. If other specialists are involved, a general briefing meeting will ensure everyone knows exactly what is required of them. The PRO should then let everyone get on with their jobs. A point to watch is the delivery of a product or material to the studio. Very often this will be coming from a different department, which should be alerted in good time. Check with the photographer that the material has been delivered a day or so before the appointed date. This gives you time to chase it up if there have been any hiccups.

Live Interest : On location or in the studio some subjects are just not very interesting, and anything which can be used to add interest will be helpful. Human or animal interests almost always improve a picture, but the subjects should be used in a way that is relevant and which helps to explain the subject. Children playing with toys, men putting up prefabricated house units, a family in a holiday resort or a woman using a knitting machine are all likely to enhance the original subject. People in the picture should be concentrating on what they are doing. They should not merely look decorative. A blonde in a bikini does not enhance a jeep nor a cuddly dog a power drill. Sometimes people are used to give an idea of scale. A man standing beside a combine harvester or an earring photographed with a close-up of the head will help to convey the size of the object.

Last-minute Checks : Always check the final composition before the photograph is taken and ask yourself the following questions:

1. Is the picture relevant to the story?
2. Is it self-evident what the subject is or does?
3. Does the picture tell the story without the need for a long caption?

The next step is to check the detail, and this will need more experience. If the shot is to be sent out in black and white the colour must be ignored and the shot viewed in terms of tones of grey. This means that the sharply contrasting colours green and black will look just the same in the black and white print. It also means that the choice of background colour is vital. An experienced photographer should have pointed out these things but it is sensible to acquaint yourself with some basic knowledge. A black and white polaroid will also help.

Composition can also present many potential pitfalls. One highly experienced PRO tells the story of her first photographic foray. The product was discreetly set out towards the back with the label half turned away. The picture looked attractive and showed a new use for the product. The only trouble was that the photograph was so arranged that it would be very easy for a picture editor to crop the product out of the picture altogether.

Checklist for Setting up the Picture

1. Brief appropriate managers that the session is to take place and arrange for any special facilities or sample product.
2. Brief the photographer in detail on the purpose of the photograph and its destination. Visit the site if possible.
3. Brief any supporting specialists in a similar manner.
4. Look for relevant human interest angles and action in the photograph.
5. Take the photographer's advice on what will and what will not make a good picture.
6. Check any technical points in advance and if mistakes could be made make sure an expert is present
7. Keep disruption to a minimum and try to keep any live models as relaxed as possible.
8. Make a final check on the photograph before it is taken to ensure that it will do its job. Does the picture show the subject off to best advantage?

If you are satisfied with the answers to these questions then go ahead and authorize the picture.

Mechanics of the Picture : The first point to consider is the number of shots which need to be taken. This will depend partly on the requirements of the interested publications and partly on technical considerations such as variations in lighting and the medium being used. If the subject of the photography is a new type of ballpoint pen, for example, at least two shots will be required, one for the retail trade press and one for the consumer press. The former could include attractive packaging or promotional material, but this would be quite unsuitable for the consumer press. Here a shot showing someone using the pen would be much more appropriate. If the PRO felt that a number of different editors were interested in such a picture he might decide to take two or three different shots: one perhaps with a child drawing or learning to write, another in an office setting and another in the home with a woman writing a shopping list.

If the photography is in black and white the photographer may be working with reels of film rather than with plates, in which case he or she will be able to take many more shots without inflating the price too much. But for some forms of still life, for example, and for colour work the photographer will be working with plates, which are expensive in themselves. These technical aspects of the shoot should be discussed with the photographer in advance and the decision may be made, in the light of the budget as well as of the PR requirements, to put a specific limit on the number of shots.

Editors' Demand : Quite apart from wanting pictures to enhance the pages of their magazine and which will interest their readers, editors need pictures of the right size and printed on the right sort of paper.

Editors want sharp, well-focused prints which are glossy but not glazed. They should usually be whole-plate size but half-plate pictures, if they are well cropped before being sent out, are equally acceptable. Pictures for television should be 10"x 8" matt, preferably in colour. Transparencies can usually be accepted from 33 mm upwards, but it may help the magazine if plate sizes are agreed before the pictures are taken.

Topicality can be important here. Nothing irritates a daily newspaper picture editor more than an allegedly topical photograph sent through the post. Pictures must be delivered to these newspapers on the day they are taken. If you think there is a good chance of a daily newspaper using one of your pictures but don't feel they are likely to send their own staff photographers, a phone call to the picture editor could arrange the delivery of exposed film immediately after the event.

Take care with the choice of prints. If the photographer has used a reel of film ask for a set of contact prints with the photographer's own choice of two or three of the pictures enlarged. Check all the pictures and crop if necessary. Do not allow the photographer to stamp the back of the photograph. You are sending the picture out and are the contact for further information. Remember too that in times of industrial strife it is possible that the photograph could be blacked if the photographer is not a union member.

Sending out Prints : All too often 50 or more prints are ordered from black and white photography and sent out indiscriminately to complete sections of the media list. Some PROs have even been known to send pictures out to radio stations. This is extremely wasteful and reinforces the inefficient image of PR executives.

However, there are some occasions when sending a photograph to a radio station is not such a bad idea. It could make it much easier for the presenter to describe an unusual item, and here perhaps a sample of the article itself might make life even simpler. Photographs can also be used to arouse interest in an event which would not otherwise bestir the news editor to cover it.

A good example comes from the PR agency for a hair preparation manufacturer. This company holds a national hair colouring competition every year with regional heats, and radio had shown little interest either in covering the event or in interviewing the winners. However, when shown pictures of the amazing results achieved by the winning entrants, most of the local radio stations near to the regional heats interviewed the regional winners.

Photographs should only be sent if you are absolutely sure that the recipients will be able to use them-even to the press. If only a small number of publications are involved and you are not sure about photographs, ring up and ask.

Some organizations print a sheet of miniature photographs so that editors may choose which, if any, they would Tike to have. This can be expensive and if a large mailing is going to regional newspapers, for example, it may be more sensible to reproduce one or two pictures on the release and invite editors to request prints, or simply state that photographs are available on demand.

Make sure that all pictures leaving the Press Office are properly captioned and that they are well protected. Pack with cardboard or with hard-backed envelopes and make sure that there are no paper-clips to pierce the prints and that the address is not written on top of them in ballpoint pen.

Checklist for Sending out Photographs

1. Decide the number of shots on the basis of the budget and the interested media.
2. Choose prints carefully and crop where necessary.
3. Have the photographs processed to the right size and on the right paper.
4. Take particular care to get the topical pictures to the daily media the same day.
5. Only send photographs to publications you are reasonably sure will want to print them. Offer photographs to other publications by phone or by stating on the release that photographs are available on request.
6. Take care to protect pictures in transit.

Copyright : The copyright in a photograph rests with the photographer, not with the person, who commissioned the picture, nor with anyone who is shown in it. If you need to have the copyright for some reason this must be negotiated separately for an extra fee or royalty.

On an important assignment it makes sense to draw up a contract with a photographer so that you are both quite clear about how the photographs are to be used, Consult the *ABC Guide to Copyright,* a publication every PR office should have. It was drawn up by the British Photographers Liaison Committee and is available from the Association of Photographers, 9-10 Domingo Street, London E1Y OTA. Tel: 0171 608 1441 Fax:0171 253 3007.

Photographic Libraries : There exist, chiefly in London, a number of photographic libraries which will supply prints and transparencies on topical or historical subjects where exclusivity is not a requirement. They charge a fee for the use of their material. You are unlikely to be using their services for material to send out to the media, though they could be a useful source of illustrations for internal publications, but you may be able to place some of your material with them for use by other organizations. The Central Office of Information is another organization which may be able to use your photographs.

However, you are more likely to have your own photographic library with reference shots of all plant and personnel and a collection of possible feature material. Too often this library' is a mound of photographs, some without captions, in a single folder or drawer. A secretary or executive has to plough through them all to fulfil every media request.

To be really useful the photographic library should be carefully organized by subject and the system should indicate the following:

1. The date the photograph was taken.
2. The photographer who holds the negative.
3. Availability in colour as well as black and white.
4. The copyright holder if different from the photographer.
5. Brief caption details.
6. The current whereabouts of the picture if you are expecting it to be returned, and a regular reminder procedure.

7. Any restrictions governing publication, such as the correct acknowledgement. It is useful to hold at least two prints of all black and white negatives and to re-order as these are sent out, and to keep black and white and colour libraries separate. A photographic library needs constant updating. Pictures of the chairman ten years ago or the old plant before the renovations are only of interest for the company history and are definitely not for current use. So check from time to time whether pictures should be retaken rather than re-ordered.

Colour transparencies are expensive and, extra care needs to be taken to ensure they are not lost through carelessness or neglect. Every loan should be followed up after a certain period of time. Some companies insist that journalists or other borrowers sign a form to say they will be responsible for any photographs borrowed and they will pay for it in the event that a photograph is lost or not returned before a certain date. This seems to be carrying things a little too far. A number of circumstances in which a transparency could be lost or damaged would be quite beyond the control of the borrower.

You will soon get to know those publications which are regular users of your transparencies, and provided the pictures usually return safe and sound there is no need for such formal contracts. After all, your organization is benefiting from the continuous exposure of its products.

Transparency Selection

Right Transparency

1. Select a transparency with the right colour balance. Its colours should be a correct combination of hue-the property of a colour that distinguishes it from other colours, of saturation-the relative purity, vividness or intensity of colour, and of value the property of a colour that makes it seem light or dark. Its tonal separations should be rich and distinct so as to result in quality reproduction in multicolour.

2. Select a transparency which is sharp and crisp, containing minute details and nuances. Even separations made on a scanner cannot reverse m inherent lack of sharpness in the picture although it can correct colour casts and improve upon desaturation and poor tonal separations.
3. Select the right format size of transparency for your job. In a 35 mm picture that is enlarged for instance, the grains are enormously magnified in the final reproduction and are almost 3000% bigger in size. Magnification also often results in a loss of detail and clarity in the final picture.
4. Select a transparency that has been correctly exposed. The leeway for altering colour balance during processing cannot alter the quality of a transparency that has been under-exposed or over-exposed during photography or developing.
5. Always use the original transparency for the best printed results. A duplicate generally has more contrast than the original, which has to be reduced by flashing, masking and the use of special film for duplicating. Make sure that the identical size of the duplicate is used.

Wrong Transparencies

1. Reject a transparency with colour casts. The sensitivities of the emulsions in each film are balanced to reproduce colour as human vision is prepared by experience to see them. Any mismatch of this with the light source leads to an unnatural colour cast. If for instance film balanced for professional studio lighting is used in daylight, the transparency will have a blue cast, daylight film used under artificial lighting causes an orange cast. The final result, an unnatural rendition of colour in print.
2. Reject a transparency in which the grains are evident these particles form a developed photographic image on the film and become even more visible upon enlargement and subsequent reproduction.

3. Reject a transparency with shadows cast by the objects photographed. Human vision interprets such shadows as black and dark grey, while colour film records shadows as blue.
4. Reject a transparency in which glare or polarised light produced by smooth light reflecting surface such as water or glass has dulled the colours and reduced the detail recorded by the film.
5. Reject a transparency with spots. These would stand out upon enlargement in the final reproduction.
6. Reject a transparency with finger prints and scratches.
7. Reject a transparency that is badly mounted. Crude hand mounting results in a transparency acquiring jagged edge fibres.

Process Camera : The process camera plays a very important part in offset lithography. With the advancements in science and technology, the process camera has also undergone a great degree of change. A survey of the Indian Printing Industry would reveal that cameras of all sorts and kinds are being used. Thus we have the old, wooden, manually operated gallery type with a bulky dark slide and the modern, sophisticated, steel frame version fitted with interchangeable lenses, integrator and densiprobe. The old model is still capable of giving a fine performance if handled scientifically so far as black and white reproduction is concerned. For colour reproduction, the scanner seems to have dug its feet in. Colour separation by electronic means is quick, sure and reliable and in this field cameras are making way for the scanners. Costwise, scanners are very expensive and every lithographic plant cannot afford them. Such plants may borrow scanning services from elsewhere for colour separations and use their own cameras for black and white line and screen reproduction.

Photography

The function of the camera is to form a sharp, well defined image of the copy in desired size. This is possible provided the camera is fitted with a lens free from major aberrations and having a high resolving power. For practical considerations, the camera lens is built up of several elements instead of a single piece. The composite lens is a convex or convergent lens as only such a lens is capable of forming a real image. (A real image is that which can be brought upon a screen. Your image in a mirror is not real but virtual).

The camera operator is given necessary instructions regarding the size of reproduction, the ruling of the screen etc. It is interesting to note that it is possible to obtain a sharp image at the back of the camera without looking at the ground glass and without any built-in focussing device. This needs some elaboration and explanation. The distance between the plane of the copyboard and the lens is called 'copy distance' and is represented by the symbol u. The distance between the lens and the plane of the ground glass is called 'camera extension' and is denoted by v.

If the focal length of the camera lens is f, the following relationship is found to exist:

$$1/v + 1/u = 1/f \quad (1)$$

(All the distance-u, v and f have been taken as positive)

The ratio v/u is called magnificent and it is denoted by the letter 'm'. If the value of m is one, the image has the same size as the object. However, if m is greater than 1, the image is enlarged and if less than 1, the image is reduced.

If we multiply the equation (1) by u and v separately, we get two more equations as below.

$$1 + u/v = u/f$$

or $$f\,(1 + 1/m) = u \quad (2)$$

and $$1 + v/u = v/f$$

or $$f\,(1 + m) = v \quad (3)$$

Now suppose the focal length of the process lens is 48 cm (You will find it printed on the lens mount). The camera is required to be set in such a way that the image has 50% linear reduction i. e. m = 112,

From equations (2) and (3).

$$u = 48\ (1 + 2) = 144 \text{ cm}$$

$$v = 48\ (1 + 1/2) = 72 \text{ cm}$$

Hence, if you set the copy distance u equal to 144 cm, and camera extension v equal to 72 cm, you will find the image in sharp focus upon the ground glass screen and in fifty per cent linear reduction.

If you want to employ this technique in practice, you have to scale the camera first. This is done as given below.

1. Put any line copy on the copy-board preferably a printed scale.
2. Focus the image manually and visually to same size. Lock the camera.
3. Take a long measuring tape. One end of the tape should touch the Surface of the copy-board. (One of the assistants may be asked to hold the tape like that). Measure a distance equal to 4f from the copyboard surface and make a mark in the back panel of the camera coinciding with this distance as shown in the figure. Let this mark be 'c'.

Find the middle Point of the distance AC and let it be 'B'. Mark the positions of 'B' and 'C' on the lens panel and back panel respectively. The camera has now been scaled. Here is how it operates. Suppose the linear reduction desired is 75% i.e. m = 3/4.

Now, according to camera optics,

$$u = f\ (\ 1 + 1/m \text{ and } v = f(1 = m).$$

Hence putting f 48 cm and m = 3/4, we find that u = 112cm, and v = 84 cm. The distance AB is therefore set equal to 112 cm and BC equal to 84 cm. You may now switch on the illuminants and check the definition and the size of the image. To your surprise, you find that it is in sharp focus and fairly accurate in its degree of reduction.

Illuminants for the Camera : Having already compromised with the inevitable that colour separations would be prepared on the scanner and that black and white work would be taken up on the camera, the necessity of using carbon arc lamps or an expensive substitute can be dispensed with. Mercury vapour lamps may be used, you can even use day-light fluorescent tubes-four on each side and get fairly satisfactory results. For accuracy in exposure, you have to ensure that the intensity of light emitted by the illuminants is more or less uniform. A voltage stabilizer will be found very useful. A light integrator will almost make the exposures one hundred per cent correct since the exposures would be correlated to units of height and not to units of time.

The Densitometer : Normally, the densitometer is not a part of the process camera. However, modern cameras are often fitted with a small 'densiprobe' for evaluating the tones of the copy and determining its density range. The densi-probe can be used for setting the illuminants in such a manner that there is no tonal variation in the plane of the ground glass if a white sheet of paper is put on the copyboard. Illuminants so set will illuminate the copy very evenly. Determination of the end-densities and density range of the copy will enable you to decide the correct detail and highlight exposures and, of course, the flash.

Hints for Development : If you are not using an automatic processor and doing development in a dish or tray, here are some useful tips to keep in mind.

1. For best results, the development must be done at a temperature between 20 degrees to 25 degrees C. If the darkroom can be maintained at a temperature within this range, you will also need a development chart as given below.

Measure the temp. of the developer and develop in accordance to the chart.

Development temp. (in C)	20'	21'	22'	23'	24'	25'
Development time (in mts.)	31/2	31/4	3	23/4	21/2	21/4

This chart should be prepared by you by trial and error.

2. The developing solution should be agitated by tilting the dish both in the long and short directions.
3. The amount of developers in the dish must be sufficient to keep the film covered with the developer during agitation.
4. Do not use exhausted developer for development. Formation of yellow colour in the developer is a warning that exhaustion is setting in.

And finally-do not prepare solutions in the darkroom. The dust from the chemicals may become a part of the environment of the darkroom and hence affect the film while you are loading it in the camera. You may later find intense black spots after development which may seem inexplicable to you.

Many printing plants now have automatic film-processing machines to perform the developing, fixing, washing, and drying functions for film and for some specialized papers. Information on processing times and temperatures, and on methods for handling photographic chemicals in processing machines, is available on request from kodak graphic arts technical sales representatives. Mixing instructions for machine processing chemicals are packages with the chemicals themselves. However, even if you do own an automatic film processor, knowledge of the principles of tray processing is invaluable for setting up a quality-control programme for proper processor function.

In a Tray : Process the exposed film in a developer, a stop bath, and a fixer; then wash it in running water. You control each step by time and temperature,.

Time : The developing time and the recommended developer are stated in the instruction sheet packaged with the film.

Temperature : You can adjust the temperature of the developer to the recommended 68F 20oC by floating the tray of solution in a larger tray of either cold or warm water for several seconds. Don't put water into the developer itself to adjust temperature. The handy Kodak Tank and Tray Thermometer may be placed right in the tray of solution.

Illumination : You must handle the film exposed or unexposed, in a darkroom illuminated only by the safelight recommended in the instruction sheet packaged with that particular film (most films with the same basic colour sensitivity-orthochromatic or blue-sensitive for example-require the same safelight). The safelight provides light of a colour and intensity that will not affect the film if darkroom work is carried out with reasonable care.

Proper safelight illumination includes lamp-to-film distance and bulb wattage, as well as the safelight filter itself. To check your safelights for safety with orthochromatic emulsions (red safelights), view the safelights through Filter, a dark green gelatin filter. If you can see white light transmitted through the filter, then the safety of the safelight should be questioned. A more accurate safelight test Would be this:

— Make a simple halftone exposure of any piece of copy on Ortho Film.

— Place the exposed but unprocessed film facing up on your work bench. Cover one-half of the image with an opaque card or masking material.

— Place the exposed but unprocessed film facing up on your workbench. Cover one-half of the image with an opaque for 3 minutes. Then process the film.

— Examine the processed halftone image. If you notice a change between the masked and unmasked areas, then your safelights are unsafe and may be contributing to apparent changes in film speed.

Equipment : The above controls require the following equipment:

Timer	Safelight filters
Thermometer	4 Trays
Safelight lamp	Tray siphon

Preparing the Solutions

Developer	Into one tray pour about a 1/2-inch to 1-inch depth of Developer, mixed carefully according to directions.
Stop Bath	Into a second tray pour about 1/2-inch to 1-inch depth of an acid stop bath, such as Stop Bath
Fixer	Into a third tray pour an inch or so of Fixer. The latter permits shorter fixing times and as a liquid, is easier to mix.
Wash	Fill a larger tray with water and keep the water running. Circulation and replenishment of water by advice such as the preferable.

Place the exposed film in the developer. Do this by dragging the film face-down through the developer and then quickly flipping it over, face-up. Agitate the developer continuously as follows: Raise the left side of the tray about ½ to 3/4 inch; lower it smoothly, and then immediately raise and lower the far side similarly; next, raise and lower the right side, and then the near side, These four operations constitute an "agitation cycle," which requires a total time of about 8 seconds, most operators form a habit of uniform agitation, so that they can more nearly repeat their results on successive negatives. Continue agitation until the recommended time has elapsed.

When a developer solution is used for a large number of negatives, it gradually becomes exhausted. A gallon of developer can develop a film area equal to about 30.8 x 10-inch sheets of film. You should increase gradually the developing time during the useful life of the solution. Discard the solution when you have reached a 50 percent increase in development time, necessary to produce a good negative, when exposure is normal.

Handle the wet film by a corner or edge to avoid damaging the image. Lift it up and let it drain for a few seconds; then quickly transfer it to an acid stop bath. This stops development more quickly than does a water bath and helps keep image uniform. It also prolongs the life of fixing both. After several seconds of vigorous agitation, transfer the film to the fixer.

Significant Prints

When your hands have been in solutions, always rinse them in clean water before wiping them on the darkroom towel or before touching anything. This will prevent spots on films caused by contamination from solutions and dry chemicals.

Agitate the film vigorously in the fixer until the film appears to be clear in the unexposed, light areas-usually after about minute in a fresh fixer. Then leave the film in the fixer for the recommended time, to remove the last traces of unexposed light-sensitive material. You can turn the room lights on at this time.

To preserve the image, the film must be washed as recommended in the instruction sheet. After washing wipe it gently with a soft rubber squeegee and hang it upto dry. The film dries more quickly if both of its sides are squeegeed onto a rigid surface such as glass or plastic.

Development by Inspection : Line negatives are often developed by inspection. When development is nearly complete, you lift the negative briefly from the sink. A magnifier will help you inspect fine detail. By observing the density of the black background, you can learn to judge when development should be stopped.

Assuming proper development, density is largely determined by exposure. You should, of course, estimate the camera exposure as accurately as possible. However developing by inspection does permit you to compensate for some exposure error by stopping short of the recommended developing time or by developing a little longer, whichever is indicated by inspection.

Checking Exposure/Development Conditions : Density scales are used to check many factors which influence photographic behaviour, such as light sources, safelight fog, developers, developer exhaustion and the fundamental properties of the sensitized material. There are, of course, many more applications for density scales in photography. The need for quick visual reference for checking exposure/development changes (intentional or unintentional) can be met by using the opposed gray scale. This guide is made by first cutting a gray scale in two, lengthwise; the sections are then joined again, but in opposing directions.

Opposed Gray Scale : To make the opposed gray scale, cut about 5/8 inch from the edge of the Separation Guide gray scale. Next, cut the 5/8-inch piece into two 5/16-inch strips. Then, join the two strips together in the opposed position so that the 0.30 step is opposite the 0.50 step. Place transparent tape on the back of the strips to hold them together. To square the guide, trim away the high densities on the ends. If convenient, the steps can be numbered or otherwise identified for easier reference.

By including the guide with all camera line copy, you should be better able to match line width rendition from similar copy, confirm normal exposure and development for certain copy, and control development compensation when processing in a tray.

Opposed Gray Scale Guide : After you have made the test exposure from the line copy target and have determined which exposure work best with each type of copy, make full-sized exposures of each type of copy and place an opposed gray scale next to the copy. These exposures establish the density value at which certain exposure and development conditions will produce the most significant density change in the scales. The term "break" is commonly used to describe the point at which a line negative of a gray scale appears to have lost most, if not all, of the tonal separation between the steps and shows a major shift in density. This is especially true with very high contrast materials, in which density values in the copy are essentially reproduced as either black or white. Consequently, the guide will look different at the "break" as exposure is adjusted to suit the different types of copy. If the copy has coloured filter is sometimes used to get improved black-and-white separation. The use of a coloured filter may cause slight changes in the "break point" that has been established as being ideal for good line copy without such a filter.

The Graphics : Lithography is a comparatively young process; it being well under 200 years since those famous Senefelder discoveries occurred. As a result lithography has developed alongside established printing processes. Let us look at the way in which a job travels through the lithographic department:

(1) Planning, (2) Reproduction, (3) Camera, (4) Camera Enlarger and Colour Scanners, (5) Processors, (6) Retouching, (7) Layout Assembly, (8) Step and Repeat Machines, (9) Colour Proofing System, Cromolin, etc., (10) Graphic Arts Input Materials.

Importance of Planning : Planning has always been an important stage in the lithographic process. With the increasing range of platemaking machines, high material and labour costs, the planning stage has become an important contribution to the production programme.

Many planners may be restricted to the simple planning techniques which are related to the class of work or type of equipment available. The importance of establishing high standards in planning is seen in the speed of the later stages of production.

The class of work may vary tremendously from simple book work assembly to multi-colour work. Planning therefore not only demands considerable skills of hand and eye, but perceptual skills in knowing how the job should be approached. This will require decisions concerning the correct techniques to be employed and the selection of materials. Planning also demands an attitude of conscientious responsibility and high standards of cleanliness and accuracy. An appreciation of typographic design and page layout should be a necessary attribute of the planner.

Originals for Reproduction : The basic requirement of any original is that it should be an accurate representation of that which it portrays. No amount of skilful retouching or correction can compensate for bad copy. All artwork should be carefully checked to ensure that the proportions are correct and if reduction or enlargement is required, sizes and proportions must be clearly marked. Copy for reproduction normally falls into one of the three categories. These are either Reflex (Flat) or Transparency:

(a) Line, (b) Continuous Tone, (c) Colour Work

Line : Preferably the line copy should be prepared in Black regardless of the colour of ink to be ultimately used in printing and it is essential that it is clean, dense and sharp. Other line copies are Chinese Black ink drawings; pen & ink sketches, artpulls of type matter, scraper board, quarter tone; tincs, stipples and bleach out drawings, etc.

Continuous Tone : Continuous one copy, usually in the form of bromide prints, should have good tonal separation from shadows to highlights throughout the range of the original. No amount of correction or retouching can put this right at a later stage. Other originals are wash crayon from and are normally made of glossy paper.

Colour Work : Flat copy in colour can be easily reproduced. Colour transparencies in size 35mm and 120mm must be absolutely sharp and of normal contrast, i.e., density range of not more than 2.0.

Copies are often presented in the form of dummies and layouts to indicate the nature and position of separate illustrations for an advertisement or composite printing surface. The term "copy" includes all subject matter. Thus a layout of the required complete work is essential either as a visual rough or something more detailed and comprehensive.

The Camera : Having produced a suitable original, the next step is to photograph it on a large process camera which does not differ fundamentally from the hand cameras used by general photographers. Modern cameras are precision instruments with critical tolerances, sleek styling, anti-vibration precautions, short focus wide angle lenses to save floor space, electromagnetic shutter, integrating light meters, spot on registration devices and reset location controls using dial micrometer gauges with measure to within 1/1000 inch. The cameras are primarily of two types:

(a) Gallery Camera, (b) Darkroom Camera

Gallery Camera : These are of the horizontal type and are still in use. These are not attached to a darkroom and stand in a special studio system requiring the dark room to the camera and vice versa after exposure.

Darkroom Camera : These are both horizontal and vertical. Vertical cameras are also of two types. Film loading end of the camera is built into the wall in the case of horizontal cameras, and vertical cameras are positioned in the darkroom itself. The following points are considered whilst selecting process cameras to suit your needs.

Camera Size is determined by the maximum size of negative or image area that can be exposed. The most common sizes are 12" x 15", 16" x 20", 20" x 24" and 30" x 30".

Normal range of process cameras is upto X2 enlargements and X4 reductions. Vertical cameras have a range from 20% to 500%, it comes in size: 16" x 20" and 20" x 24".

The copyboards are suitably provided to cover the entire range and hold different types of copies. Copyboard is supplied as standard, holder and transparency holders on gallery cameras are optional.

Optics used on these cameras and other process cameras correspond to the size of the camera. Apochromatic lenses (suitable for colour reproduction), prism is mounted in the lens (or in modern camera optical reversal unit incorporating front coated mirrors replaces prism, etc.) as and when reverse negatives are required for block-making and despatch plate-making.

Light source for copy used to be provided by set of four arc lamps, suspended in pairs on either side of copy, distance from the copy and angle of the light source is adjustable according to the size of the original being reproduced. The arc lamps have been replaced with Halogen lamps and Xenon lamps in most of the cameras being produced these days.

Filter Holder : Provision for inserting gelatine filters in the lens are also available in all makes of cameras. The modern cameras have filter turrent electric-operated for selection of filters etc.

Flash Lamp : Darkroom camera are also equipped with a flashing device, switching device, switching on-off through electronic timer.

- Magnetic shutter for precision.
- Exposer timings, the same works in conjunction with the Electronic Timer.
- Modern cameras offer programming facilities computerised auto-focus, auto-size, density correction, online densitometer, etc.
- Focussing screen (ground glass) is provided for checking of focus manually.
- There are Roll Film cameras, Plate Maker cameras for small printers.

The environments and working conditions must be strictly adhered to and maintenance procedure should be followed as:

(a) Optics must be protected from chemical fumes and humidity, a bag of celicagell must be placed near the optics.

(b) Dusting of the camera should be done with the help of a vacuum cleaner.

(c) Mechanical adjustment of the camera, i.e., squaring and parallelism between Copyholder, Lens Column and Vacuum Back, must be checked, corrected for error, collometer or a sizing stick provided by some manufacturer should be used for squaring.

(d) Antivibration mounting and levelling should be periodically checked.

(e) In case of Arc Lamps, these must be cleaned daily and serviced fortnightly. Whilst using Xenon or Halogen lamps, a log-book should be maintained to record burning hours for having replacements arranged within working life of the lamps.

(f) All moving parts and Vacuum/Suction Pumps to be lubricated weekly.

Colour Scanners : Camera Enlarger as a photographic reproduction instrument stems from the increasing use of colour transparencies for reproduction including the miniature 35mm and 57 X 57mm, (2 1/2" x 2 1/2") which provide a deciding factor in its development. It occupies less floor space and is simple to operate. It incorporates latest in technology, i.e., Lens Turret, Xenon Lamps, Vacuum Base Board, Filter Holder, Punch Register System on Base Board and three point location in the transparency Image plane. Cold Cathode lighting, Electronic Flash and Computerised Controls makes it a completely self-contained Camera Reproduction Unit.

Colour Scanning is an alternative to photographic masking methods for the correction of colour originals. The manufacture of photographic masks, to adapt the colour separation to the characteristics of the process colour inks, is replaced by electronic calculation of the requirements involved and the immediate production of separations suitable for screening and platemaking.

The Processors : Automatic film paper processors are required by units using phototypesetter, colour scanners and for high speed and high volume work in the graphic reproduction departments.

With dish or tray development, consistency is difficult on account of the problem of controlling the solution and standardising agitation. The chemicals are discarded after use, hence the process is uneconomic. Machine processing using film processors whilst involving initially a large outlay of capital, are money savers, in that one machine can process work of Camera, Scanner and Contact Printers, eliminating darkroom bottlenecks and cutting chemical cost by 50%. Valuable flo space, previously occupied by sinks, drying cabinets, etc. is saved. The machine functions efficiently after 30-45 days or more, after that the chemistry is normally changed and the machine emptied for complete cleaning and servicing.

Retouching and Contacting

Retouching : Hand corrections for monochrome or colour work consists of adding or removing density from the photographic image. The most important method is the dot-etching of screen positives made from continuous tone negatives and in some instances, depending upon the quality of the original and the continuous tone negative, retouching is carried out at this intermediate stage.

Special Retouching Desks can be installed which consist essentially of a adjustable light box with opal perplex sheet or ground glass. A pair of tungsten lamps provide the necessary even light without straining artist's eyes.

For preparing multiple, same size positives from one master negative exposing half-tone positives from continuous tone negatives and contact screens. Composite positives are very often required to be made from two separate negatives for exposing positives for deep-etch platemaking.

All the above operations are carried out on the contact Printing cabinet. The Contact printer should consist of face-down vacuum frame mounted on a cabinet. The vacuum of the frame is adjustable to suit different thicknesses of Films. The height of which is sufficient to provide even illumination from point light Source. Provision should also exist for adjusting the brightness of the lamp with a dial as a guide for repeat exposures. Timer should be incorporated for accurate exposure. Safe light should also be incorporated for positioning the negative and film etc. The cabinet should be lighttight so that when exposure cycle commences the operator could open unexposed film without fear of fogging material.

Layout Assembly and Stripping : The layout is the working basis of all subsequent planning operations. It is a full size technical drawing which indicates the various image positions as they will finally appear upon the printed sheet. It will also include "aids" such as register, collating, fold and trim marks, star targets, signal strips and colour control blocks. These will assist the specialists engaged in subsequent operations such as the printing, folding, collating, trimming and punching operations. The aims of an accurately produced layout will be to facilitate the positioning of various images, the register of multi-colouring work, ease of production in the later stages, economy in the use of materials and machinery at all stages. In order to fulfill these aims the necessary information must be readily accessible. Good liasion should therefore exist between the planning, production, camera, pressroom and finishing departments

The planner must consider factors, e.g., sheet size; sheet grain direction; type and size of plate used; plate clamp allowance; Paper-grip allowance; arrangement of individual images of varying sizes; areas of critical register; ink distribution over the sheet.

When selecting a table for planning and ruling up no expense should be spared to obtain the best equipment. Layout accuracy in lithographic planning is essential at this point for the production cycle since little can be done at later stages to put bad planning right.

The planner should select a table which is:

— Versatile in use and of solid construction for accuracy for drawing of impositions and layouts.

— for checking of press sheets and assembled flap.

— provision for scribing of negative film or cutting of masking materials.

— adjustable tables allow for varying working postures.

— suitable Glass top to accommodate largest layout sheet.

— stainless Steel Straight Edges with finely engraved scales with facility for locking arrangement.

— layout grippers for holding the Astrafoil.

— table illumination-Fluorescent light tubes for even distribution of light.

Lining-up Table

The tables should be placed at level to avoid distortion. Each of the two chain driven straight edges can be aligned to move the straight edges parallel across the table and at right angle with Vertical Straight Edge. It is necessary to check this adjustment periodically.

8

Inks for Printing

Printing by the rotary letterpress method from rubber stereos originated in the last years of the nineteenth century and inks for the process consisted of aniline derived dyes dissolved in alcohol or water; hence the adoption of the generic name of aniline inks. Since 1935 development in printing machines and ink formulations has been dramatic and the range of substances printed has increased so that the term "aniline" has been rendered obsolete. The term "flexographic inks" came into use in 1952 and the use of the word "aniline" together with its chemical associations of toxicity and odour largely disappeared. In recent years the quality of print produced by the flexographic process has improved greatly. The process was originally limited to the printing of paper bags and sacks, but with recent progress in the design of printing presses, stereos and substrates, excellent decorative tone work can be produced.

Special Ink

A flexographic ink consists of three basic types of ingredient: solvent, resin, binder and colour. The selection of these is dependent on the end use of the print as well, the substrate to be printed and the type and speed of the printing machine. The ink must be low in viscosity in order to be distributed adequately in the simple distribution system, and yet remain on the surface of the stereo, thus producing a clean print. Many flexographic printing presses are capable of production speeds of 300 metres per minute, and print from reel to reel. The inks have to be formulated to dry at this speed. When the substrate being printed is non-absorbent, it is essential that all the solvent is removed from the print prior to re-reeling if set off is to be avoided. The solvents used must not attack the various types of rubber or plastic used to form the stereo, the resin system selected should ensure adequate adhesion to the substrate during the life of the print, and the final print is usually required to be odourless.

Substrates : Before considering the basic formulation of flexographic inks it is desirable to consider the types of substrate printed by this method. This will enable a relationship between the ingredients selected and the end usage of the print to be developed.

The types of substrates may be divided into three groups: paper and board, film and foil.

Paper and Board : The range of end uses of flexographic printed paper is vast and includes paper bags, waxed bread wrappers, parchment for fat wrappers, coated papers for labels, kraft liners for corrugated cartons. All may be printed on reel to reel presses and the inks may dry partly by absorption as well as evaporation. The range of ink specifications varies widely and may require resistance to light, resistance to wax, fat, etc. In general there is no problem of adhesion to the surface of paper though the rub-resistance of a print may be important.

Board is usually printed on a sheet fed press. Large quantities of corrugated board for subsequent case making are printed flexographically. The major requirement is for rub-resistance during transportation.

The surface contour of papers and board influences the quality of the print achieved. Tone printing using fine screen is only possible on smooth surface, and it is more common to print tone designs on film and foil surfaces than on paper when using the flexographic process.

Films : The use of film for flexible packaging has developed rapidly in recent years. Accent is placed on the production of flexible films which have excellent barrier properties and which can be handled by a variety of packaging methods and machines. The two major film types have been based on regenerated cellulose and polyolefin films. Uncoated regenerated cellulose film has poor resistance to moisture. The use of a coating based on cellulose nitrate and wax increases the moisture resistance of the film and enables it to be heat sealed. An improvement in moisture and gas barriers can be achieved if a coating of polyvinylidene chloride (pvdc) is applied.

Polyethylene and polypropylene films have excellent moisture barrier properties, and it is possible to coat polypropylene with pvdc to improve the barrier properties.

Inks cannot be absorbed into the films, so that adhesion to the surface of the substrate must be obtained by the resin system and the solvents must be removed during the printing operation. When certain coated films are being printed, it is possible to improve ink adhesion by heating the web, thereby fusing the ink to the coating, but care should be taken to ensure that no film distortion takes place as a consequence of the heating.

Other films which are printed flexographically include polyester, nylon and polyvinyl chloride.

Foil : Aluminium foil used for flexographic printing is usually no thinner than 0.009 mm when unlaminated. Thin gauge foils may be used for confectionery wrappers, thicker gauge for certain lidding operations, and laminated foils for a wide range of package protection.

In certain cases, aluminium foil may be washed with a primer which prevents oxidation and promotes ink adhesion. In view of the non-absorbency of the surface, inks must be based on resin systems having excellent adhesion properties. The inks must be very flexible, have good solvent release and exhibit no tendency to block in the reel.

Basic Ink Ingredients : Flexographic inks are composed principally of colourant (dye or pigment), resin and solvent. The ink types may be classified in general terms by sub-dividing according to the main types of basic ingredient. It is usual for the ink manufacturer to market inks under trade names pertaining to the resin type used, as this selection is closely linked to the properties and end use of the ink. Inks may be considered by colourant as (a) dye type and (b) pigmented inks. In certain cases, blends of dye and pigment may be used in the same ink; for example, a combination of titanium dioxide and dye. Such an ink type is classed as semi-pigmented. Water based inks may be considered as a sub-group of pigmented inks.

Dyes : The dyes most commonly used in flexographic inks are salts, usually the hydrochloride, of basic dyestuffs. They are soluble in alcohol and many of then) are soluble in water. The dyes are usually "laked" with tannic acid or a similar product. This process increases the solubility of the dye in methylated spirits, develops colour strength and greatly reduces solubility in water. The tendency to bleed in wax, glycerine and other treatments is also reduced. As a general guide, in amount of tannic acid equal to the weight of dyestuff should be used in the ink formulation. The lightfastness of the dyes is improved by laking, but it is still poor (Blue Wool Scale 1). High acid value resins of a phenolic type may be used in place of, or in combination with tannic acid as a laking agent, thereby reducing the amount of additional binder which may be required in the ink formulation. It should be noted that the use of a particular laking agent may affect the shade of the dye Solution considerably.

Dye based inks are widely used on paper for bread wrappers, bags, etc. where no lightfastness requirement is demanded. Because of their almost Newtonian behaviour, low viscosity inks of high colour strength may be formulated enabling clean printing to be obtained. The migration tendencies of basic dyes do not encourage their use on plastic films or in contact with a wide range of products.

The dyestuffs most commonly used are:

Auramine	Victoria blue
Magenta	Rhodamine G
Malachite green	Methyl violet
Rhodamine	6G

Soluble dyes having considerably greater lightfastness and resistance to fats, etc. are available and may be used for special applications. The dyes vary in solubility and in general are much less soluble and of lower colour strength than the basic dyes. Suppliers' specifications should be consulted before using certain dye/solvent combinations. The main uses for these lightfast dyes are for foil printing, where the transparency of the dye can give striking decorative effects. Many of these dyes are metal complexes of which the following are examples:

Solvent Yellow	19
Solvent Yellow	45
Solvent Red	102

Because of the wide scope of work printed flexographically, the range of pigments used is broad. In general terms the requirement of the pigment is that it shall have low oil absorption, high colour strength, economic price, and stability in the appropriate resin/solvent combination.

The rheological behaviour of the pigment in a flexographic system is influenced by the method of preparation of the pigment, the incorporation of wetting agents, the conditions of precipitation and washing. Pigments of apparently similar chemical constitution may have vastly differing flow and storage characteristics in the same resin system.

The main types of pigments used for general purpose work are :

Organic

hansa, and benzidene yellows

permanent red 2B

PMTA blue, violet, green, pink

phthalocyanine blue, green

lithol reds

permanent red 4B

lake red "C"

Inorganic

lead chromes	molybdate orange
titanium white	carbon black
bronze blues	(iron blues)

For particular specifications, e.g. soap resistance, other pigment types will have to be used and some of the above may not be suitable for all resin systems and substrates. It is important while formulating ink that the stability of the ink during storage be examined in addition to the more obvious requirements of flow, adhesion, product resistance, etc. Accelerated tests should be conducted to establish the viscosity and shade stability of ink systems.

Resins : The function of the resin component of the ink is to act as a dispersing medium, carrier and adhesion promoter for the pigment. In the introduction it was noted that adhesion to the substrate may be entirely physical, as in the case of ink penetration into paper or board; or physical/chemical, adhesion being obtained either by hydrogen bonding to or chemical reaction with the Substrate surface. Resins of various chemical type may therefore be used, but a prerequisite is that they shall be soluble in suitable solvents for the printing process and they will release the solvent rapidly during the drying stage. Resins may also be divided into two broad classifications: non-film forming and film forming. The latter provide a continuous dry film on the surface of the substrate, examples being cellulose nitrate, ethyl cellulose, and polymeric resins.

Formerly, the basic resin used in pigmented flexographic inks was shellac. It has good wetting properties for the pigment, has adhesion to a wide range of substrates, and is soluble in methylated spirits. However, shellac has slow solvent release characteristics, low heat resistance, and has recently become very expensive compared with other resins. Alcohol Soluble maleic resins have largely replaced shellac in systems which require the use of hard resins obtainable at a more economic price.

Of the film forming resins, cellulose nitrate is the most commonly used in solvent based flexographic inks. It has excellent pigment wetting characteristics for almost all pigment types, and has excellent solvent release and heat resistance. The fact that it is compatible with a wide range of synthetic resins allow its use in inks for a variety of substrates. Pigmented dispersions in cellulose nitrate, known as chips, may be prepared which can give excellent gloss and transparency, which may be of advantage when surface printing on non-absorbent films and foil. Cellulose nitrate may be used in conjunction with other resins to produce curing ink systems, giving heat resistant formulations more resistant than conventional inks.

Ethyl cellulose is also used widely in solvent based inks. Though the pigment wetting and flow characteristics are not as good as cellulose nitrate, ethyl cellulose has excellent solvent release, low tack, good film forming properties, and is especially useful in dye inks when no resin-dye interaction takes place.

Polyamide resins have excellent adhesion to a wide range of substrates, including polythene, polypropylene, foil and pvdc coated film. Particular care must be taken to ensure that the solvent system required for a particular grade of polyamide resin is compatible with the stereo material being used.

The use of acrylic resins has increased in two specific areas. The advent of the use of pvdc coated films for good packaging and the consequent requirement for heat resistant inks with good gloss necessitated the use of acrylic resins, which have good compatibility with cellulose nitrate and cellulose esters, and have solubility in suitable flexographic solvents. Disadvantages of acrylic systems are their tendency to "string" at the printing stage, causing dirty working, and the problems of solvent solubility and resin compatibility.

The use of acrylic resins in water based systems has increased, mainly due to the rapid increase in the price of shellac.

Other resins used in flexographic inks include polyvinyl butyral, polyvinyl acetate and polyvinyl chloride, all of which are used for specific purposes. The skill of the ink formulator is in the selection of the appropriate resin combination to meet the printer's and the end user's requirement.

Solvents : The function of the solvent component of the ink is to dissolve the resin and enable the ink to be handled in the ink duct, transferred to the stereo, thence to the substrate. When non-absorbent substrates are being printed, the solvent must be entirely removed during the drying operation of the printing press. The choice of solvent is dependent on:

(a) the resin system selected, which may be pre-determined by the substrate and the end use requirements.

(b) the substrate being printed.

(c) the composition of the stereos.

(d) the flow characteristics of the ink.

(e) the speed and drying capacity of the printing machine.

(f) restrictions which may be imposed by operators' or end users' requirements or legislation.

The most common solvents used are: water, methylated spirits, ethyl isopropyl and normal propyl acetates, iso-propanol and normal propanol, and 2-ethoxyethanol ("Cellosolve").

In certain cases aliphatic and aromatic hydrocarbons (SBP solvents and toluene), and ketones may be required to enable the satisfactory solution of particular resins. When these and high concentrations of ester solvents are being used, special precautions in the use of stereos must be taken.

With the advent of the photopolymer plate, restrictions on the use of certain solvents are even more severe.

The following table indicates the suitability, or otherwise of various types of stereo materials when used with solvents. "R" indicates that the material will give satisfactory performance. Those marked "C" maybe used with care, when print quality is less critical, and stereos made from another material would be undesirable. The materials marked "N" should not be used because the stereo may be severely swollen and even disintegrated by the solvent.

This table should only be used as a general guide. Most inks are not based on single solvents, and stereo materials may vary in composition. In case of doubt, further information should be obtained from the stereo manufacturer.

Additives : These are used to modify the ink system to meet the final requirements of the print.

Plasticisers are particularly important when printing on plastics films and on foil. Being in effect a non-drying solvent for some resin systems, they impart flexibility. However, the addition of plasticiser lowers the heat resistance of a resin and when added in excess can give rise to blocking. The correct selection of various plasticisers can improve ink adhesion on certain substrates.

Waxes are incorporated to impart resistance to rubbing and scratching. They may be included in the ink either as a pre-dispersed medium or by the use of a micronised form stirred or milled directly into the ink. The most commonly used wax is polyethylene. For certain particular requirements or non-blocking characteristics, silicone fluids or fatty acid amides may be included in the formulation.

Solvent Resistance of Stereo Materials

Solvent	*Natural rubber*	*Nitrile rubber*	*Butyl rubber*	*Photopolymer plate*
Alcohols				
ethyl alcohol	R	R	R	R
iso-propyl alcohol	R	R	R	R
n-propyl alcohol	R	R	R	R

Esters				
ethyl acetate	N	N	R	N
iso-propyl acetate	N	N	R	N
n-propyl acetate	N	N	R	N
Ketones				
acetone	C	N	R	C
methyl ethyl ketone	N	N	R	N
methyl cyclohexanone	N	N	R	N
Glycol ether				
'cellosolve'	R	R	R	R
Aromatic hydrocarbons				
toluene	N	C	N	N
xylene	N	C	N	N
Aliphatic hydrocarbons	N	R	N	N
Water	R	R	R	R

R = Recommended C = Caution N = Not recommended

Water based inks require special attention, the two problems associated with inks of this type are foaming in the ink duct and during the manufacturing operation, and the possibility of mould growth. There are various anti-foam products available to the ink maker, many based on silicone derivatives. The two areas of concern are whether the anti-foam is effective in the resin system being applied, and whether the anti-foam may affect the printing stereos and the print quality. Certain compounds may effectively eliminate bubbles from the surface of ink being agitated in a duct circulating system, but may also cause craters in the ink film which are transferred onto the stereo immediately prior to printing. Anti-foam additives may contain hydrocarbon solvents which severely attack stereo rubbers, causing swelling and Subsequent print distortion. It is recommended that non-harmful fungicides be used to eliminate the likelihood of mould growth in water based inks during storage.

Preparation of Ink

Three distinct groups of ink type will be considered initially:

(a) Dye based inks

(b) Water based inks

(c) Pigmented inks-solvent based.

Dye Based Inks : These have been developed from the original aniline inks. The inks are formulated from solutions of basic dyestuffs which are laked to increase alcohol solubility, colour strength and reduce water solubility.

The main solvent used in dye based inks is denatured ethyl alcohol (methylated spirits). Both 64 overproof (op) and 74 op grades are used, and the former contains approximately 5 per cent of water. This small amount of water helps to stabilise the dye solution, but too much would cause precipitation of the dyestuff. Dye based inks are usually used for printing on paper, the end product being general purpose bags, wrappings, waxed bread wrappers and sweet wrappers. They are rarely used on plastics films due to the tendency of the dyestuff to migrate into the film. The inks produced have low viscosity and high colour strength, and can print at very high machine speeds due to the penetration of the ink into the paper stock. Should the drying rate of an ink need to be increased, acetone or ethyl acetate may be added. Retarding of ink drying may be achieved by the use of glycol ethers, though it must be realised that the retention of any solvent in a print may give rise to objectionable odours. The problems of set off caused by retained solvent and other factors will be discussed later.

The adjustment of an ink for drying rate is dependent on the drying potential and printing speed of the machine, the area of type face, etc. The best results are achieved by correct initial formulation in co-operation with minor modification by the printer at the press side. For instance, some printers may wish to add 5 per cent of retarder to an ink to maintain clean printing from a small type-face, and others would complain that this addition would slow down the drying rate of the ink so that the production speed would have to be reduced.

A typical formulation is:

Dye Based Waxed Paper Ink

10.0	victoria blue dye
2.0	methyl violet dye
12.0	tannic acid-or equivalent
6.0	shellac solution (50 per cent in 64 op meths)
5.0	"cellosolve"
65.0	methylated spirits (64 op)

When auramine yellow and rhodamine B dyes are being used, it may be found necessary to increase the amount of laking agent used to minimise the wax bleed of the dyestuffs. Inks intended for use on sweet wrappers which may have to undergo a glycerine treatment to improve flexibility, should be tested for resistance to water and glycerine.

Inks may be formulated on 74 op methylated spirit, provided some additional water is included. The use of resins improves ink transference from the stereo and hardens the ink film, in addition to being considered as possible laking agents. The incorporation of small quantities of ethyl cellulose may reduce the tack of the ink and assist in overcoming ink penetration through very absorbent papers.

Ink based on more lightfast dyes are most often formulated for adhesion to aluminium foil. The dyestuffs require no laking agent to adjust their resistance properties.

A starting formulation for a lacquer for shellac washed foil would be:

45.0 methylated spirits (74 op)

15.0 ethyl acetate

5.0 "cellosolve"

5.0 plasticiser

20.0 cellulose nitrate

10.0 shellac varnish (50 per cent resin)

Dye based inks are manufactured by making solutions of the dye and laking agent in the solvent, either by cold or hot blending on high speed stirring equipment. It may be necessary to allow the solution to stand for a period to allow undissolved particles of dye to be settled or be filtered. The solutions may be prepared in concentrated form for subsequent blending with other varnishes and solvents or, alternatively, by mixing dyestuff, laking agent, varnish and solvent, thereby eliminating the manufacture of the concentrated solution. Dyestuffs are fully transparent and therefore do not give bright colours when used on coloured papers, e.g. brown kraft. Some opacity may be imparted by including a percentage of a titanium white base to the dye ink. The medium into which the white is dispersed must be suitable for use with the dyes. These semi-pigmented inks may also be used on lightweight papers, which may become very transparent when waxed.

Other pigment/dye mixtures are used either to produce specific colour effects, or to increase the colour strength of a fully pigmented ink with a low viscosity dye concentrate, though the possibility of interaction of the dye with the pigment must be closely investigated.

Water Based Inks : Fully water based inks must not be confused with water reducible inks. The latter may consist of inks based on organic solvents which may be partially reduced with water. An essential feature of these is that the resin used must also be soluble in the solvent/water system.

Water reducible systems are not widely used, but interest is shown when supplies of solvent are limited or when the use of water as a slow drying solvent may assist in obtaining good print quality. The scope of water based inks will be discussed more fully.

The traditional water based inks consist of resin systems which are dispersed in water. Naturally occurring resins such as casein are readily soluble in water and may be suggested as an ink vehicle. However, it will be observed that the resistance of a print of this type of ink to water will not be satisfactory. The ideal formulation is that which although water based, will have acceptable resistance to water when the print is dried. Traditionally, shellac is the main resin used, which can be made water soluble in an alkaline solution. Suitable alkalis are caustic soda, ammonia, or triethanolamine. The resulting varnish usually has a pH between 7.5 and 9.0. Because the varnish consists of a soap rather than a true solution, water based inks are very sensitive to water reduction. The use of certain pigments may be precluded because of the effect of the pH of the varnish system.

The advantages of water based inks may be summarised as follows:

Excellent press stability is achieved because of the low evaporation loss from the ink duct. The print quality is not impaired by ink drying on the stereo.

There is no solvent attack on the stereos, and photopolymer plates may be used.

Obvious economies are obtained in using water as reducer and cleaning solvent, both for price and availability reasons.

There is no fire hazard.

Typical water based flexographic inks may be based as follows:

Red Water Based Ink

19.0	calcium lithol red
60.0	alkali solubulised shellac-water varnish
5.0	polyethylene wax compound
15.75	water
0.25	silicone oil

Blue Water Based Ink

12.0	phthalocyanine blue
10.0	barium sulphate
65.0	solubilised acrylic resin-water varnish
5.0	polyethylene wax compound
7.75	water
0.25	silicone oil

The disadvantages are the poor level of gloss and the slow drying rate which, if conventional methods of drying are used, restricts the use of water based inks to highly absorbent substrates. Developments are proceeding to establish the feasibility of using radio frequency drying equipment in conjunction with water based inks on plastics films and foils.

The main uses of water based inks have been in the paper sack and carton field, where highly absorbent papers are used and the non-inflammability property is a major advantage. High press speeds are obtainable and the print becomes satisfactorily water resistant shortly after printing.

Due to the high increase in the cost of shellac, various synthetic resins have been used in waster systems. A wide range of acrylic resins is available from which water/alkaline solutions may be obtained. Solid resins may be soluble at pH 7.5 to 9.0, and certain emulsions may be solubilised at this degree of alkalinity.

Extending pigments are used to reduce the raw material cost of inks. The use of lead chromate pigments in water based inks is frequent in view of the advantages of low cost and high opacity. The use of these toxic pigments may be restricted by local regulations, and the pigments may be affected adversely by the pH of the vehicle or alkaline adhesives used in board manufacture. The wax compound is necessary to provide a rub-resistant print, which is particularly required for the corrugated case and paper sack market. Various materials may be recommended for use as anti-foam additives. In certain cases it may be found necessary to include in-can preservatives.

The temptation to include solvents in water based formulations should be avoided, particularly when problems of fire hazard may arise. High concentrations of pigments in water paste form are available, from which water based inks may be manufactured by a stirring technique rather than the grinding of dry pigment into a suitable vehicle system. This method should show manufacturing cost savings for the ink maker.

Heat Transfer Inks : In recent years there has been a major development in the use of inks which are suitable for heat transfer from a carrier web (usually paper) to fabric. This is based on the use of disperse dyestuffs which sublime at high temperatures. The requirements for the print are for good print quality, low initiation cost, ability to print wide webs, and a water based flexographic system is often used as the vehicle for these dyestuffs. The main property of the print on the carrier web is that the resin used does not interfere with the subliming properties of the dyestuff. The formulation of ink is a very specialised technology; the selection of the dyestuff is influenced by the composition of the fabric and the resistance properties required from the transferred print. Advances in the technology have produced ink systems which are suitable for heat transfer printing onto most synthetic fabrics, and more recently onto natural fibres.

A typical starting formulation for a heat transfer ink would be:

10-20 per cent	disperse dyestuff
60-70 per cent	solubilised acrylic resin
5 per cent	wax medium
15 per cent	water

Pigmented Solvent Inks : This classification includes the widest range of resin and solvent systems. As indicated earlier in the chapter, the choice of resin and solvent is always influenced and often predetermined by the substrate to be printed and the specification to be met by the print. It is therefore appropriate to consider the resin system in parallel with the substrates indicating the basic formulation types and the requirements which may be stipulated when using certain substrates. It is important to realise that certain ink systems may be satisfactory for use on a wide range of materials with only minor modifications. Others may be restricted in use because the formulation is too complex or too expensive to be used for relatively low performance requirements.

Ink Performance : Web offset heatset presses are running faster and faster every year. Production speeds will reach 3,500 feet per minute by the end of the 1990's. This will be a significant improvement over the 1,200 to 1,400 feet per minute generally accepted as the standard in the early 1970s. But speed alone is not a valid criterion for measuring efficiency in today's rapidly changing pressroom. Productivity and paper waste reduction are increasingly important factors which must be considered.

One basic question which must be answered is what does productivity really mean? A good working definition for most printers would simply be excellent press and ink runability combined with minimum downtime for web breaks and blanket cleaning. There are, however, several external factors which affect ink performance in the drive to achieve high productivity.

These variables include paper, distribution of the fountain solution, plant water quality, solvents, plates, blankets and rollers. These variables play pivotal roles in how well ink will, or will not, print. But none are more critical than the paper surface, the chemical characteristics of the fountain solution and their combined compatibility with the ink chemistry.

Use of coated paper for web offset heatset publication work has increased substantially during recent years, but has not kept pace with the 33% growth of the printed insert market from 1981 to 1986. In 1986, more than 16 billion flyers and inserts were printed on uncoated stock. They were produced for a wide range of end-use markets but most were related to advertising.

This parallel growth in productivity and printing has increased the burden on the paper substrate. The most important characteristics of paper are absorptivity, roughness, surface strength, brightness, wet strength, caliper, pH, conductivity and sheet formation. It is very important that paper stock be consistent from roll to roll, have good gloss and ink holdout along with a lack of blistering and delamination. It is absolutely essential that the paper does not contribute to blanket contamination. It is obvious that the testing of inks and coated and uncoated stocks is necessary if one is to predict what final properties of the printed surface will be achieved on press.

After paper, the second most important variable is the dampening system and how effectively it controls the fountain solution. The principal function of the dampening system is to transfer a constant thin film of solution to the non-image area of the printing plate and to assist in emulsifying water into the ink to form a proper, stable emulsion. Dampening systems can be divided into low energy types, medium energy systems, and high energy brush and spray equipment. All of these systems depend upon controlling the lithographic dampening or fountain solution whether it is acidic or neutral. The solution contains many ingredients, ranging from buffering salts to use of protective colloids and emulsifying agents.

What does productivity really mean? A good working definition for the printer would be excellent press and ink runability combined with minimum downtime.

The main functions of the fountain solution are to keep the non-image area of the plate clean and to form a micro-emulsion .of water in the ink. This provides the press with a cooling and purging effect. While fountain solutions have other functions they all focus on controlled emulsification between the ink and the fountain solution. This emulsification must be carefully performed to allow the transfer of ink to the form rollers of the press and plate. Without proper emulsification, water can breakout and stripping can occur.

Emulsions are formed through both chemical and mechanical action. It is essential that the proper formulation of ink resins and vehicles be selected for compatibility with wetting agents in the fountain solution. It is also important that the press and the dampening system design be such that the amount of energy exercised does not interfere with the stability of the emulsion. The stability of a water-in-ink emulsion can be of prime importance as opposed to an inverted emulsion.

It has been discovered that the shape of a curve that is obtained when one plots the concentration of fountain solution in an ink vs. time axes study can be helpful when attempting to predict printability. The stability of emulsions and the shape of curves can be drastically altered when substances such as isopropyl alcohol are substituted for the glycol ethers generally found in the solutions. Many of the ethers, such as butyl cello-solve tend to alter paper coatings by solubization and to act as peptizing agents on the gel structure of the inks.

Other important considerations are conductivity and pH. Conductivity, which in its basic definition is the ability to conduct an electrical charge, can vary due to extractions from paper, ink, plant water, on any change in dilution of the fountain solution. pH can cause an interaction between the paper and the fountain solution, which in turn, can affect drying time and ink receptivity. It has been proven that careful monitoring of these two variables can improve print consistency.

Effect of Ink : Discussions about paper, fountain solutions and emulsification are very useful but they lead to the most important subject of all. That, of course, is ink and how it is affected by these variables.

Lithographic ink has remained basically unchanged since it was first developed hundreds of years ago. The main ingredients have remained constant, except for concentration and chemical nature. It still consists of pigments, resin or solvent vehicles and additives. Most ink chemists would agree that the composition of lithographic ink, whether it is being printed at 1,200 feet per minute or 3, 500 feet per minute, is similar, except for rheological structure, that is its floor characteristics. The fact is that for many years, resins have been utilised, including modified rosin esters and functional hydrocarbons. So have the long oil linseed alkyds and aluminium gallants. Also, petroleum-based solvents and slip additives are still used. One is prompted to ask, if this is the situation, what has changed to enable us to print at higher speeds on today's variety of substrates? The answer is quite simple. It is not so much that the composition of the building blocks has changed but that the structure has been rebuilt. The corner stone, in this case, is rheology.

There are several factors involved with rheology, but the most important are tack, viscosity and yield value. It has been discovered in recent years that those inks which have excessively large increases in shortness (yield value divided by viscosity) after emulsification are likely to show poor performance on press regardless of the shape of the emulsification curve.

Another conclusion drawn from studies and rheological measurement on fountain solution/ink studies is that thermo-dynamic stability of such emulsions is necessary for optimum press performance. In particular, the shear and thermal stability of ink/fountain solution emulsions is generally desired for optimum lithographic performance and can overcome some deficiencies of press mechanical condition.

There have been some major advancements in pressroom equipment and raw material design. But there is still no single factor that affects printability more than the rheological characteristics of a printing ink and it is there that ink manufacturers are concentrating their research.

Testing and Control : Good press performance of an ink relies largely upon the optimum selection of raw materials, and upon correct fabrication. Once this selection has been carried out, the continuing operational performance of that product will then depend upon the maintenance of standards, both in raw material quality and manufacturing.

The extreme value of testing and controlling raw materials and finished inks is thus apparent, and it is proposed to examine this area in the detail that is necessitated by its importance.

Methods of testing belong essentially to two distinct types:

(1) Numerical determinations-those that can be expressed in identifiable quantities such as tack values, acid values etc.

(2) Comparative tests based on simple non-quantifiable tests of factors such as shortness, degree of flow etc.

As many of the properties of printing inks are either ill-defined, or not well understood, it is not surprising that many tests fall under the second category.

In some cases, it is necessary to check the product in the form of a laboratory print. This invariably involves visual assessment, and highlights the still dominant reliance upon the human observer, who is more efficient in many ways.

As long as the ink maker is not less critical than the printer, printer's customers or other assessors, it is likely that his decisions will be acceptable, particularly as his method of assessment will be the same as the others.

Any planned testing programme should first involve an estimate of the testing required. In estimating, certain questions need answering, such as:

(1) Is the test realistic?

(2) Can the length of time required for the test be justified?

(3) Is the test necessary?

(4) Is the testing adequate?

(5) What are the limits of any test?

If these points are covered in the planned programme, then problems arising as a result of fluctuations in raw materials, which can be a major source of problems if left uncontrolled, will be minimised.

It is thus the primary objective of any new product development to include a testing program that adequately covers both a quality performance test on that product and more fundamentally includes an assessment of raw material quality.

Various Techniques

In order for raw material testing to have any meaning, the sample taken from a delivery of material must be representative of the bulk in all respects. This is a simple and perhaps obvious statement, but if the sampling is not carried out efficiently, then a batch may be incorrectly assessed and this could possibly result in costly repercussions at some future date.

A single delivery of material may contain several drums with the same batch reference number as well as others with a different reference. Ideally, samples should be taken from all containers and each tested accordingly. But where this is not considered practicable, one may take a calculated risk and examine samples taken at random from containers of nominally the same batch.

The following is intended as a guide to sampling different kinds of material:

> Resins which are delivered in lump form, may well also contain some smaller pieces and fine powder. A composite sample should then be taken which is representative of the proportions of each grade present. It must also be remembered that there is a specific reason for resins being delivered in lump form (usually to prevent oxidation) and so they should only be crushed, where necessary, immediately prior to the actual raw material testing.

The vibration in transit of a cask of pigment may well have caused some segregation of particles of different size. Hence, the cask should either be tumbled before opening or several samples taken at varying levels in the cask with a special auger-like tool.

The Liquids : Liquids should be thoroughly stirred or the barrels tumbled before opening to ensure that no separation into distinct phases has occurred.

Selection of Tests : Quality control sections, whether concerned with raw materials, intermediates or finished inks, carry a great responsibility for the efficient working of a company. Decisions must be made in all testing departments on the tolerance limits required: if these limits are too narrow, then ink production can be impeded and late deliveries could ensue, whereas too wide limits can, of course, have a detrimental effect on both quality and reproducibility. For commercial purposes, a working compromise must be reached: some testing will be regarded as essential, and further testing, while desirable, may be uneconomic. The ink formulator must bear a great responsibility in setting these limits as he alone is fully aware of both the final ink specification and of the raw materials which are essential to the success of his particular formulation.

Comprehensive testing of raw materials has the advantage of reducing the range of tests needed at the finished product stage, and hence a faster service to the consumer. However, this advantage is partially offset by the necessity to test deliveries of some of the more versatile raw materials in a wider range of formulations than those in which the batch may eventually be used. The individual ink companies must, therefore, balance their testing resources to give the most advantageous results.

In the remainder of this chapter, a relatively comprehensive guide to the testing of both raw materials and finished inks has been attempted but it is impossible in the scope of such a section to include all the highly specific tests which could be carried out. Where standard test methods are included, only the salient points have been given and the reader should refer to the published test procedure for the practical details. References are also quoted throughout the chapter for the reader to further his background knowledge in specific areas of testing procedure.

Quality control of pigments is particularly difficult as a single pigment can be used in a wide variety of vehicle systems to give inks for many different end uses. Hence, the testing procedure must be selective and it can logically be divided into three sections. Firstly, limited testing can be carried out on the dry pigment itself to ensure the batch meets the specification for shade, strength, particle size, oil absorption, moisture and volatile content. The second and possibly most important consideration is to compare the ink making characteristics of the batch against the master standard in the ink maker's own vehicle systems. Finally, provided the batch meets the specification to date, prints from the sample and standard inks are checked for their resistance properties.

Tests on the Dry Pigments

Particle Size : Since the pigment particle size will affect such fundamental properties as strength, hue, rheology and stability of the finished ink it would seem desirable to check particle size or at least the average size distribution as part of the quality control procedure. However, in the size range of most pigments (less than 1mm) the majority of the standard techniques for sizing (e.g., gravitational sedimentation, optical microscopy) are slow and inaccurate. Only two methods are suitable for particle size measurement in this range: electron microscopy and centrifugal sedimentation. Electron microscopy is an expensive method and requires an experienced operator but is capable of producing very accurate readings. The disc centrifuge is now the preferred technique and results compare favourably with those obtained using electron microscopy. However, neither of these two methods is simple and quick enough to be used as standard quality control procedure on each batch of pigment and the ink maker therefore places greater emphasis on the dispersion of the pigment particles in the finished ink.

Oil Absorption : The oil absorption of a pigment will depend on:

(1) The type of pigment (i.e. whether it is a lead chrome or barium lithol).

(2) Particle size and size distribution.

(3) Particle shape.

(4) Surface characteristics of the sample, such as those obtained by treatment to improve wetability or even simply due to absorbed moisture.

If the oil absorption of the pigment varies from batch to batch then formulation changes will have to be made to the inks and clearly this is undesirable. Since the factors affecting oil absorption cannot easily be measured, the test is reduced to a purely empirical comparison between the batch and master standard. The actual test method is given in BS 3483, Part 137; 1974, the result being quoted as the mass (or volume) of oil required to wet 100 g of pigment. Alternatively, the sample and standard can be dispersed in a measured amount of oil and the relative consistencies of the two samples can then be compared.

Moisture and Volatile Content : Absorbed moisture may affect the ease of dispersion of some pigments and this should be determined on each batch of pigment according to the method in BS 3483, Part 6; 1974. A temperature of 105° C is chosen for this test as at higher temperatures volatile matter may be lost which is an essential part of the pigment: this is especially true of carbon black and pigments on an aluminium hydrate base.

Ink Making Characteristics : All pigments should be checked wherever possible in the vehicle systems in which they will be used in production, but in certain cases where the pigment is used in several different types of inks this will result in a lengthy testing procedure and a selective range of formulations must then be chosen. This should include oil and liquid ink formulations (where appropriate), a vehicle system which is used in bulk with the test pigment and one which is a more difficult medium for ease of dispersion. The method of dispersion in the laboratory should:

(1) Simulate production milling methods.

(2) Be rapid and comparative.

(3) Utilise small quantities of pigment so as to retain a single master standard for testing as many batches as possible.

For example, bead mill dispersions with liquid and oil inks can be simulated in the laboratory by a high speed stirring technique using a standard weight of beads or steel balls in a known amount of ink. Small triple roll mills can of course be used to represent their larger production counterparts, but care must be taken to avoid any alteration to the roller settings in between milling the standard and batch pigments.

The first test must be to ensure that the batch of pigment disperses at least as readily as the standard and to an equivalent degree so that costly production milling time will not be lost. Dispersion is measured on a fineness of grind gauge. This is a hardened steel block containing a shallow groove which is graduated in depth from zero to, for example, 25 or 50 microns. A sample of ink is placed at the deep end, drawn down with a steel blade towards the shallower part, and the dispersion is taken as the point at which the continuous ink film breaks down across the groove. However, care must be taken in interpreting the result if discontinuity in the ink film occurs higher up on the gauge due to the odd oversize particle. It is then important to determine whether these scratches are caused by undispersed pigment particles, or by, for example, wax or dried ink, and this can be confirmed by examination of a smear of the ink under a microscope.

Once the correct dispersion level has been attained, the trial ink can be compared with the standard for strength, hue, gloss and flow (or consistency). Firstly, the flow is checked as it is impossible to obtain meaningful comparative prints unless the batch and standard have very similar consistency. Liquid inks having near Newtonian flow properties can be compared by viscosity measurements using any of the standard techniques (e.g., Ford and Zahn cups). Oil inks, however, are more difficult to assess by instrumental measurement and for the present purpose are probably best compared by checking their consistency with the aid of a palette knife, and by a comparison of their relative flow properties on a vertical glass plate.

The strength of the trial pigment is then assessed on a drawdown at full strength and at reduced strength as a 'bleach'. The drawdown is carried out by placing small quantities of the standard and test inks about one inch apart on the top sheet of a securely held pad of paper and firmly scraping them towards the operator with, for example, a 3 inch wide blade. Initially, the blade should be held nearly vertical to reproduce a film thickness comparable to a printed film weight and then finally the blade should be brought almost parallel to the pad to give a thick film weight-the mass tone of the ink. The drawdown should be carried out on a semi-absorbent paper on which a broad black band (19 mm wide) has been previously printed so the opacity (or transparency) of the batch and standard pigments can also be compared.

The bleach technique involves dilution by mixing (not grinding) a coloured ink with a much larger quantity of opaque white so as to eliminate any minor differences of gloss and hue. In the case of yellow inks, the eye cannot differentiate small strength differences and so sufficient blue is added to the bleach to bring the hue into the blue-green region.

Hue and gloss can be measured by instrumental techniques but normally a visual comparison of a drawdown and print is sufficiently accurate. The undertone and top tone of the inks can be assessed using the thin film of the drawdown and the thicker mass-tone respectively. Gloss can also be checked on the drawdown but, more accurately, by examination of a print of the batch versus standard on an appropriate stock.

Resistance Tests : Provided the pigment matches the standard on the tests conducted to date, the appropriate resistance checks are carried out. Many of the characteristic properties of a pigment are a function of its chemical nature and hence are unlikely to vary from batch to batch unless an impurity is present. Pigments are, however, coated to provide easier dispersion in different vehicle systems and this can give rise to batch variation especially when the pigment is obtained from an alternative supplier.

All the resistance tests are carried out on prints of the batch and standard inks rather than on the dry pigments themselves, but it is important that an appropriate vehicle system be chosen, e.g., it is pointless to try and check the heat resistance of a pigment when a low softening point resin is present.

Lightfastness : As the lightfastness of a pigment is a function of its chemical nature, it is only necessary to carry out random spot checks but attention should be paid hereto pigments used in inks where lightfastness is an important criterion, e.g. wallpaper inks

Pigments will show higher lightfastness at full strength and therefore it is important that a realistic strength print be submitted for test. For example, a PMTA pigment should rarely be tested at full strength, since its main application will be as a toner pigment. As pigments for use on wallpapers could often be used in tints, it is advisable to test these at both full and tint strengths. Prints should be prepared on a good quality paper which does not yellow on exposure to light or contain artificial brightening aids which are destroyed by ultra-violet radiation.

The exposure of prints to daylight is too lengthy a procedure to be suitable and the use of an artificial source is therefore adopted. The only light source to have an emission spectrum close to that of daylight is the xenon arc and provided a filter is used to reduce the amount of ultra-violet radiation a result comparable to the daylight exposure is obtained in a much shorter time. Other light sources such as the carbon arc and mercury vapour lamp are not recommended as the results bear little comparison to those obtained under daylight conditions.

Another factor which greatly affects the lightfastness figure is the effective humidity which is dependent on the relative humidity and temperature of the surrounding air and the surface temperature of the pattern. The average effective humidity value for daylight exposure in Britain is 45 per cent and therefore the test apparatus should be capable of approximating to this figure.

In order to numerically classify the lightfastness results obtained the prints are compared with a set of eight pieces of wool, each dyed with a different blue dye which has been carefully graded to fade after a set of exposure to light. This is known as the Blue Wool Scale and the scale ranges from one (poor lightfastness) to eight (excellent) according to the number of the wool dyes which have test method. The procedure for mounting and assessing samples is given in as 4321:1969. But it is worthy to note that the term 'fading' includes not only a reduction in strength but also changes in hue, brightness, darkening or any combination of these factors.

Heat Resistance : Heat resistance of pigments is a critical factor in the areas of tin printing inks (and other metal coatings) and wallpaper inks which will be subjected to hot embossing. The pigments are simply tested by placing prints in a suitably heated oven for a set period of time, the actual conditions depending on the end usage of the print. The prints are then compared with an unheated sample for changes in strength, hue and brightness.

Soap and Detergent Resistance : Pigments to be used in soap and detergent wraps should be checked to ensure no impurities are present which are liable to cause bleed problems. Although test methods for both soap and detergent resistance are given (BS, 4321 Test methods 6 and 7 respectively) the manufacturers of these products have their own test methods which are generally more severe than the British Standard tests.

A typical soap resistance test as provided by a leading manufacturer, is as follows:

> A 25 per cent soap gel is made up and allowed to set. The gel is moistened and the print to be tested is first soaked in water to prevent curling (one minute for paper and five minutes for board). The print is then placed face down in the gel and left for 15 minutes, after which time it is examined There should be no sign of bleeding at this stage. The print is then replaced and left for three hours before being further examined. After this period there should be preferably no bleed, although a slight bleed could be considered acceptable.

Testing for detergent resistance is becoming more complex with the advent of the enzyme powders and more recently "solvent" powders. Provided a pigment passes the above test, it is unlikely to fail with the standard soap powders and therefore detergent resistance should be assessed with an enzymic powder. (Note: To date no standard test has been published for resistance to the "solvent detergents").

A typical detergent test resistance is as follows:

> A five per cent solution is made up using the appropriate enzymic detergent in water. Two filter papers are soaked in the solution, one is placed on a glass slab and the print to be tested is placed face down on filter paper. The second filter paper is then laid on top and a further glass slab provides a sandwiched effect. The print is then examined after three hours and there should be no bleed although a slight bleed could be considered as acceptable.

Alkali Resistance : This test can be conducted either by streaking dilute sodium hydroxide solutions on to a print (e.g. 2,3 and 5 per cent) and examining the dried streaks for discolouration or as in the British Standard test (BS 4321 Test method 5) by sandwiching the print between filter papers previously soaked in a dilute alkaline solution. In this case, the filter papers are dried after a set contact period and then the degree of staining is assessed with the aid of a grey scale.

Acid Resistance : Acid resistance can be carried out in a manner similar to BS4321 Test method 5 above but replacing the alkaline solution with either dilute hydrochloric acid or dilute acetic acid. The latter reagent is normally used where the print could come into contact with vinegar or pickles.

Wax Resistance : Wax resistance is essential for inks on waxed paper bread wraps, ice cream cartons, certain vending machine cups and similar applications where the substrate is made more water resistant by immersion in molten wax (usually paraffin wax). The standard test (BS4321 Test method 10) involves immersion of the print in the molten wax for five minutes after which the wax is allowed to run over the margin surrounding the print. The margin and the wax in the basin are then examined for discolouration.

Deep Freeze Resistance : This test is becoming increasingly important as more and more products are being stored under deep freeze conditions. On carton board, the vehicle system (or overprint varnish) will normally provide adequate deep freeze resistance and testing of the pigment is not necessary. However, for polythene printing the deep freeze resistance of the finished pack is a function not only of the vehicle (usually straight or modified polyamide) but also of the pigment as well. The deep freeze resistance of the pigment in these cases is not so much a function of its chemical nature but of the pigment coating and therefore quality control of each batch of pigment is essential for this application.

The severest conditions met by the print is not when the pack is actually under the deep freeze conditions, but during the stage of thawing on removal from the refrigerator, and hence the test normally conducted is one of water immersion.

A typical test is as follows:

> The print is immersed in water for a period of at least one hour and a maximum of five hours. The print is then flexed between the knuckles ten times and should show no more than five per cent removal. A second portion of the print is then blotted dry and should show no more than five per cent removal when checked by the Scotch tape test.

9

Production Tasks

Every newspaper is designed to meet the needs of its customers. Although more or less all newspapers now-a-days get the same news, yet their presentation differs according to the requirements of their readers. The readers of a quality newspaper require detailed articles. On the other hand, the readers of a popular tabloid require more visual impressions and the spoken word. In a Tabloid newspaper the photographs and the headlines are given more space whereas the text is short. These headlines and the pictures can convey the story of a news at a single glance. Thus, we see that the layout and type faces of a newspaper are very important along with the contents of the information.

Various Types

It is said that there are 5,000 different type faces in the world which are used in the various alphabets of different languages. Of course, a journalist is not concerned much with the typography. But this is the main tool of the sub-editor of a newspaper. A fount of type is a collection of letters, numbers and other devices such as punctuation marks etc., all of the same character and belonging to the same family. In fact, a series of type faces consists of several founts in different sizes. A family of type is a collection of founts and series all of the same basic design, but in different sizes and weights or widths.

The weight of a type face is referred to by its x-height. In each family of type there are certain letters that project upward from the main body of the letter. For example, b, d, and h. Still, there are certain letters that are projected downwards like g, j and p. Similarly, there are other letters that are shaped entirely within the main body like a, e and x. And the height of these letters is known as the x-height.

Type faces are measured in points. A point in the system used in most English speaking countries, is 0.0138 inches or 1/12th of a pica (0.166). There are approximately 72 points to the inch. The point sizes refer to the measurement of the body of the letter. The text sizes most commonly used in newspapers are from 4-3/4 to 12 points. For headlines 14 to 96 points are used. A variety can be given within the body type by using a contrasting type face within the same family—usually either bold or italic. Some papers also begin a story or sections of stories with a larger letter, usually two or three lines, known as a drop letter.

Designing and Style

Sometimes, to give importance to the beginning of a news story, the introduction is set across two or three columns in a larger point size than the story that follows it. For this, sometimes a contrasting type can also be used. Generally, if a bold type is used for the first two or three sentences of an introduction, then the story should go into an intermediate point size of the standard body type for the next two sentences which should be set across either two columns or in a single column, depending on the layout of the page.

The type faces which are used in the printing of a newspaper determine its character. Some newspapers even have a specially designed type character. Although most of the newspapers may not have a definite character, yet they also have a planned series of type faces which are available to the sub-editors. Every newcomer must try to know the type faces which are used in his newspaper.

Newspaper Layout

The number of type faces which are used in a newspaper should be small enough so that people are able to handle them in a hurry. Still, the number should be sufficient enough for different effects. Very large and very bold faces are needed only for special occasions, when some really big story is to be published. Generally, modest type faces are needed to headline the usual run of stories.

The layout of a page is very important in the production of a good newspaper. The layout should be such that the greatest amount of information is printed on a page to give variety. But, this may be kept in mind that it should not create any confusion. There is no doubt that every paper has its own style. Some of the newspapers have now-a-days moved from a vertical make-up to a horizontal style. Generally, the horizontal style is only useful, when the number of lengthy articles on a page is small. In such a case, lengthy headlines across four to six columns can be given. But one thing should always be remembered that a page should give the look of being clean and neat from the top to bottom.

10

Binding

The binding (finishing) operation has been grossly dependent upon the skill and efficiency of the manual work-force. The skill normally acquired through years of experience gained under the expert guidance of senior members of the family as the binding has been a family oriented craft\trade.

Binding or Post-Press Operation being one of the most important functions in presenting and preserving the printed material, can be described as follows:

(1) Pre-Press Binding or warehousing

(2) Post-Press Binding/Finishing

Warehousing/Pre-press Binding

White-paper warehouse

Printed-paper Warehouse

Binding/Finishing Warehouse

White-Paper Warehouse

Paper is stored and cut before being issued for Printing. Equipment required-Guillotine/Cutting Machines.

Printed-Paper Warehouse

Printed sheets are stored awaiting instructions for Finishing. Book printing invariably involves binding in parts thereby saving additional expenditures of binding.

The Warehouse : Simple forms of finishing (cutting & trimming) e.g. pamphlet and magazine binding including packing and despatch functions are performed.

Equipment required-Guillotine/Cutting Machine, Wire stitching and Dab-Press etc.

Extensive range of Cutting Machines (Guillotine) are available as follows:

(a) Hand Clamp and hand-levered Cutting action with 4-5" opening; Size: 26", 32", 36" & 42".

(b) Semi-automatic heavy duty with Foot-clamp and motorised Cutting action with manual or motorised back-gauge movement with upto 5" opening; Size: 26, 32, 36, 42 & 48".

(c) Automatic with self-clamping, motorised back-gauge, safety device, 5" opening etc. Size: 33" & 42". Optional Magnetic Clutch and electronic Photocell safety device.

(d) Automatic with Hydraulic clamping and Cutting action, Safety device, digital display, Air cushion table etc. Programmable. Size: 33", 42" & 48".

The modern machines should incorporate the following features for accurate cutting efficiency and reliable trouble-free performance:

(i) The knife fall is so engineered that the cut is made at 90 degrees with the table and provision for adjustment to take up wear etc.

(ii) Clamping should be adequate and adjustable to various levels to suit different types of stock. The clamp action should be complete before the knife strikes the paper.

(iii) The back gauge must be easily moved by hand or be powered. It should be easily locked in position and when locked immovable. The back gauge should be parallel to the cutting line and adjustable both vertically and horizontally.

(iv) Knives should be of good quality and of good depth to allow many regrinds: easy and swift knife change facilities with fine setting adjustments.

(v) Cutting sticks should be easily adjusted, changed or turned.

(vi) Side plates should allow the cutting of small areas accurately.

(vii) There should be accurate gauging and presentation of the cutting distance in a position which is easily read.

(viii) Suitable safety guards in, accordance with the rules & regulations of Factories Act.

(ix) Other facilities e.g. micrometer settings, air-cushion tables, illuminated tables, power-operated back-gauge, photo-cell operated guards and Programmable for multiple Cuts.

Post-Press Binding/Finishing

Folding

Scoring & Creasing

Gathering

Insetting

Collating

Wire Stitching/Stabbing

Thread Sewing and Stitching

Binding Terminology

Styles of Binding

Perfect/Adhesive Binding

Spiral wire and Plastic-comb binding

Embossing, Die-cutting, Round-cornering, Varnishing & Laminating.

Folding

One of the most common and important operations. Folding may be done by:

(i) Hand

(ii) Machine-Semi Auto/Auto.

A sheet of paper has to be folded in accordance with the agreed imposition so that the printed pages will appear in correct sequence. A sheet of paper may be folded in various ways and the folds may be at right-angles, parallel or a combination of both right-angle and parallel folds. (See Illustration 'A').

Folding is an important operation because the final appearance of a job may be spoilt by inaccurate folds causing uneven margins which cannot be rectified in subsequent operations.

(i) Hand folding-Sheets are folded by hand with a bone of folding stick, when the number of sheets required to be folded does not justify setting up a Folding Machine or when the scheme of imposition is unsuitable for machine folding.

(ii) Folding machines of various patterns and capacities exist, and these are capable of folding sheets at speeds greatly in excess of those possible by hand-folding. The method of folding is by either knife-blade or buckle-fold principle or combination of both. The capacity of a Folding machine is determined by the size of sheet to be folded and the number of folding units. Folding machines are either hand-fed or fitted with automatic feeder (Simple Pile feeder or Continuous Paper feeder). Different thicknesses of paper stock and any alteration in the size of sheet entail adjustment to both the folding mechanisms.

The following characteristics of the printed sheet will effect the folding quality:

(a) The forme should be centered on the sheet, unless there is a good reason for it not to be so.

(b) Back-up should be accurate, the back mark in correct position and signatures properly located.

(c) Sheet size constant with clean edges.

When thick material, such as board, thick cover paper, manilla etc., is folded, its surface becomes damaged and ragged at the fold unless it is scored or creased before being folded. This is done on a rotary scoring machine or a bender scorer by making a blind impression into the material to compress and stretch the fibres so as to produce a score or crease which will permit the material to bend without its surface being broken and the fold becoming ragged.

Gathering : When a job consists of more than one section, the sections, which have been folded separately, have to be collected together in complete set ready for binding. This operation is known as gathering. In order to distinguish one section from another signatures are used. Signatures are generally capital letters or figures printed at the foot of the printed matter on the front page of each section in alphabetical or numerical order so that the sections can be gathered in correct sequence and later checked. A gathered job consists of separate sections collected together in correct order as complete sets of signatures.

Insetting : The placing of one section within another is known as Insetting. For example, if an 8pp. section is inset in the middle of another 4pp. section, a 12pp. section results. The smaller section being wrapped round the larger section. The pages have to be imposed accordingly otherwise the folios will not be in correct sequence.

Insetting is an operation which has to be carried out with more than average, care as insetted sections cannot subsequently be easily checked. An insetted job is one in which the centre section forms the middle round which all the other sections are wrapped. Inset should not be confused with an insert which is a loose piece of paper or board inserted between the leaves of a book/pamphlet and not secured in any way.

Collating : After folded sections have been gathered, they are collated, which means that they are examined to ensure that they are complete and that the signatures are in correct sequence. On machine-gathered or cheap work, this examination is often dispensed with.

Collating marks or 'back marks' are sometimes printed on the back folds of gathered jobs and in this way the operation of collating is simplified because any displacement of sections or other errors in gathering can be seen at a glance.

Wire Stitching/Stabbing : The cheapest and fastest method of binding single section or insetted work and the method most widely used for magazines and pamphlets is wire stitching. In this operation one copy of the insetted sections, opened at its centre, is placed on the saddle of the machine. Wire, fed from a reel is automatically cut to the correct length for the stitch and driven by the stitching head through the back fold, being clenched beneath at the centre to form a staple which holds the sections firmly together.

Gatherer stitchers are more elaborate machines having an endless chain feed device on which the separate sections are placed, either by hand or by automatic hopper feeders, before being carried under one or more stitching heads. This type of machine permits the insetting of sections to be carried out at the same time as stitching and greatly increases output as the operation of the stitching heads is automatic.

Gathered work, consisting of separate sections, is stitched through the side at the binding edge from front to back. This method is known as stabbing, side wire stitching or flat wire stitching

Round wire is generally used for saddle stitching and flat wire for side stitching. The wire is usually galvanised steel, but brass or copper is used when non-rusting wire is considered desirable. The gauge of the wire varies according to the thickness being stitched and the hardness of the paper. Stitching machines are available in India as single-head or double-head power-operated for a capacity ranging from 5" to 1.25". Paddle-operated machines are capable of handling stock upto 9/16".

Thread Sewing and Stitching

Gathered sections are sewn and insetted work is stitched through the back fold, just as wired jobs are stabbed or stitched, but linen thread is used instead of wire.

Sewing is used in better quality magazine work and in bookbinding, and may be done either by hand or on a sewing machine. Machine sewing is quicker than hand sewing and has the advantage that stitches are independent of each other so that every stitch must be broken before a section can be removed, whereas a single break in the thread of hand sewn work is sufficient for removal of a section because each stitch is made with the same piece of thread.

Modern machines using straight needles may be grouped into hand-fed, semi-automatic and automatic versions.

Binding Terminology : Certain terms are used in connection with bindery and warehouse work, some of the same are quoted as follows:

(a) Head or top is the edge of a page or book parallel to and above the printed matter or used to indicate the upper positions on any form of binding.

(b) Tail is the edge parallel to and below the printed matter or the lower positions on any form of binding.

(c) Back, spine or binding edge is that portion of a book or pamphlet where the sheets are secured together by thread, wire or other means or corresponding external portion of a book/pamphlet.

(d) Foredge is the edge of a book or pamphlet opposite the back, spine or binding edge.

(e) Cover is any material cut to size for the binding of a book or pamphlet.

Styles of Binding

(a) Edition Case Binding

(b) Letterpress Binding

(c) Stationery Binding

Edition Case Binding : Today the majority of books having stiff cloth covers are bound in this style. This method of binding is known as casing because the cover is prepared separately from the sections making. (See Illustration B & C).

Operations in Binding a Cased Book : Cutting Printed Sheets and Folding; pasting End Paper; Gathering and collating sections; sewing collated sections; smashing; trimming edges; gluing of back; rounding and backing; back lining; Case making & Blocking.

Letterpress Binding : This is the name given to those styles of binding used for reading books as distinct from books used for written records such as accounts books. Edition Case binding is a branch of Letter-press binding. (See Illustration 'D' for Extra letter Press binding and Illustration 'E' for library style binding).

The work of letterpress binding may be divided into sewing, forwarding, covering and finishing.

Stationery Binding : This includes the binding of account books, manifold and duplicate books, receipt books, cheque books, and memoranda books, loose-leaf books, punching and creasing sheets for loose-leaf binders.

The style of binding books which are to be used for written records of either a temporary or permanent nature needs to be different from that for books printed for the purpose of reading.

Perfect Binding : A type of Binding which has become very popular due to its economy and flexibility. What can be easier than gathering loose sections to form book blocks, jogging these, preparing the spines, gluing them and applying a cover.

Perfect Binding or Adhesive Binding can be defined as a method of binding books with adhesive as the only binding medium not involving thread for sewing or steel-wire for saddle stitching.

The development of a fully Automatic Adhesive Binding Machine began in the latter part of the nineteenth century, but it was not until after World War II, with the development of suitable adhesive that the process became popular.

Perfect Binding holds a challenge to book binder and machine manufacturer alike. There really are considerable differences between producing large quantities of thin paperbacks as economically as possible, binding bulky telephone directories or mailorder catalogues in such a way that they will stand-up to frequent use over long period.

For achieving best results with adhesive binding, it is essential to study the size of the book, type of paper, grain of paper and the cover, these variable factors are required to be balanced for selecting the most suitable glue and parameters of machine setting accordingly.

Adhesive binding, also known as 'Perfect', 'Patent' or 'Threadless' binding is being used extensively in binding industry because:

1. It produces flat-opening books of any thickness.
2. The books can be either paper covered or cased-in.
3. Adhesive-binding can be done in an un-interrupted work flow.

Process of Perfect Binders : The Perfect bound book passes through the following stages:

Gathering : Loose sections or sheets are gathered (manually or mechanically) to form book-blocks and transferred for feeding manually for slower machine and mechanically in-line for faster machines.

Jogging : Built-in vibrating mechanism helps the book blocks to have even spine.

Preparation of Back-Bone

The back-bone (spine) of the book is prepared by mailing-out a section of the spine leaving about 3/4" of the head and tail uncut thus providing a paperhinge. The cutters make a serrated pattern on the surface of the back-bone and roughening cutters prepare an ideal spine for a strong adhesive bond. The paper dust is removed with the help of a vacuum pump to avoid any dust particles transferring to Glue-Tank.

Gluing : The characteristics of adhesive used in perfect binding are fast drying, flexible and strength to with-stand constant use. The three basic glues used are: (i) Cold Glues, (ii) Animal Glues & (iii) Hot-Melt Glues.

(i) Most Cold-Glues are polyvinyl acetate with plasticizers which form a tough flexible film that dries slowly therefore require additional drying energy.

(ii) Animal Glue is a fairly fast setting gelatine that becomes brittle within a short period of time once the liquids of which the glue is formulated have evaporated.

(iii) Hot-Melt glues have no wetting agent but rather are melted by applying high temperatures. Once applied to a book and cover, the hot-melt adhesive cools rapidly to a solid flexible state that lasts indefinitely.

Cover Feeding : Paper covers can be scored (creased), aligned and applied to the back-bone immediately after Gluing.

Nipping : The back-bone with the cover pasted is nipped from the bottom and the two sides.

Delivery : The bound-books are delivered on their spine with help of stacker arrangement. Belt delivery can be attached for faster transfer.

11

Printing Industry

Journalism ad : Communication is a process involving sorting, selecting and sending of symbols in such a way as to help a listener perceive and recreate in his own mind the meaning contained in the mind of the communicator. Communication involves the creation of meaning in the listener, the transfer of information and thousands of potential stimuli-communication enables us to do important things, to grow, to learn, to be aware of ourselves and to adjust to our environment.

Mass media together comprise a new social institution, concerned with the production and distribution of knowledge in the widest sense of the word, and having a number of salient characteristics, including the use of relatively advanced technology for mass production and dissemination of message; the systematic organization and social regulation of this work; and the direction of the message at potentially large audiences who are unknown to the sender and free to attend or not.

Open Institution

The mass media institution is open, operates in the public sphere to provide regular channels of communication for messages of a kind determined by what is culturally and technically possible, socially permitted and in demand by a large enough number of individuals.

It is usual to date the beginnings of mass media from the first recognizably modern newspaper, in the early seventeenth century, which in turn was a new application of the technology of printing, already in use for over 150 years for the multiple reproduction of book manuscripts.

This history of media development is more than a record of technical advance and of increasing scale of operation. It was a social innovation as much as a technological invention, and turning points in media history are marked by major social changes. This history of the newspapers, as the first mass medium, illustrates the point very well. Its develoment is linked to the emergence of power of the bourgeois class. It became an essential instrument in subsequent economic and political struggles, a necessary condition for economic liberalism, constitutional democracy and, also, revolution and bureaucratic centralism. Its development thus reflects political and economic forces on the one hand and major social and cultural changes on the other.

Early social science views of mass media reflect some of these circumstances. Commentators were struck by the immense popular appeal of the new media and by the power which they might exert in society. Views divided sharply on whether to welcome or regret the new instruments of culture and information.

The first period of scientific investigation of mass media undertaken between the mid- 1930s and the late 1950s resulted in a much more modest estimate of media effects than was previously assumed. Since the 1960s there has been further development in the assessment of mass media effects in the direction of a renewed belief in their potency.

Role of Newspapers and other Media : Good newspapers are essential if individuals are to function effectively in an increasingly complex world, and if the democratic system is to prevail. Other media can complement, but not replace newspapers.

Traditionally, the newspaper's basic roles have been to inform, influence, entertain, and foster the development of the nation's economy through advertising; those roles are still important. But changing audiences, and potential audiences, have suggested the addition of a fifth basic function : to serve people and help make their lives better.

The Advantages : Compared with other media like television, radio, magazines, etc., and with the latest technology development it could be said that there are many advantages still enjoyed by newspapers. First, newspapers provide a wider variety of news and information than the other media and they present far more details than the electronic media. A second advantage is that they fit into the consumer's schedule more easily than the broadcast media. In the third place, newspapers, along with other print media, are particularly suited to the communication of what has been described as linear or sequential information. Human beings today must assimilate an astounding amount of information to keep pace with a rapidly changing world. They do this by continuously programming their brains, which can be compared to highly sophisticated computers. The printed word can be used for more efficiently in such programming than the spoken word. Fourth, newspapers can present certain types of entertainment such as the crossword puzzle much more effectively than the broadcast media. Fifth, newspapers can present certain types of advertising far more effectively. Finally, it can be noted that newspapers are particularly effective in presenting information, developing issues and motivating action at the local level. They can give meaning and perspective to community life not possible through the other media.

A newspaper's responsibilities vary with the size, frequency of publication and intended audience of individual publications. The responsibilities of the metropolitan daily, the country weekly and the college newspapers are not the same. Each must determine its particular functions and perform them as best it can. Nevertheless, there seem to be some common responsibilities that apply to all. Newspapers must:

(i) lead in the search for truth;

(ii) in a democratic society, help make democracy work;

(iii) help individuals and communities adjust to change and improve themselves; and

(iv) remain free, independent and solvent.

The history of the development of newspapers must begin with the first efforts to produce them. But a better perspective may be obtained if newspapers are discussed as a major development in the story of man's efforts to communicate with other men. Communication grew out of a need and became more sophisticated. Symbols and materials for communication were developed, and the information of news concept evolved. At first, men relied on gestures and crude sounds. Then they developed the use of objects such as knotted cords and notched sticks to serve as records and reminders. Later they began to record information and ideas through the use of pictures carved into stone tablets or on the walls of caves.

Egyptians are noted for their sacred writings, or hieroglyphics. The Babylonians and especially the Phoenicians pioneered the development of writing. The Greeks modified the Phoenicians' system somewhat. The Romans, and subsequently the Anglo-Saxons, produced the modern alphabet of 26 letters. These were the symbols of communication.

Meanwhile, improved materials for communication were being developed. At first the stone and clay tablets. Then the Egyptians discovered that the papyrus plant could be used as a writing material. The Greeks and Romans used tablets with wax on them, and the Romans developed the use of animal skins for writing. The Chinese developed a form of paper from cotton, rags, hemp and tree bark by the second century after Christ, and its use gradually moved westward. But it was not until the fourteenth century that paper became common in Europe.

Most information was transferred to paper, skins or tablets by hand until the fifth or sixth century when the Chinese developed a form of block printing. Under this system, images and words were carved into blocks, inked and pressed against the paper or printing material. Block printing became common in Europe by the fifteenth century.

At the same time the concept of disseminating information, or news, was being developed. As the need for communication increased, the symbols, materials and methods of providing it became sophisticated.

Origin and Evolution

Johann Gutenberg provided a major breakthrough about A.D. 1450 when he developed the means to cast and use movable type word, but the idea was not quickly transmitted to Europe. Gutenberg developed brass moulds to cast individual letters, and he developed an improved ink out of lampblack and oil. He printed his communications on a press.

The development of movable type opened the way for the development of mass media. Hundreds of copies could be reproduced in a short period of time. Numerous publications, including some newspapers, were produced in Europe in the sixteenth and seventeenth centuries. But the breakthrough in publication potential was not accompanied by an immediate breakthrough in press freedom. On the contrary, those in power who had sought to monopolize earlier forms of communication sought also to control the development and use of printing. Kings and princes realized the potential of printing and sought to use it for their own purposes. The modern struggle for press freedom was soon joined.

England, which provided the model for American journalism, was ruled by a succession of autocratic monarchs during the early development years of modern printing. The absolutist Tudors came to power shortly after printing was introduced into England and remained in power until early in the seventeenth century. Gradually, they used the new methods to further their own interests.

By 1603, when the last of the Tudors died, the people had a surfeit of autocratic rule and wanted individual freedom, including free speech. The Stuart century, which ended in 1714, was thus one of great conflict and change. Out of this conflict, and in response to the needs it created, developed the first newspapers of the English press, and later magazines. Although neither entirely free nor consistently responsible, the early newspapers did provide a vehicle for wider expression of opposing views as well as a medium for other news and advertising. Similar needs and conflicts later resulted in an American press.

The first publication generally designated as a newspaper was a controlled publication founded in 1665 by the head of the Crown's printing monopoly.

It was first called the *Oxford Gazette* and later, after being moved to London, the *London Gazette.* It was the first English newspaper.

England got its first daily newspaper, the *Daily Courant,* shortly after the turn of the century. England's first magazine, *The Review,* was started about the same time by Daniel Defoe, a writer better known for his story of Robinson Crusoe.

The best known publications of the early eighteenth century were the *Tattler* and the *Spectator* of Joseph Addison and Richard Steele. Other English writers also produced models for their American counterparts or provided them with arguments to use in their own battles for press freedom and representative government.

The Press in England remained severely restricted throughout most of the eighteenth century. Parliament enacted a tax in 1712, sometimes called the Tax on Knowledge that hampered Press growth for a century and a half. It was not until late in the century that the Press got some protection against libel and greater freedom to cover the activities of Parliament.

The first colonies developed in the South, but the first newspapers were started in New England because people there had a need for them sooner. Newspapers were not developed sooner in the colonies because they were not needed. Most persons knew already what was going on in their small communities. They received other news from the English papers that were shipped to the colonies periodically, and there was little business or commerce in the early years to support local publications.

The need for better communication was growing in the late seventeenth century when Benjamin Harris decided to start a newspaper in Boston. He was stopped because he sought to publish without the approval of the government and indirectly offended the government. After the suppression of Harris' paper, no one tried to start another for almost 15 years.

The first successful effort to publish a newspaper without permission in the colonies came in Boston in the early 1720s. The paper was called the *New England Courant,* and it was published by James Franklin, elder brother of Benjamin Franklin.

James Franklin's younger brother, Ben, also made a substantial contribution to colonial journalism. He was the most successful, financially and otherwise, of all the colonial journalists. Franklin did everything well and became publisher of the principal newspaper in Philadelphia. He made that newspaper, the *Pennsylvania Gazette,* into one of the colonies' best publications, carrying both news and literary comment. His success can be measured in terms of advertising, circulation, number of pages published, and similar figures as well as in influence. Franklin was also instrumental in the development of many other newspaper ventures, including a number of foreign language newspapers. Above all, he demonstrated that a printer journalist could serve his community and earn a good livelihood at the same time. John Peter Zenger started his *New York Weekly Journal* in the early 1730s in part to provide a voice for the rising merchant class in New York.

Through their advocacies and their reporting of opinions and events, newspapers helped to create a new government in America. During the revolution itself they helped rally Americans to the cause and helped them sustain their purpose through difficult times. The newspapers did a remarkable job of reporting events and unifying the patriots.

Newspapers continued to play a vital role after the fighting ceased. They grew and developed with the nation they helped create and sustain. The first daily newspapers were started in Philadelphia in the middle of 1780s, and others were begun in other major cities in subsequent years.

The Constitution as amended almost immediately by the Bill of Rights (First ten Amendments) outlined at least in a general way the path that the new nation should follow. The continuing value of newspapers was recognized in the First Amendment, which reads in part, "Congress shall make no law... abridging the freedom of speech or of the press..."

President Thomas Jefferson's view of the press, its roles and responsibilities, are particularly noteworthy. He is generally regarded as one of the great champions of a free press. Said Jefferson : ' 'The basis of our governments being the opinion of the people, the very first object should be to keep that right; and were it left to me to decide whether we should have a government without newspapers, or newspapers without a government, 1 should not hesitate a moment to prefer the latter. But I should mean that every man should receive these papers and be capable of reading them."

Benjamin Day founded the first of the penny papers in the fall of 1833. He called it the *New York Sun.* James Gordon Bennett started the *New York Herald* a year or so later. The *Herald* became the nation's leading paper in circulation, and perhaps in influence. Better known than Bennett was Horace Greeley, who founded the *New York Tribune* in 1841. The daily edition never attained the circulation of the *Herald,* but the weekly edition by the 1850s was reaching 20,000 readers through the East and Middle West

Henry J. Raymond made a major contribution in founding the *New York Times* in 1851. The *Baltimore Sun* became famous for its coverage of the nation's capital, and the *Chicago Tribune* was a leader in the development of Middle West. The *New York Herald* provided the most extensive coverage of the war presumably the Civil War, and it probably caused President Lincoln some sleepless nights. The *Herald* was read by most persons in England and other foreign countries for news about the United States.

Newspapers experienced a second revolution in the latter decades of the nineteenth century. They did not alter their basic function, established in the 1830s and continued to emphasize news. But their methods of collecting, processing and presenting it were changed substantially. Many of the changes came as a response to the rapid expansion of business, industry, government and population. More persons needed more information, and they needed it more rapidly.

Some of the key developments included the Linotype, the half-tone engraving, the stereotype, the web-fed rotary press, colour printing techniques and wood pulp paper used in the mechanical department, and the type-writer and telephone used in the news and advertising departments. Technological development made the rapid expansion of newspapers in the late nineteenth century possible.

Pulitzer was one of a number of editors in the late nineteenth century who pulled together the new techniques in reporting and editing and the new technology to relate bigger and better newspapers to serve an increasing number of persons. Pulitzer at the *St. Louis Post-Dispatch* and especially at the *New York World* showed what amounted to new journalism. He bought the *New York World* in the 1880s and made it the USA's most successful newspaper.

One regrettable extension of the new approach suggested by Pulitzer was the yellow journalism that evolved in the 1890s. Yellow journalism is a term used to describe extreme sensationalism. The term itself evolved from the struggle between Hearst and Pulitzer over a comic strip featuring a character called the Yellow Kid. Hearst hired away the cartoonist who drew the strip for *Pulitzer's World.* Pulitzer then hired another cartoonist to draw a similar strip. Some of the other newspapers thought this struggle typified the unfortunate practice of the time, and dubbed the two offending newspapers "yellow journals" and much of their content "yellow journalism ".

The most important development of the early twentieth century newspapers was the introduction of a more responsible journalism in the founding of the *Christian Science Monitor* and the rejuvenation of the *New York Times.* Of the other New York newspapers, *The World* and *The Tribune* probably were the most successful in the early twentieth century.

Some of the larger newspapers could afford correspondents of their own in Washington and in some of the major capitals around the world. But an increasing number of newspapers came to rely on one or more of the wire services and syndicates which developed in the early twentieth century for coverage of distant events and a wide variety of features. Wire services such as Associated Press, United Press and International News Service provided immediate coverage of the news. Syndicates such as King Features and United Features, and others provided a wide variety of news, features and other materials, including the increasingly popular comic strips.

After World War I a new type of newspaper, the tabloid, was born. The tabloids symbolized the era and were characterized by a smaller format than most newspapers, displayed big pictures and big headlines, and laid emphasis on sensational stories.

The first and most successful of the tabloids was the *New York Illustrated Daily News.* The *Daily News* received tabloid competition in the middle 1920s from the *Daily Mirror* and the *Daily Graphic.* Newspapers achieved new significance and influence in the 1930s with an increasing emphasis on interpretative reporting. Some newspapers employed specialists of their own to explain government, business and other developments. Others relied on the syndicated columnists who rose to prominence in the 1930s.

Many newspapers joined with other newspapers, wire services, magazines and radio to provide extensive coverage of the events involved in World War II. Coverage of the War was extensive and generally impressive. Many correspondents were cited for their efforts. Ernie Pyle particularly effective in reporting the human side of the war, was killed while covering the action in the Pacific. President Truman said : "The nation is saddened again by the death of Ernie Pyle. No man in this war has so well told the story of the American fighting man as American fighting men wanted it told. He deserves the gratitude of all his countrymen. "But also in peaceful time, journalism has claimed its victims.

Another major breakthrough in newspaper operation was the improved and expanded use of offset printing. Since offset usually involves cold type and photography, it fits in nicely with the new photo-composition devices.

The press itself became the subject of criticism, sometimes deserved, often not. Newsmen were accused of stirring up trouble by their very presence at events and demonstrations. Newspapers were criticised for biased reporting, particularly by young reporters who felt they should join the marchers as well as report the march. In late 1969 Vice-President Spiro Agnew launched an attack on both broadcast media and newspapers for abusing their powers. He charged that too much power over public opinion was concentrated in the hands of the television networks and a few large Eastern newspapers such as the *Washington Post* and *New York Times*.

There are about as many types of newspapers today as there are newspapers. No two are exactly alike, even though they may be part of the same group or one of two owned newspapers in the same city. Most will differ primarily because their purposes and audiences are different. Even group-owned newspapers will have different cities, especially if those cities are in different parts of the country, and jointly owned newspapers in the same city will have morning and evening editions. Newspapers will differ to some extent simply because the persons who publish them are different.

Each newspaper has its own functions and its own staff to perform those functions.

Many groupings can be employed to place newspapers into better perspective. They may be grouped according to purpose, such as general and specialised; according to frequency of publication, such as daily, weekly, semiweekly and biweekly; according to time of publication, such as morning and evening; according to circulation, such as large, medium and small; according to geography such as national, regional, metropolitan, suburban and rural; according to method of production, such as letter press and offset: according to format such as standard and tabloid; according to achievement such as good, fair, poor and bad. Other groupings could be suggested and most newspapers obviously could be placed in several of them. Newspapers are most easily categorized by frequency of publication. The two broad groupings are dailies and non-dailies.

The Newspaper is a Business Institution. Today's newspaper owner is constantly challenged by his publication's dual role as quasi-public institution with special privileges and responsibilities and free enterprise operation with a need to pay expenses and show a profit. The newspaper must serve the needs of the public for facts and opinion in an unselfish way if it is to justify its special status; yet it must succeed as a business enterprise in the information field if it is to exist and serve the public in any way.

The organisation and operation of newspapers will vary somewhat with their size and historical development. But certain basic functions are common to all. The jobs could be: owner(s) and corporate officers, publisher or general manager, business, production and news and opinion (editorial and editors). Business will include office activities, advertising, circulation and distribution, personnel and promotion.

The editorial section is vital to the development of a good newspaper. Someone has suggested that the news section is the heart of the newspapers and the editorial section is its soul. The editorial page sets the tone of the newspaper and expresses its character on a continuing basis. Basically, the editorial section performs two functions. First, it provides a continuous expression of the newspaper's opinions on important issues. Secondly, it provides a form for the expression of opinion by others on these issues.

Newspapers have contributed, through their search for truth, to more honest behaviour from government officials and to ethics not only in the USA, but in many other countries where the press could be considered free. The Watergate story unfolded in 1974 and the Iran-contra affair in 1986-87 are cases where this can be seen. Another case was the NASA contracts investigation. It is true also of Peru and many other countries of the new world.

Journalists have asserted with some success that the right to publish without prior restraints, and the right to obtain information about government are essential to the success of the democratic system. Both rights are asserted on behalf of the public at large. Anyone should be able to publish without prior restraint, provided he is responsible for what he publishes; anyone should have broad access to information about his government.

Disagreements have arisen over the specific procedures to follow in administering the rights and the extent to which reports concerning crimes, persons accused of crimes, and judicial procedures can prejudice juries and make fair trials impossible. Newspapers and citizens generally have a great deal of freedom today to provide information and commentary about public officials, public figures, and other persons involved in matters of public interest. Libel laws vary from country to country and even within the same country. This is an area of great discussion and disagreement as well as complication because of definitions of terms like: actual malice, privacy, fair use, etc.

The continuing success of newspapers will depend to a great extent on their ability and willingess to develop and adopt new technology to carry out their information functions. The use of new methods and new technology is essential to their success if not their survival. Newspapers that change with the times can continue to be an important source of printed information and vital participants in the continuing human story.

There is much that newspapers can do in today's complex world. They can still influence, entertain and foster the development of the nation's free enterprise system through advertising. But their opportunities and responsibilities for service go far beyond their basic functions. The life of the nation itself depends on the continued development of a free and responsible press.

Print Media

The printed word is no longer regarded by the educators as "non-communicative" or ineffective. In the words of Holmberg, "By far the most important medium in distance education courses is the printed word. This applies to conventional correspondence study, as well as to highly sophisticated multi-media presentations like courses of the open university." Though we said earlier that the choice of media depends on the subject matter to be covered, the value associated with the print medium seems largely objective and independent of the nature of the subject-matter. Print medium has proved largely effective in cognitive, affective and psychomotor domains, and there will hardly be any educator who wants to belittle or ignore the place of this medium. As Charles Zuber of the University of South Pacific said : "Any medium ... can generally be regarded to a greater or lesser degree as support for course material in the form of print care must always be taken that this existing and fundamental medium should not be overlooked."

In my opinion, the words of Zuber are representative. Yet there are occasions when experiments show that the printed word is more effective in certain domains than in another. In Nashif's opnion, "... if the objective is cognitive, involving analysis as a philosophy, the printed word will probably be more effective."

Secondly, accepting the indispensable value the printed word carries cannot ignore two evident shortcomings of the print media. Print media lack the personal touch and secondly are not flexible or open enough to allow for dialogue. This makes us state the need for supporting the printed word with the non-print media.

Mass Media

The world appears to be in the midst of an information explosion, A recent advertisement for IBM said that we are living in "The Age of Communications." And, indeed this seems to be the case, even to a casual observer. Satellites relay television signals around the globe. Magazines, newspapers, books, and radio bombard us with facts and opinions. Films offer both information and entertainment. Together, then, the mass media provide us with information more easily and quickly and in greater quantities than ever before. But what are the mass media ?

First, the mass media are the instruments of communication that I have just mentioned : books, such as the one you are reading now; magazines and journals of opinion, like the *Illustrated Weekly of India* or *India Today;* newspapers, like *The Hindu, The Times of India, The Statesman;* television and radio, like Doordarshan and All India Radio; and films from the Films Division of the Government of India and private films producers which are generally distributed in many parts of the world. In essence, these are tools that extend our ability to talk to one another. A conversation between one another serves as a model of communication; someone sends a message, and someone else receives it. Because messages the media disseminate reach thousands and even millions of persons, the media are instruments of mass communication.

But obviously, these "instruments" or "tools" are not at all like the tools we are accustomed to. In the art of painting, for example, the word "medium" (the singular of "media") refers to the liquid substance in which pigment is suspended as well as the liquid used in applying paint. Depending upon the characteristics of the medium — whether it is oil, water, egg tempera, or acry the artist will achieve different effects.

The first surge in modern communication began about 1440 when Johannes Gutenberg, a craftsman and inventor in Mainz,

Germany, developed movable type. Sometimes before 1455, Gutenberg printed his greatest work, the Gutenberg Bible, on a renovated wine press. The method of printing that Gutenberg devised — printing from movable type — was used without any major changes until the 20th century.

The invention of the telegraph and telephone in the 19th century marked the start of a second major surge in communication —the rise of electronic media. By 1835, a painter, Samuel F.B. Morse, had made the first working model of an electric telegraph. By 1838, he had developed the system of dots and dashes known today as the Morse Code, and by 1839, the first telegraph line in the United States came into being.

Radio started as a medium of entertainment but soon became an important source of information. By the 1930s, bulletins broadcast by radio stations had begun to displace newspaper "extras". Radio, however, was soon overtaken by television, which rapidly became the most satisfying source of entertainment.

Practical Aspects

The primary role and responsibility of the "press" is to report what is going on as honestly and as accurately as possible, to inform the public of the good, the bad, the interesting as well as the not-too-interesting and, by doing so, to play a definite and constructive role in bringing about a better informed and more alert, interested citizenry.

The mass media try to persuade as well as inform. The media's power to persuade, however, is generally exaggerated. People are more likely to be influenced by their friends and relatives than by the media. The media cannot easily change deeply rooted opinion.

People also turn to the media for entertainment. The media also stimulate the economy by carrying advertisements for goods and services. To survive, the media must have money. Too often, the public—and even some journalists — forget that most media are private businesses and must earn a reasonable profit in order to remain in business and retain their independence. The media serve as watch-dogs over our society, and journalists believe they have a special responsibility to examine critically the performance of the government. They are often criticized, however, for bias and a lack of credibility. The scepticism towards the media, as towards other entrenched institutions, is healthy in a democratic society.

Inevitably, the media will continue to change. The field of journalism is highly sensitive to changes in its environment: to advance in technology and to changes in the nation's political, economic, and social systems. Media that have become stagnant — that failed to adapt to the times — have been forced out of business.

Journalism is so much a part of the political system that it influences the structure of the system itself. Without mass media, there would be no political system as we know it. And as the source of so much of the information we have about the world around us, including the world of politics, the media have great power to influence what we think about. Some of the older sources of information and influence, such as the school, political party, and religious institutions, seem to be diminishing in importance as politics becomes more media-oriented. But traditional sources of influence such as the family and social environment remain more powerful in influencing political behaviour and voting than exposure to the media.

Fundamental changes in a political system, like revolutions or changes in party dominance, come about slowly and are surely aided by the mass media but hardly caused by them.

Partly because they enjoy more leisure, people are devoting more time to the media. Few media, however, seek a truly mass audience. Individuals differ, and most of the media appeal to specific sub-groups within our society. Newspapers attract better educated and sometimes a wealthier audience than radio and television. Few readers, however, look at every story in a paper. Like restaurants and department stores newspapers offer a wider selection of items.

Social Role

(i) A newspaper should cover government at every level. It would devote special attention to the government agencies in its area — not only by covering meetings but by critically examining the activities of the agencies. Recognizing its role as a check on government, a newspaper should present the views of the critics of government spokesmen.

(ii) A newspaper should go beyond government news and bulletin-board journalism to reveal the equality of people's lives and the human fabric of its community. This can be achieved through several techniques, and stories that provide a local dimension to important national and international issues.

(iii) A newspaper should attempt to publish, as best it can, a complete and balanced presentation of local, state, national, and international news. Obviously a metroplitan paper cannot be judged by the same standard as a small-town paper that prints only four pages a day and is bought for its local news. But papers of all sizes must emphasise the news of continuing importance at all levels — international as well as local.

(iv) In an age when the medium is said to be the message a newspaper must attempt to present its news as effectively and as attractively as possible. Page layouts, photographs, charts, type selection, graphics — all must help guide the reader to the news that is most important and encourage him to read what he otherwise might overlook.

(v) A newspaper should stand for something. Its editorials should take a position on the important local issues. It should clearly, logically explain its point of view. Editorials need not argue forcefully each and every day, but regularly the reader should sense that the editorial writer truly cares about what he is saying. A paper also should encourage diversity of opinion, including letters to the editors that criticize the paper.

(vi) A newspaper's management — as well as its news staff— should operate the paper with integrity; the news columns should be free of bias; employee policies that avoid conflicts of interest should be enforced; pay and working conditions should encourage the professionalism of the staff.

Discussions about the media's responsibilities often overlook two factors of fundamental importance: financial incentives and the related responsibilities of our Indian public. Hope for more responsible media rests not only with journalists, but also with a more informed and discriminating audience — an audience that patronizes the best that the media have to offer.

Most persons including journalists generally agree upon the characteristics that are desirable in news media, but they disagree over questions of who should define the media's responsibilities and whether those responsibilities should be enforced. Journalists reserve the right to determine the standards for themselves. Except for government regulations, there is no clear evidence to indicate that they would succeed. In the broadcasting department, for example, critics contend that the government's efforts to exercise indirect control have stifled the very characteristics which it should encourage.

Selection of News Stories : Because the news media do not have enough time and space to report all the information they receive, they report only the stories that are most important, interesting, timely, and unusual. They also emphasize stories that affect large numbers of persons and that involve their local communities. The media's selection process is also affected by their traditions, sources, and advertisers. Several studies have found that reporters have only a dim or generalized image of the audience they are expected to serve, and that they are more anxious to please themselves, their colleagues, and their editors than the public. Policies — particularly the problem of political bias— are still a factor in the selection process but are declining in importance. The major services and other prestigious media serve as models for the nation's journalists and often influence their decisions. Many media are becoming steadily candid, but there is still a tendency to avoid material that might offend large segments of their audiences.

The problem of good taste varies from one medium to another. Numerous other variations between the media are also evident. Persons who understand the media and their selection process are able to attract more publicity by manufacturing the types of stories that the media are more likely to report. Only a few of the factors involved in the selection process are acknowledged by conceptions of news.

Current Issues : Because of threats to their credibility, the media try to eliminate conflicts of interest, and many now try to ban the acceptance of favours that used to be common. Even as such issues are resolved, however, new and seemingly more serious issues will inevitably arise. So there will always be problems and reasons to question the media's performance. The issue can play a beneficial role, however, since they force the media to re-examine their traditions and adapt to society's changing needs.

Media and Politics : Three different and often contradictory theories attempt to explain the relationship between the media and government: the watch-dog, partnership and participant theories. Even though the watchdog theory does not always predominate, some conflict between the media and government is inevitable because of their different perspectives and different roles in our society. Government officials in other parts of the world attempt to unify their nations and win public support which is vital to the success of their programmes and discuss alternatives suggested by the officials' political rivals. In our country, of late, our political rulers make all-out efforts, first, to entrench themselves in power by hook or by crook so much so that the media with objective and honest traditions find themselves in uneasy situations.

Journalists are concerned about the government's use of publicity and secrecy and its ability to manufacture consent.

Nevertheless, journalists appear to rely heavily upon the government's publicity releases. Some additional information comes from leaks and background briefings. Although never specifically authorized by the Constitution, secrecy has become common, particularly in the areas of national defence and foreign policy. Journalists do complain, oftentimes, that the government also uses secrecy to hide its own mistakes.

The Quality

Before evaluating the quality of news coverage, it is essential to consider standards of evaluation. Nothing is good or bad in itself; it is good or bad with respect to some standard. The following are the most important of the many standards that have been proposed and used by the media and media critics :

Profitability : The Indian mass media are, for the most part, privately owned and privately financed barring some public limited companies and trusts. Unless they earn a profit, they will fail.

A newspaper, in imminent danger of failure, is unlikely to spend much money improving its news operation. This is generally more common in India than in many other countries of the world. A mass medium that earns a lot of money still does a poor job covering the news. But one that loses money almost always does a poor job.

Audience Satisfaction : Like profitability, audience satisfaction is a necessary but not a sufficient condition for media quality. If nobody reads a newspaper article it can accomplish nothing—but many articles are well read and still accomplish nothing.

Accuracy : An inaccurate news story is always, without exception, a poor news story. Most editors and reporters know this, and strive mightily to spell the names right, even if they do not fully understand what their sourcesare saying.

Objectivity : Nearly all responsible journalists aim at objectivity, and quite often they fail. Words have connotations as well as denotations; they imply more than they say. As long as reporters must work with words, complete objectivity is impossible. And even an "objective" reporter must decide whom to interview, what to ask, and which facts to include in the story. Fairness is a reasonable standard to ask of journalists, literal objectivity is not.

Underground editors and other committed journalists often complain that where one side is right and the other is wrong, objectivity is a false god. Was objectivity a good thing during the decla ration of Emergency in India by the then Prime Minister who expected the media to be "fair" to her ?

Unusualness : Most editors urge their reporters to find stories that are distinctive, dramatic, or in some way unusual. If overused, this standard becomes more a definition of sensationalism than of news. If the media ignore what is typical and stress what is weird, they inevitably present us with a weird picture of the world. Nonetheless,' 'man bites dog" is still a bigger story than "dog bites man ".

Relevance : Relevant news is important news. What kind of stories are most relevant ? Those that are local, timely, and directly useful to the audience. This standard, too, is sometimes overemphasized. The most local, timely, and useful stories around, after all, are the supermarket ads.

Completeness : *The Times of India, The Hindu* followed by *The Indian Express, The Statesman, The Amrit Bazar Patrika* can be considered to be very near complete newspapers in India. But not for everything — they are somewhat weak in management, science topics and editorial cartoons. And is the most complete medium always the best medium ? A three-hour TV film show is hardly three times as good as a one-hour show, especially if You are waiting for a special feature. When we demand completeness, what we are really asking for is a sample of the show that is adequately large and appropriately varied.

Independence : However a medium selects its news, its judgements should be its own, and should not be influenced by outside pressures. If a newspaper kills a story because a big advertiser insists on it, then it is a poor newspaper—not because it killed the story (may be it didn't deserve to run), but because it deferred to the wishes of an advertiser. Independence is absolutely essential for good journalism.

Propriety : The mass media have an obligation to keep within the bounds of propriety and good taste. But what are those bounds? Some business executives think it is in poor taste to report declining sales figures. Some revolutionaries think it is good taste to report do-it-yourself bomb- making techniques. Most editors disagree on both counts.

Comprehensibility : As the world grows more complicated, it becomes less and less adequate for reporters to stick to bare facts in their reporting. Interpretation is essential to put the facts into a meaningful context, to make them comprehensible to the reader or viewer.

Uniqueness : Democracy is predicated on the assumption that all kinds of news and opinions are available to the public, competing in the free market of ideas: The trouble with this assumption is that most of the media today are not ideological competitors. They all say pretty much the same things, and that is not healthy. I, therefore, propose the standard of uniqueness. Any mass medium that is significantly different from its competitors is in this sense "better" than that which is undifferentiated. Calcutta City is better off with both *The Statesman* and *The Amrit Bazar Patrika* as also *Business Standard* than it would be with two papers like *The Statesman.*

The eleven standards listed above are by no means exhaustive. But the broad ones touching the core of the topic have not been overlooked. Standards, like these, can be set in hundreds. The point to be recognized here is that judgements of quality are meaningless without explicit criteria.

You, as public relations persons also involved in journalism to a reasonable degree, can go ahead and criticize the mass media.

You are as qualified as anyone else. But make sure you know what your standards are.

Policy : It is not uncommon that the owner of a mass medium would like to control news coverage. There are three reasons for doing so. Each reason dictates its own policy. Thus

(i) the economic interests of the company dictate a "business policy ";

(ii) the individual likes and dislikes of the owner dictate a 'personal policy"; and

(iii) the ideological convictions of the owner dictate a "political policy."

Newspapers tend to show their bias in three ways :

(i) They give large headlines to the favoured party.

(ii) They give more prominence to articles by the favoured author.

(iii) They print more quotations from the favoured party, and more remarks praising that party.

Competition : For one thing, a newspaper which is not competing against a rival can present news in better balance. There is no need to sensationalise.

Competing newspapers live in fear of each other. They maybe stampeded into excesses by their fear of losing circulation to a competitor less burdened with conscience.

Monopoly Control : The unopposed newspaper can give its reader relief from the pressures of time. Deadlines no longer loom like avenging angels just this side of the next edition. There is more freedom from financial pressure on the business side. A single ownership newspaper can better afford to take an unpopular stand. It can better absorb the loss of money in support of a principle.

If it is ture of natural laws, reasoned the philosophers of the "Enlightenment," it should be true of people's laws as well.

If men were free to inquire about all things to form opinions on the basis of knowledge and evidence, and to utter their opinions freely, the competition of knowledge and opinion in the market of rational discourse would ultimately banish ignorance and superstition, and enable men to shape their conduct and their institutions in conformity with the fundamental invariable laws of nature and the will of God.

Media Relationships : An enterprising and result-oriented public relations manager is one who pins faith in the following points with respect to media relationships :

- He loses no opportunities to give them service.
- He answers all questions fully, honestly and promptly.
- He would treat a newsman as he would treat a customer.
- He knows his own organization, its details, its spellings.
- He is never a barrier or obstruction; the public relations professional is not a "suppress" agent.
- He honours a legitimate "exclusive", however much he is tempted to balloon it into a more general break.
- He is impartial between one medium and another.
- He does not bluff, misrepresent, exaggerate or pad.
- He makes every effort to provide a story for a newsman who desires one.
- However much provoked, he is not abrupt with a newsman.
- He is as energetic in helping the media cover an adverse story as any other kind.

Newspaper's Job ? : First and most important, newspapers should help build the superstructure of democracy—an informed electorate. Thomas Jefferson said "... and were it left to me to decide whether we should have a government without newspapers or newspapers without government, I should not hesitate a moment to prefer the latter."

No ordinary mortal can attend every city council, local government, and zonal meeting and still have time to brush his teeth, much less hold a job and rear a family. The newspapers and their broadcast cohorts must cover for us. Day in and day out newspaper reading should tell us whether health and sanitation codes are enforced, whether the State Government is firm in dealing with unreasonable demands on the Public Transport Undertakings, and so forth. If a community problem is festering on a sidestreet somewhere, the newspapers should tell us about it long before the lid blows off and disrupts the town.

In short, newspapers should not only tell us *What is Happening,* but must undertake the much more difficult task of giving us a picture of the community itself, a picture of the changing background against which things happen.

This is a rough assignment. Rougher still when you consider the covering of newspaper problems.

Glamorous Competition : Since the advent of radio and television, newspapers have resembled a graying matron vying for her fair share of attention at a dinner party full of movie starlets.

Rising Costs : Rising costs and burgeoning competition for advertising revenue have the tendency to squeeze the "news" publication.

Complexity : In a world that seems more complicated every morning, newspapers must daily report and interpret everything from railway accidents to archaeological digs and do it fast, be objective, make it clear.

If we agree with Thomas Jefferson that newspapers are an essential ingredient in democracy, it follows that we should support our local newspaper.

Here are three good ways to do so :

1. Read it carefully.
2. Honour its best efforts.
3. Criticize it fairly.

Misleading Headlines : Most state and national news comes into the local newspaper office from wire services. Metre after metre of it (without headlines) rattle off the teleprinter and into the desk of the wire editor who must decide what to discard and what to print. Then the news editor looks at dummy sheets showing the day's advertising and decides where to put major stories.

Next, the copy editor writes the headline to fit the number of columns the story should run.

If an important story carries a misleading headline in the newspaper, it is due to a local news judgement error. If it happens often, you have a legitimate complaint.

Important stories are buried in the back of the newspaper. Any newsman will tell you, newspapers don't place stories in descending order of importance throughout the newspapers. In a newsman's eyes, the story on page 7 may be every bit as important as the one on page 9. Don't forget, newspapers sell ads throughout their paper on the basis that you will read every page.

Newspapers invariably try to have a balanced front page to draw people into the newspaper. People are enticed this way to read the paper before they can tell newspapers what they need to know.

Too Much Sensational News : The argument is that the masses in general look for such news to read through over their morning cup of tea served by the tea shop.

Too Much Advertiser Influence : Standard papers with a national reputation will not be swayed by the "advertiser" influence on their additional content — that is a basic tenet of journalism; advertising revenue supports newspapers, and some newspapers have more integrity than others when it comes to backing a disgruntled advertiser.

The press should take care to see that reporting on incidents do not turn into riots.

Newspapers Slant News by Selection and order of Facts in a Story : Complete objectivity is almost impossible, In the facts newsman select stories, and reporters are subjective. They should announce their position in the beginning and promote it rather than preserve the fiction of objectivity.

Perfect objectivity is impossible; perfect anything is impossible. But a reporter would think he has done a pretty good job if he has given the reader the facts he needs to disagree with him.

Freedom of the Press never rested on the idea that a single reporter could write ten columns of universal truth every time he sat down at the typewriter. It rested on the idea that he was supposed to try... and that out of free and honest discussion, the truth would emerge.

Getting criticism from all sides is perhaps the surest sign that newspapers are doing a good job. But it will certainly worry them if people criticize them for the wrong reasons. Perhaps criticizing for the right reasons is the citizenship skill that can help our democracy most...and the best way we can support our local newspaper.

" A free Press is the unsleeping guardian of every other right that free men prize"— Sir Winston Churchill.

News and Features : "News is the statement of freshly ascertained facts about something of interest that has happened, is happening, is about to happen, or that, contrary to expectation, has not happened, is not happening, and probably will not happen."

— Paul White, in his book, "News on the Air", page 171.

"News is an accurate and timely report of some event, situation, condition or opinion... a report which will interest the particular persons for whom it is intended."

— Dowing Leatherwood, in his book, "Journalism on the Air", page 171.

"News may be defined as an accurate unbiased account of the significant facts of timely happening that is of interest to the readers of the newspaper that prints the account."

— William S. Maulsby, in his book, "Getting the News".

News can be read with greater interest if the news stories are written effectively. To make stories effective, attention must be given to the form of lead used with them. The lead is the first part of the news story; it gives the gist of the entire account. In short, it is the first unit of the news story in an epitomized form.

Lead : A good lead not only indicates the tone and temper of the story, but also answers questions likely to arise in a reader's mind on learning of a certain event. It is attractive and observes the principles of good news writing. There are numerous types of leads. The most important of that uses the 5 W's and the H. Here are examples :

The 'Who' Lead : Smt. Indira Gandhi has been declared the leader of Congress (I) party to head the National Government this morning...

The 'What' Lead : The murder of the housewife at Indira Nagar, Madras, remained a mystery. So too the tracing of the murderers while the victim was buried today at....

The 'Why' Lead : To save his mother's life Appukuttan Nair left his bank job in Madras yesterday and flew to Trivandrum just in time to give her a successful blood transfusion.

The 'When' Lead : Not until Monday or Tuesday will new applicants be able to enrol at the Bhavan's College of Mass Communication, Madras, as the Honorary Principal is faced with piles of applications, notably for the Diploma Course in Public Relations, the Registrar of the College announced here today.

The 'Where' Lead : In the Guruvayur temple in Kerala State, Smt. Indira Gandhi, the Prime Minister of India, was weighed in sugar today to respect the vow taken by the party leader who had prayed to the presiding deity for her success as the Prime Minister.

The 'How' Lead : Mr. Devraj Urs's prompt action in stepping down from the Chief Minister's post in Bangalore has not only created a favourable image of him but also precluded the possibility of being ousted from the post by the newly elected political party, Congress (I).

Once the lead is selected, the building of the rest of the story develops naturally if the news writer remembers to put first what is more important. A convenient way to remember the proper structure of a news account is to arrange the facts to be reported in the form of a triangle standing on its point.

Feature Writing : In writing a feature one has to depend on the eye and the ear, sentiments, feelings, emotions and observation. The difference between "News Writing" and "Feature Writing" lies in approach rather than in subject matter.

A newspaper man writing on the beggar problem in India, especially on the life of the pavement dwellers in Bombay and Calcutta, will have to dig facts from records, relate them to each other, marshall them and draw his own conclusions. But if he were to describe the tragedy of the beggar and pavement dwellers of all sorts, he must spend some time with the beggar and pavement dweller, interview him, his friends, his wife and children if any. At the same time, the feature writer cannot dispense with study.

Feature writing has yet to develop fully in India for many reasons. Illiteracy is greatly responsible for this. Demand creates supply. There is not very much demand for features, because 80 per cent of the people cannot read newspapers. Furthermore, feature writers need to get more guidance to compete with their counterparts in the West. We have yet to establish traditions in feature writing. Whatever ideas feature writers have about their craft have been gathered from reading British and American papers.

Even language papers are now showing keen interest in features. They run women's pages, children's pages and the like, but miss the spirit of feature writing.

While writing a feature one should try to write a striking introduction which may arouse the reader's curiosity and interest. How to end a feature is as important as how to begin it. Sometimes the technique of short story writing may be successfully employed to write a feature.

News and Puffery : A study of what is called product publicity will help to show the difference between news and puffers.

In the 1920'sand 1930's when early newspaper advertising for commodities and services was better known as "puffing", it was hard to tell editorials from advertisements because in the art of displaying advertisements, sophistication was yet to come. It belonged to the day when the space broker found it was easier and more profitably to sell space if he also had creative talent and especially a gift for writing slogans.

In the early 19th century advertisement copywriters were famous authors and poets like Charles Lamb. Puffery was the available aid to marketing although much despised by men like Carlyle who could not understand that a trader or manufacturer must make known in order to sell, and that newspaper advertising was our economic means of broadcasting a sales message to buyers distant from the mill or factory.

To the newspaperman, puffers have continued to mean literary advertisement, and the attempt to present advertising as news has incurred the wrath of editors who were convinced that their editorial columns were being invaded and misused, although a great many things advertised are also of news value.

A puff or a free puff, as it is more often described, means an unmistakable advertisement appearance in the editorial columns. It is the term used by an alert editor when he thinks that somebody is trying to gain from a reference in his columns. It is also used less specifically by advertisement managers responsible for selling space who regard editorial mention as announcements improperly occupying space which they could or should have sold. For these reasons we frequently see the absurdity of a legitimate news story from which all commercial names have been obviously deleted, usually to appease the advertisement manager. The Press is regrettably inclined to be dominated by the advertisement side rather than the editorial, for the simple reason that many publications exist very largely on their advertisement revenue. However, with competition from TV and radio, high production costs and reduction in advertisement revenue due to economic crisis, income from cover prices is becoming more important, thus encouraging greater editorial independence. And unless the editorial secures adequate sales, the advertisement manager will be unable to sell his space. A good editor may well rely on good officers providing him with materials which help him to achieve a successful journal.

12

The Organisation

Newspaper Organisation

Editor : (a) relations with owner, individual proprietor; partners; private or public limited company or charitable trusts; relations with publishers, printers and public; (b) need for clear line of authority and division of responsibility for policy and production process, relations with staff of Editorial Department and with the Business Section (advertisement, circulation and accounts); Promotion (public relation); Circulation (readers' preferences) and Printing Department (for flow of copy, etc.);

Structure depends on nature of organization : (a) single edition; (b) multiple edition (printing only), multiple edition (chains); multiple-language editions—Joint Editor, Managing Editor, Associate Editor, Executive Editor, Guest Editor — (for book page, arts, fashion, etc.);

Editorial Conference : Editor and Assistant Editors (News, Views, News-Views, Magazine, Art, etc.); News Editor;

News Editor : Deputy, Chief Sub, Senior Sub, Sub-Editor, Sports, Conference Editor — managerial function (flow of copy to press, make-up etc.); editorial function; liaison with reporting section; selection and distribution of copy to sub-editor with instructions on length, headline, etc., coordination; and

Sub-Editor : main tasks—qualifications (general, technical), need for alert mind, quick decisions, cool temper — relations with other colleagues, with superiors and the printing department; rights —Working Journalists Act; professional training; efficient discharge of his tasks, whatever his position in the hierarchy, decides his progress—individual and professional.

Editing General Principles

News editing : Process by which information is presented to readers in entertaining way for their enlightenment on current affairs—rush of modern life newsflow varied and of complex implications —extraction of relevant material from this vast newsflow.

Reader's requirements : News is what man is interested in as an individual and as member of a society — food, shelter, clothing, transport, religious and social differences, national and international problems, differences of publication owing to differences in locale, complexion of population, etc., variety of publications — for laymen and experts, etc., — Form Follows Function.

Fourth Estate : Fourth Estate is the press of England. What are the other three estates ? Lords, Temporal and Spiritual and Commons — modern newspapers not mere chroniclers of news but interpreters as democracy requires well informed and enlightened public opinion —catering to popular interest not enough, public interest must be considered.

Basic responsibilities : Salesmanship aspect — reader as customer — financial viability — advertisement and circulation — warning on threat to freedom of press and hazards of journalistic profession for advertiser's pressures and public lobbying— responsibility to reader —reliable information, entertaining presentation, and enlightenment.

Code of Ethics

Reporter vs. Editor : Why editing ? Reporter gathers news and is primarily responsible for selection and bright and brisk presentation — but editor makes sure the account is well stressed, organized, uses aids like headlines, pictures, charts, sketches etc. to draw the reader's attention — reporter not infallible, rush in getting news makes report defective — editor acts as second mind.

Five W's and one H : Main Factors—what, who, when, where, why and how—editor rearranges details to dramatise value — meticulous examination of details—eliminates editorial expression from news—news is sacred but comment is free — check-up on details —simplicity of language and style deletes trivia, absurdities, irrelevancies, emotionalism, propaganda —care to avoid identification of the speaker and reporter. Coordination with other news of the day.

Warning : In rearranging and rewriting reporter's copy.

Editor should preserve the spirit and personality of the reporter and as far as possible, the words of the reporter—no change for mere changes sake — change only to make the news element a unity, cohesive and emphatic, for greater impact on the reader.

Copy Matter

Copy Received by : 1. post; 2. telephone; 3. telegram; 4. cable and wireless; 5. teleprinter circuit — news agencies; 6. monitoring of radio and television programmes; 7. lift journals.

Types of Copy : 1. City — local news from own reporter or news agencies; 2. District and mofussil correspondents; 3. State and Union capitals; 4. Foreign news from abroad; 5. News, Views, News plus Views:— special articles from own correspondents — Letters to Editors, official information, crime, education, etc.

Copy Content : 1. political, economic and social developments; 2. statements and speeches — press conferences and interviews; legislature proceedings; 3. arts, film, drama, etc.; 4. sports; 5. commerce; 6. gossip — personal cloumn; 7. births and deaths-accidents-sickness-morgue; 8. weddings — birth anniversaries, etc.; 9. human stories from occasional correspondents.

Sources of Copy **:** 1. Government, the biggest source in India — Secretariat and other offices, Collectorates; 2. Public sector and private sector firms — industries; trade unions; 3. Political parties and politicians; 4. Economic and social organisations; 5. Universities, College managements and students, teacher bodies; 6. Syndicated copy articles, comic strips, etc.; 7. Public utility services; 8. Embassies of foreign countries.

"Tasting" copy for "Slant", Colour and Advertisement passing off as "News"

Distinction between News and Propaganda **:** Difficult to draw a line, while suppression as well as overmuch publicity will hamper the journalist's service to his readers, total withdrawal is bad; essence of propaganda is selection and spread of ideas or news to induce a desired belief or action — transmission or opinion to influence people — the selectiveness pertains not only to content but also to the decision in what page, in what proportion and in which position and with what typographical emphasis the news should appear.

Propaganda Devices **:** They are *Amoral* like any other tool of knowledge — either for or against particular cause, person or event —1. Name Call, 2. Glitter, 3. Transfer or usurpation of ideas, functions like fast, Crusades; 4. Testimonial from VIPs—Tyranny of minority opinion, 5. Band Wagon — use of religious symbols, colours, music and slogans — tyranny of majority; 6. Card-stacking giving selective stimuli; and 7. Conspiracy of silence.

If these devices do not accord with the responsibilities of the journalists, they should not be adopted. If the propaganda is harmless, or helpful and does not affect professional standards and is subversive of the above responsibilities, then they may be considered innocuous and used.

Distinction **:** Distinguish between colourful and coloured reports.

Advertising Passing off as News : What was mentioned above is what the journalist should avoid. What follows is what he should guard against, that is, in the above, he should avoid making the readers victims of his propaganda; and in what follows, he should avoid becoming a victim ofpropaganda by others.

Who Supplies Information and Why : 1. Handouts — picked news; 2. Made News — circumstances are created to give publicity to an idea, to a prominent person or organisation etc.; 3. Hoax; 4. Camouflaged publicservice; 5. Polluted news; 6. Free publicity, professional publicity-mongers— problem of inclusion of who gave the news and why — the inclusion will remove the poisonous effect of such propaganda.

News or Advertising : Buying space for advertisement should not be confused with the pressure to invade news columns — difficulties in drawinga strict line — should hotel names be used in accidents or receptions, so also hospitals, lawyers, doctors, etc. — police reports require mention of police personnel if they are news sources.

News Value

Relative Nature : Change from region to region, state to state readership differences even within the family, influence of edition time, place of occurrence, developing news, essential and non-essential aspects, advt. and dummy.

Gatekeeper's Function : (a) What item should go into the publication; (b) in what detail and length; (c) where it should go on page; (d) with what typographical emphasis; (e) role of aids like pictures, cartoons, sketches, tables etc. How to make the reader concentrate on what the editor thinks is important and should be read immediately.

Responsibility : For selection of news relates to the specific aims of the publication, maintenance of standards of the profession and catering to the tastes and interests of the readership — popular versus public interest.

Criteria for Selection of News : Immediacy or timeliness, immediate import of interest, writing about strikes etc., preparing the reader to meet an eventuality, background information about what has happened or is about to happen — Cauvery waters and famines etc.

Proximity : (a) geographical news from one's own birthplace of where one studies or works: familiarity; (b) ideological: one's interests, ideological affiliation ; specialists etc.

Prominence : Activities of prominent people, ministers, actors, etc., events in prominent localities: overshadowing nature in Indian Press.

Conflict and Consequence : Physical conflicts like communal and caste clashes, wars among nations, war against diseases, inventions and discoveries produce changes, beneficial or harmful — fibre replaces cotton, automation renders people jobless, reservation, dissatisfaction.

Development and Progress : Removal of slums, new slums for old, pangs of progress, new problems.

Surprise and Suspense : Events for which the reader is least prepared— if Smt. Indira Gandhi announces retirement from public life etc. — suspense over actor's condition — snags in spacecraft will be concern to people till the snags are removed.

Sex : Issues like sex education, sexual jealousy, murder, etc.— discoveries about sex motivation — use of sex hormones.

Oddity : Odd behaviour of prominent persons — millionaire willing away his fortune for gods; ear-boring ceremony for cat etc.

Human Interest : Role of emotions, issues of universal interest —suffering elicits sympathy, but false sympathy is dangerous — a man sacrificing his life for another, animals in distress, prevention of cruelty to animals in drug industry, should it be done or not. News of value may not always be apparent. It has to be sought after.

Creation of News Interest : Editorial campaign for the benefit of the community.

Crime and Policy : How much and what kind of crime news should be printed ?

Newspapers probably are reproached more for reporting crime news than for any other reason. The critics say that newspapers make crime by reporting crime.

Crime News : The factors which make crime news may be summarised as follows :

Prominence of Persons : Wealth and position count in any kind of story, but especially when there is proof of wrong doing.

Prominence of Place : The same test applied to familiar things and places whenever they serve as background.

Property Loss : If all other factors balance, the property loss gauges the news value.

Action and Crowds

Mystery and Suspense : As long as the police are baffled, news interest thrives and expands. The moment the case is solved, interest dies.

Unique Circumstances : Anything. startling, novel, or peculiar especially if it relates to the motive that promoted the act, strengthens the news bond.

Emotional Pull : Police reporters probably unearth more human interest stories than any members of the staff, with the possible exception of reporters.

Gruesomeness and Melodrama : The first lesson a crime reporter learns is that he must eliminate repellent details from his copy. If he fails to do so, the sub-editors will do it for him. This means little colour.

News Desk : There are two kinds of news editors. There is the passive news editor who reacts like a chief clerk in a government office through whom everything must pass, but who does not initiate or inspire any action. Then there is the active news editor who initiates and directs the operation of news gathering. The active news editor's work produces the news on which the paper exists; the page for topical features; the inspiration for dramatic pictures, cartoons and illustrations; and the occasion and theme for the commentaries, columns and leaders.

An active news editor's job is to sell his readers what his fellow beings have been doing since the last issue of his newspaper appeared. How can a news desk be made active ? Mainly in checking the stock sources of news :

1. Government and official news; News about the head of the State, Cabinet, the Legislature and the Administration.
2. Meeting of the legislature, local bodies and subsidiary agencies of Government such as State, Corporation, etc.
3. Functions attended by Ministers, Officials, V.I.Ps.
4. Activities, movements and statements of people already known to the public or interesting to the public such as businessmen, entrepreneurs, scientists, educators, sportsmen, filmstars, cul tural and religious leaders, etc.
5. Accidents, crimes, litigation, police.
6. Health and hospitals.
7. Births, marriages and deaths.
8. Money and business.
9. Cultural and religious events.
10. Science and economic news.

These ten themes span a wide range of human activity and interest and should be rigorously exploited to develop news possibilities.

A fundamental general rule for active news editors to remember. It is not enough for a newspaper to report what the Government and the public does. It must report what the public feels, thinks, hopes and fears.

News Photography : Our newspapers make nothing like enough use of illustrations. This makes them weak in two fundamental ways. They are not telling the news as effectively as they could. And they are failing to use one of the fundamental means of bringing colour and variety : the forbidding greyness of their newspapers.

The old Chinese proverb is still true today : One picture is equal to a thousand words. Not all photographers are genius but an ordinary run-of-the-mill photographer will respond and can produce good news pictures if he is told what to look for. But to begin with, he must, of course, have sufficient technical knowledge to take good pictures.

The newspaperman has to bear two things in mind when he considers photographs for publication. He has to consider the photograph's technical value and also its editorial value. Since you will almost inevitably lose some of the detail in your photographs in reproduction, what you want, technically, is a picture with sharp detail and large pattern. Look for a picture that shows crisply the various gradations of grey —the halftone — that bring out the contents on a face or a building. This sharp detail is called "contrast".

What can you do with pictures which do not meet the technical tests? : With a mediocre picture, "crop" for the most interesting part and enlarge that for reproduction. The best motto here is one used by the staff of the *Vancouver Sun :*

> "If a picture is great it deserves to be played big." If it's an ordinary picture it needs to be played big.

It is far easier to get a photograph technically suitable for reproduction than to find one worth printing on strict editorial values. Judgement comes into this of course but there are a number of useful tests you can bear in mind.

Does the Picture Live ? Every news picture must tell a story at a glance. The best pictures show life happening. They show suspended animation, you might say. They capture something that is there one minute, gone the next.

Is it posed ? In the very best news pictures the subject is not conscious at all of the camera. Then the people in your pictures must be active. Not the "line up" or "firing squad" pictures. You know the sort of thing a group of people lined up like condemned men facing a firing squad. They look straight into the camera. They do nothing else. What kind of story does the picture tell ?

Can you see anything ? Another reason why you should avoid the ordinarily squad group pictures is that most times you cannot even see who the people are in them. If you must use a group picture (say, of a football team) you must make it big or otherwise the individual faces will not reproduce in the newspaper.

Edit pictures for size, shape and detail. A strong vertical stress is an effective shape of picture for a newspaper.

A strong horizontal stress is also striking. Almost invariably you should make the picture bigger than you first thought.

Most newspaper photographs are improved by "cropping" — cutting out unnecessary background detail.

Crop pictures for two reasons: First, you will be getting rid of a good deal of fussy clutter.

Secondly, crop because it will give you more space to display the main points of interest.

Captions : All the rules of news writing apply to writing captions. Captions should be written in short, pithy sentences. They must tell who is in the picture, what they are doing, where they are doing it, when were they doing it, why were they doing it. Give full names to identify everyone in the picture; and be accurate.

Captions should supplement what we can see with our eyes. A caption of a picture showing Mrs. Gandhi speaking should not just say "Mrs. Gandhi speaking." We can see that. The caption should say, even in a sentence, what she addressed the people about.

Overlines or Titles : The caption supplements what we can see with our eyes. The overline never does that. It merely sums up what we can see in an arresting fashion.

News in our Time : Mass communication has given us a window on the world, and we often might not like what we see through it. But without the news, we would be without the means to correct the ills and injustices of modern-day life.

In his recent book *Eyewitness to History,* the distinguished English professor John Carey tells of how a correspondent from *The Times* of London was sent to France to cover the Franco-Prussian War of 1870. After the decisive battle of Sedan, he rushed back to England by train and ferry boat, staying up all right to write his account of the German victory. He arrived only to find that competing newspapers had published reports of the event sent by electric telegraph two days earlier. *The Times* had literally blundered into a new era in western society — an era in which the news from almost everywhere is available to almost everyone every hour of every day.

The improvement in the transmission of the news coincided with improvements in printing and paper making technology which made possible the speedy production of huge quantities of daily newspapers that could be sold at minimal prices. Meanwhile the spread of literacy owing to compulsory education was opening up a mass market for the "peny press". Soon the ordinary people of the United States, Britain and Western Europe had a ready means of learning what was going on in the world, a privilege once reserved for a relatively small literate minority. Public access to the news had been established : from there on it was merely a series of technological steps to today's 24-hour television news by satellite.

"Arguably the advent of mass communications represents the greatest change in human consciousness that has taken place in recorded history," Carey wrote. "The development, within a few short decades, from a situation where most of the inhabitants of the globe would have no day-to-day knowledge of or curiosity about how most of the others were faring, to a situation where the ordinary person's mental space is filled (and must be refilled daily or hourly unless a feeling of disorientation is to ensue) with accurate reports about the doings of complete strangers represents a revolution in mental activity which is incalculable in its effects."

Public access to national and international news has deeply influenced popular culture, politics, and even philosophy. It has given ordinary men and women a more humanistic and tolerant outlook on life by making them empathize with all of humanity. New reports force us to look human suffering in the face, and make us want to do something about it, whether to donate money to aid disaster victims or call on our governments to put pressure on other governments to stop committing injustices. In the age of the news, no man is an island. We cannot help but be, as John Donne put it, "involved in mankind".

So pervasive is the news in western countries that it has become one of life's necessities. There are, of course, times when it is absolutely necessary to know what is happening for our own well-being, as when a hurricane is heading in the direction of where we live. But beyond immediate practical information, we need the news to help us cope with the pace and complexity of modern living. As the Canadian journalism professor Wilfred Eggleston wrote: "Survival of all living creatures requires an awareness of the changing environment .... Speedy and accurate information is required for people to react."

Out of our need for news has evolved a principle which would never have been thought of in the days before the telegraph: that the public has a right to news that can be trusted. The Canadian Royal Commission on Newspapers broached this concept in 1981 by declaring that people have a "to inform themselves" which is inseparable from their right to express themselves. Canada is one country where the right to the news is enshrined in legislation. To hold a broadcast licence, every Canadian radio station must carry news reports.

The ability to keep track of what is happening and of what is being said is central of our system of government. "A people without reliable news is, sooner or later, a people without the basis of freedom," political scientist Harold Laski wrote.

Wherever there is no political freedom, the news is always controlled — not only internal news, but news from abroad which invites comparisons with conditions elsewhere and exposes the repressed populace to "alien" ideas. No less a tyrant than Adolf Hitler objected fiercely to free reporting. "Our law concerning the press is such that divergences of opinion between members of the government are no longer an occasion for public exhibitions," he said at the height of his power.

A man of an opposite cast of mind, the American statesman Thomas Jefferson, once declared that if he had to decide between government without newspapers and newspapers without government, he would choose the latter. At the same time Jefferson was the first to admit that the freedom of the press which he so eloquently upheld could be abused. This freedom (which today covers the electronic media as well) is by no means unbridled. News organizations are not free, for instance, to ruin a person's reputation, to invade a person's privacy, or to subject a person to 'trial by publicity'. They are prohibited from doing such things by various laws.

Despite these legal constraints, news organizations remain very much responsible to themselves, and there is plenty of room for breaches of that responsibility. Newspapers, radio and television stations carry not only accounts of events, but commentary on those events. Writers and broadcasters of opinion do not need an array of indisputable facts to blacken a reputation or throw suspicion on the motives of an organization; sufficient to mix a few suggestive facts in with a lot of innuendo. A clever writer or editor with an axe to grind can paint a biased picture even in an apparently impartial report.

At one time it was left almost entirely up to newspaper proprietors and their sycophants to decide how much restraint would be applied on their ability to play with the facts, or to publish absolute falsehoods. Their papers frequently distorted the "news" to suit their own political objectives. Sensationalism ran rampant among hotly-competitive big city dailies. The truth was often slaughtered in the crossfire of their circulation wars.

New Breed of Journalists : For better or for worse (some say worse) the new generation of newspaper proprietors in North America are for the most part detached from day-to-day operations of papers they own, running large chains from corporate head offices. News organizations have become big businesses, whether their outlet is in print or by electronic means.

The decline of the old-time imperious press barons coincided with the rise of professional journalists who insist that their first duty is not to the boss but to the reader. Sensational dailies still exist, but beneath their splashy lay-out, they will usually be found to be quite scrupulous about getting their facts straight, at least in their news columns.

Today, any news organization worthy of the name pledges itself to ensure as far as possible that the news it presents is accurate, fair and balanced. While this has always been an informal understanding among ethical journalists, many organizations have adopted formal codes of ethics, and some employ ombudsmen to protect the public interest.

By adopting such self-restraint, the media have acknowledged that the dissemination of the news is not just another business. It is a form of public trust, not only because people need information to live out their everyday lives, but because the media have so much latent power. Power must be counterbalanced by responsibility, and news organizations have chosen to exercise that responsibility themselves, rather than risk the threat to democratic practice posed by having governments do it for them.

What the Public Thinks ? : The greatest power of the media to influence public opinion lies not so much in their commentary on the news but in their selection and presentation of it. "Of course the people won't always vote the way the editorial-writers tell them on next week's sewer by law," observed the 1970 Canadian Senate Report on Mass Media; "but who decides when they'll start thinking and talking about sewers — or whether they'll worry about pollution at all ?"

Back in the comparatively simple world of 1920, the great American columnist Walter Lippmann wrote : "The news of the day as it reaches the newspaper office is an incredible medley of fact, propaganda, rumour, suspicion, clues, hopes, and fears, and the task of selecting and ordering the news is one of the truly sacred and priestly offices in a democracy."

All sorts of judgements come into play when a newspaper or new program is being produced: How long should a story be ? Should it come first, last, or in between ? Within the story itself, which points should be emphasized over others ? In a controversy, which spokesmen for which side should be quoted more prominently ? The answers to all these questions have a strong influence on what people think about issues and events.

How do editors and news directors choose what you will or will not hear about ? According to George Kennedy in his textbook *News Reporting and Writing*, there are five usual criteria: impact (what everybody will be talking about); proximity (all things being equal, something that happens a few streets away is bigger news than something that happens 1,000 miles away); timeliness (news has a short shelf life); prominence ("names make news"); conflict (as in strikes, politics, crime, sports competition); and novelty ("if a dog bites a man, that's not news; if a man bites a dog, that's news").

The yardsticks used by professionals to judge what makes news frequently come in for criticism from the public and its spokesmen. "Trouble : that's (what's) wrong with journalism's current definition of the news," complained the Senate Report on Mass Media. "There is more to life than hassle and strife, but the media's entertainment in drama, conflict and disruption prevents them from reporting it."

The trouble is that people like to hear about trouble as long as it is not happening to them, and the news is to a large extent "market driven". A perhaps apocryphal story is told in the business about a man who started a wire service which carried only good news, and promptly went broke.

It is an open question whether it is the consumers or processors of news who demand that it be delivered at great speed, but certainly any news organisation that is consistently beaten to the punch on stories would fear losing the market share to more alert competitors. Many of the failings of the media can be traced to the haste with which reports are prepared.

The scope for error is enormous when reporting is done in a rush, which is why newspapers and agencies obligate themselves to publish corrections when the inevitable mistakes occur. Speed breeds superficiality; when something is reported in a hurry, important details may be overlooked or misunderstood.

Facts and the Truth

Even when the time to prepare a report is not unduly short, there is a constant danger of getting events or issues out of perspective. At a time when life is growing even more complicated, salient facts may be lost in the shuffle of all the considerations that come into play. Also, news people see things through their own pre-conditioned perceptions, and "the observers," as communications scholar P. W. Bridgman put it. They must deal with words, and words can be slippery. They sometimes pass on their biases to readers or listeners through their choice of language.

Reporters, as opposed to opinion journalists, traditionally have tried to keep their personal feelings and opinions out of their reports, but objectivity is not without its pitfalls. There is a decided difference between the facts and the truth. It might be a fact that a person involved in a newsworthy situation says something, but what he says might not be true. Still, his words must be reported objectively in the absence of evidence that they are lies.

The school of "new journalism" that grew up in the 1960s contended that true objectivity was a psychological impossibility and should, therefore, be dispensed with. In any case, the new journalists insisted, objectivity was merely an excuse for the established media to support the status quo on questions of justice that cried out for reform.

Though it was practised in the name of democracy, subjective reporting proved to be distinctly undemocratic, which perhaps explains why it is now discredited among most mainstream journalists. Its practitioners felt free to ignore the precept that there are two sides to every story when one side did not agree with their point of view.

The Aberrant one-tenth of what happens makes the News : Worse, the freedom from the discipline of objectivity blurred the distinction between personal interpretation of the facts and pure fiction: It became just too tempting for some writers not to invent convenient "facts" when a story was (so they thought) written from such a personal point of view that no one could check up on it. In several cases, someone did check up, and found that stories had been falsified.

Although members of every profession will occasionally bring it into disgrace, the cases of fabrication seemed to confirm the views of those who regard the entire media with unwavering suspicion Such derelictions are, in fact, very uncommon. The great majority of writers and editors strive intently to ensure the integrity of the news.

People who excoriate the sins of the media frequently fail to differentiate between reportage and commentary. The media themselves sometimes contribute to the confusion by mixing the two in the form of "interpretative reporting." and not clearly identifying the line between the verifiable facts and what the writer speculates those facts might mean.

Mostly, though, people who rail against the media are indulging in the time-honoured sport of shooting the messenger. They are upset by the endless chronicle of folly and evil which journalists deliver—"the usual depravities and businesses and hypocrisies and cruelties" which Mark Twain said could be found in any morning's news. It is natural enough to want to ascribe blame for all the tumult and grief that seems to surround us. And so journalists are blamed for going out of their way to make the world look worse than it is.

This is particularly so in the case of "investigative reporting," which digs out news rather than waiting for it to happen. The public sometimes seems to have more sympathy with the subjects of revelations of misbehaviour than with the journalists who have uncovered them. "There they go again," people will say. "Why do they have to tell us these things ? Why not let sleeping dogs lie?"

The answer is that our society would be a lot worse off if media did not play such a role; the fear of being exposed is a strong deterrent to corruption. Granted, the media sometimes go too far in their pursuit of real or supposed villains. That is one reason why there are now press councils in many parts of North America. The councils are there to see that, in their lust for justice, the media do not commit injustices themselves.

The most commonly-heard complaint against the purveyors of news is that they "blow things out of proportion". In the most general terms, they certainly do. The bad news which comprises the bulk of national and international reports is out of proportion to the great mass of "good news" that is never reported. At any given hour, nine-tenths of human affairs around the world are proceeding peacefully, smoothly and safely. The stuff of headlines is the other aberrant one-tenth, or less.

Walter Lippmann said that the task of news people is to provide a picture of reality upon which men can act, but the news does not and cannot reflect the whole of reality. Still, it does give us grounds for action to build a better world. There are times when we would prefer not to know just how stupid and bad human beings can be, but if we did not know about it, we would never be able to correct the stupidity and badness. The news is a necessary evil in the advancement of civilization. It might even be said that there can be no civilization without the news.

Responsible Reporting : Open to all parties, but influenced by none.

Only a courageous publisher supported by an inspired, intelligent, and dynamic editorial staff ably augmented by knowledgeable, efficient and dedicated "reporters" can find his greatest fulfilment as a newspaper man.

A newspaper cannot please everyone every day. The newspaperman must know his public : it will help if the reader knows something of the problems of the reporter and the editors, and how they go about solving them.

The newspaper is produced for commercial gain, sold under highly competitive conditions, and must have careful business management. If it is not issued for sale so as to make a profit, it is not a distinct individual, but a part or adjunct of something else. If published to advance any cause, it is an organ, not a newspaper. It cannot be independent unless it earns its living.

The perfect newspaper will be the voice of the lowly and oppressed and forgotten people, champions of the underdog. If in discharge of its responsibility especially in the present "restless world" — it occasionally troubles the public conscience, that is not to its credit. If it is a defender of civil liberty and a friend of righteous causes it is performing a worthy service. Its chief function is to hold up a mirror to the happenings of the day. If it is careful to keep the mirror clean and as flawless as possible, the reflections will be honest, clear and interesting.

Newspaper writing and newspaper reading are not jobs for people who cannot, when necessary, look at a subject objectively. The reader needs to distinguish between knowledge and guessing, between trained and casual observation, between verification and credulousness.

The urge to play up conflict in print and in coversation is widespread, and newspapers might improve their image by curbing it.

News is accurate information about any event of public or human interest, of the record of significant acts or opinions. It tells about something that is different from daily routine.

Two attributes of the good newspaper reporter today are selection and sincerity. He knows what incident to include to give his canvas the image of life, and he cannot be induced to omit an iota of what he believes to be essential. He is neither too dainty to face facts as they are, nor too blind to discern their full significance, but he will not revel in the unhealthy or set down anything in malice. He is true to the facts whether he is writing an account of a college concert or a report of the clash of events in world politics.

The press is not free if those who operate it behave as though their position conferred upon them the privilege of being deaf to ideas which the processes of free speech have brought to public attention.

Just as the citizen tries to order his life so as to live decently, effectively and fruitfully, so a newspaper can contribute to its generation by telling the news in accord with the principles of honesty, impartiality, integrity, accuracy and fairness. The editorial writer with a sense of responsibility will try to give his readers a balanced presentation of basic facts, tell the purpose of proposed action suggest alternatives, and illuminate the whole matter by his soulful thought.

Press Release : The word press signifies newspapers, magazines, journals or dailies or periodicals in general. Subject matters to publicise or as reported in the press. Press release signifies to make news known publicly or to allow news to be made known publicly. An advertisement, for instance, is released of a product recently introduced in the market. Press release is a statement given to newspapers, reporters etc. Government corporations, institutions issue press releases to inform the public. Press and news media are powerful, and generally inflnential to project an image to the public. Indian Press is free press and the people have much faith in the press. The press can effectively communicate to the public.

The press transmits facts, figures, symbols to the readers. It is an objective announcement about a particular matter or event issued to the press for publication to inform the public in time. The press has every right to publish any news item intact or in condensed form. It all depends on its news-worthiness and importance. A press release is not confined only to news items of Government, politics, national and international events. Press releases include advertisements, appointments, legal notices, growth of industry, government notifications, guidelines, achievements, activities, marriages, entertainment, rentals, seminars etc. A press release is effective only when it satisfies qualities like information, which is concise, clear, and devoid of hackneyed publicity materials. Selection of a newspaper or newspapers for the subject matter and the circle of readers for whom it is meant are the deciding factors for the effectiveness of any press release. They are closely related with each other. Evidently the wrong selection of newspaper(s) for the publication of any fact is a matter of great significance to achieve the objectives of release. Therefore, in any press release the right selection of newspapers and its significance cannot be overemphasised.

A few illustrations of recent press releases are as under :

Illustration 1

Office of the Andhra Pradesh

Housing Board

'Gruhakalpa' Mukarramjahi Road,

Hyderabad

Press Note : In the Notification No. 13/92 issued calling for applications for allotment of houses at Ongole, the cost of application is mentioned as Rs. 35/- and by post Rs. 25/- by oversight instead of Rs. 25/- and Rs. 35/- respectively. Therefore, it is informed that the applications can be had in person by paying Rs. 25/- and Rs. 35/- by post from the office of the Regional Housing Engineer, A.P. Housing Board, Vijaywada.

For Vice Chairman & Housing Commissioner.

Illustration 2

Wanted Distributors

A company manufacturing PCs and State-of-art new generation Fax machines wishes to appoint area-wise distributors who are : Financially sound. Professionally managed. Having good track record in the field.

Apply within 10 days with full details along with bank references.

To

The Chief Executive,

XYZ Company Limited 15,

Anandha Road Alwarpet,

Madras 600018.

Illustration 3

X.Y. GROUP Requires

Two

Company

Secretaries

For Their New Delhi Offices

The candidates must be members of the Institute of Company Secretaries of India. Past experience is not necessary. Please apply with salary expected within 10 days to :

The Managing Driector

X. Y. Group Limited

12, New Colony,

Model Basti

New Delhi-110005.

Illustration 4

Steel Authority of India Limited

(A Government of India Enterprise)

Rourkela Steel Plant

Rourkela-769 011 Orissa Office of the Additional General Manager (MM)

Purchase Department Sub : Second Corrigendum

To Tender Notice No : P/Proj/Modn/4011899124 for signalling and Truck Inter Connection Package under Phase-II Modernisation of Rourkela Steel Plant.

Sl.No.2.0 First line for existing entry please read as the Tender documents will be available for sale from 30-6-1990 to 21-7-1992.

Sl.No.2.1 First line in place of 10-7-1992 please read as "31-8-1992." All other conditions of the tender notice shall remain unaltered.

Registered Office : Ispat Bhavan, Lodhi Road, New Delhi-110 003. Illustration 5

Notice inviting Tender

Sealed tenders are invited for design, manufacture, supply, erection, testing, commissioning of FEED systems for the Banbury Mixer at our Kankinara Works, West Bengal.

Tender documents can be obtained from Materials Manager (Project), at the address given below on all working days between 10.00 a.m. and 2.00 p.m. up to 21-6-90. Last date of submission of bid completed in all respects is 21-7-90.

Type Corporation of India Ltd.

(A Government of India Enterprise). 19, Jawaharlal Nehru Road, Calcutta - 700 087.

Mass Media Guidelines

1. The sacredness of human personality has to be the vital content of any mass media reporting.
2. Must ever be alive to responsible reporting in this restless world.
3. Newspapers must be open to all parties but influenced by none.
4. Only a courageous publisher supported by an inspired, intelligent and dynamic editorial staff ably supported by knowledgeable. Efficient and dedicated "reporters" can find his greatest fulfilment as a newspaper man.

5. In this imperfect world of "Man, the unknowns," people practising different professions tend to forget the Code of Ethics. Though "Journalism" is a profession, it has to be considered as a mission. Only a sincere "opposition" and an aggressive press could be the guardians of democracy.
6. From being a "reporter" he should endeavour to combine velocity and facility and become a "social scientist".
7. The perfect newspaper will be the voice of the lowly and oppressed and forgotten people, champion of the underdog. Its chief function is to hold up a mirror to the happenings of the day. If it is careful to keep the mirror clean and as flawless as possible, the reflections will be honest, clear and interesting.
8. The urge to play up conflict in print and in conversation is widespread, newspapers might improve their image by curbing it.
9. News is accurate information about any event of public or human interest, or the record of significant acts of opinions. It tells about something that is different from daily routine.
10. The press is not free if those who operate it behave as though their position conferred upon them the privilege of being deaf to ideas which the processes of free speech have brought to public attention.
11. Just as the citizen tries to order his life so as to live decently, 'effectively and fruitfully, so a newspaper can contribute to its generation by reporting the news in accord with the principles of honesty, impartiality, integrity, accuracy and fairness.

Relative Merits

Timing and Place : Not only does the newspaper have greater merit than the radio because it is the older of the two media, but also because of the special advantages and conveniences offered by it. The radio listener has to adjust himself to the timings and place of the station, while the reader can take his paper wherever he likes, go through it at leisure and re-read a part which he likes. Even the appearance of the "Radio-Newspaper" and its possible development does not alter the position because the newspaper can give much, much greater variety.

Leisure : In this era when prompt supply of news is of paramount importance, the radio sometimes beats the newspaper in the game. But even this occasional beating only whets public appetite to read more and at greater leisure about important developments in the reader's favourite newspaper. The ghost that the radio and the press are rivals has been laid to rest long ago.

Illiteracy : Illiteracy which is a large chink in our armour, is no obstacle in the case of the radio as it is in the case of the newspaper. The vast areas of the countryside can be opened up and brought under the educative influence of the radio by installing more community sets. The regional radio stations lay more and more emphasis to rural programmes.

Cost : Radio-mindedness is limited mainly by one's paying capacity. If the radio sets could be made and sold at cheaper rates and the Central, State and other local taxes on them are brought down, it will be a boon to the lower and middle classes and to people living in the villages.

Coverage : Despite competition from the radio and the TV the newspaper is undergoing a tremendous revolution not only in respect of new ideas and new methods in editing but also in the introduction of new printing procedures and machines. The major consideration of the print media today is how to catch the interest and attention of the reader so that he continues as ever to wait anxiously for the morning newspaper. There is an attempt to put greater variety in coverage, more human value stories and the lighter type of matter which may inform, instruct and provide entertainment at the same time. Newspapers are becoming more and more humanized.

Visual Look : With the printing revolution already going fast, newspapers, especially weeklies, fortnightlies and monthlies, are using modern methods of offset printing in which many colours are combined to give a better visual effect.

Ideology : A country's political system (stemming from the political ideology) is obviously related to the direction and speed of a country's total national development. If this assumption be true, then media and national development join in a kind of symbiotic relationship of a complex nature. It is this symbiotic relationship that has been consuming more and more time and effort of researchers and theorists in the related fields of journalism, sociology and political science since about the middle of this century.

Integrity : Editors and writers are a highly individualistic group who maintain fairly high standards of competence and integrity in evaluating information they pass on to their readers. Newspapers are as much a public utility as water, electricity, gas or transportation. Because they are essential to the smooth functioning of a political democracy and a free enterprise economic system, newspapers keep the public interest foremost in their day-to-day judgement of news.

Foreign Print Media

The legislature, the judiciary, the executive and the press are the four pivotal pillars on which modern democracy is built. The press, as the Fourth Estate, it should safeguard the principles of democracy by effective dissemination of information. The press plays a paramount role in a democracy, it is not known as the Fourth Estate for nothing. Secularism, socialism, democracy, self-reliance and constitutional values are the important factors to move towards liberalisation of Indian newspaper industry. There should not be any discrimination on the grounds of religion, race, caste or creed.

"The approach to foreign media has been governed by considerations of larger national interest and has ever been and ought not to be treated merely as an issue of economic policy". (N.Ravi, The Hindu).

The Controversy

There is a great deal of controversy and views on the concept of foreign print media. It is nothing but liberalisation of newspaper

industry like other economic sectors liberalised and globalised. In other words it is the presence of foreign press on Indian soil. Allowing foreign print media is giving permission to the big foreign newspaper business concerns to commence publishing in India it is a step towards globalisation with liberalisation. The free entry of newspaper and periodicals permits foreign print media to print and publish news and views from India. As a result foreigners directly print and distribute their news. Free foreign print media is possible only with the Government policy of liberalisation to the newspaper industry. The trend in media ownership in recent global village is towards large and free foreing newspapers. The concept of going global has become most popular in recent years in media industries as print, film, broadcast, cable. satellite, marketing and advertising organisations have been expanding their activities across frontiers. Globalisation of newspaper industry with liberalisation policy represents nothing more than trans nationalisation which affects substantially domestic activities.

Communication is the heart of all social interactions. Our worlds in its communication dimension consists of nations affiliated to United Nations. The basis for globalisation is that people cannot live in isolation and human solidarity.

Ban on Foreign Media : In the year 1955 the Government witheld permission to foreign nationals to own newspapers in India. In the year 1956 the Government laid down that foreign news agencies have to operate in the country by collaborating with Indian news agencies and not directly. The entry of foreign print media also had been thoroughly examined by the first press commission. The ban on foreign nationals running newspapers in the country was imposed during the period of Jawaharlal Nehru. According to Mr. Justice Sarkaria,' 'the ban was imposed in the national interest when the nation's intergrity and security was endangered by fissiparous forces operating from within and outside the country".

Problem of the Print Media : The major problems of newspaper industry in this country are :

1. Declining sales.

2. Increasing competition.
3. High price.
4. Uneconomic rates.
5. Time and language.
6. Lack of direct servicing wires to all newspapers.
7. Liberalisation policy helping electronic media to huge sums by way of advertisement revenues.
8. Multiple channel.
9. Foreign satellite.
10. Video and cable TV.
11. The advertisement rates of the Government advertisements are uneconomic and lowerst commercial rates.
12. Introduction of colour pages by some newspapers, which small newspapers cannot afford.

The recent trend is that the advertisement revenue which other wise would have gone to the print media is now being diverted to the electronic media. The advertisements rates fixed for Government advertisements through Directorate of Advertising x and Visual Publicity (DAVP) are not reasonable. Print media have been facing the problem and challenges from radio, television and is now computing with the electronic media in the form of internet, cyberspace.

For and against Foreign Media or Merits and Demerits : There has been a wide debate over the open door proposal for foreign media and its possible threat to the Indian free press. There are different opinions and wide spectrum of views. Editors, and media barons, politicians and intellectuals, and even readers form a part of the wide spectrum of views, divided down the line.

There are supportive of the entry of foreign print media and some objected the same. While some people say the entry of foreign media is not a harmful, while others perceive a threat to Indian free press. On the other hand some people adopts middle path, in view of globalisation, opening the doors to foreign publishing houses may not pose much of a problem provided adequate steps are taken to ensure that their operations are regulated and controlled to safeguard national interest.

No unanimity may emerge on controversial and sensitive issue like this, because it is a question of defending sovereignty, upholding national tradition in a multi-cultural and multi-lingual country like India. Allowing free entry of foreign print media may, however, require an amount of national consensus.

The ideas and opinions are so sharply devided over whether or not to allow the entry of foreign print media in India. There is no consensus of unanimity on the matter. Opinions widely differ between journalists, politicians, lawyers, academicians and social activities. Interestingly enough the trend is against the entry of foreign media.

It is all above theoretical proposition and it is difficult to see how the Netty of foreign media would work and help Indian press with highest level of professional conduct, standards, latest technology.

However, under the following paragraphs, the merits and demerits of foreign print media are presented.

The Merits

1. Foreign print media would help to get huge investment, new technology and varied expertise and experience. For improving the printing technology and publishing technique and for giving boost to Indian journalism, foreign media are partly recommended, it brings in capital, technology and professional advise.
2. Foreign and Indian press working together would help expand the perception of Indians on multifarious issues of global nature. The open door policy permits a wholesome view of cultural cross currents taking place, in a global village.
3. Allowing foreign print media promotes a healthy competitive spirit and entrepreneur ship in Indian newspaper industry.

4. In a free global village foreign entry into newspaper industry, anybody can own a paper .
5. Allowing the foreign print media in the country in the name of liberalisation would help expanding knowledge.
6. The advent of foreigners into a newspaper industry would bring about an improvement in professional standards of journalism and communication by way of stiff competition. The entry of foreign media would help in widening the perception of the Indians in the matters of both national and international.
7. Foreign newspapers offer higher salaries, perks, and better working conditions, better prospects, career opportunities, greater mobility, better working environment. Thus foreign media will snatch the cream of the Indian journalist by offering better monetary benefits.
8. Foreign print media promote fast declining cultural values. The presence of foreign media reflects credible global cultural revolution brought about by sophisticated printing, phototype and electronic technology.
9. Be global and by global is the order in these days of information revolution and communication age.
10. The target readership of the foreign news papers would mainly be the english reading urbanites.
11. There is no fear of professional competition. Indian journalists are professionally competent with anyone in the world. In respect of standards and professional code the Indian journalists are not lagging behind.
12. Some of the newspapers in India are tied up with some business houses which filter the news and fair views. While some newspapers are bias of political parties and religious sects. The foreign media eliminates this environment in view of competition, standards and other commercial considerations. The problem of politically biased and editorials tailored to sub-serve the politico-business interest may exit from Indian newspaper industry.

The inflow of well known foreign newspapers will not only destabilise the english language Indian newspaper, but also the regional and small language propers through advertisement revenue diversion and readership. It is not advantageous to the vernacular press which may vehemently oppose the idea of entry of foreign media which would be a total disaster as it would irreversibly damage the pluralistick and relatively independent national press.

The Demerits

Be Indian and by Indian is the Indian slogan. The father of the Nation Mahatma Gandhi advocated Swadeshi in all fields.

1. The foreign press would definitely pose a direct danger to the Indian language newspapers. In fact Indian language newspapers are the real moulders of the public opinion.
2. The concept of liberalisation and globalisation by no means have any relevance to the newspaper industryliberalisation, globalisation of newspaper cannot be equated in the same category of other economic sectors, it is a sensitive media of information and sensitive political matter. This sector is not an economic commodity.
3. The entry of foreign media would affect integrity, and security endangers by fissiparous forces operating from within and outside the country.
4. Giving foothold in the country to the outside newspaper, would endanger the free flow of information by Indian media holding different views.
5. As a powerful outside foreign may not show concern for Indias interest.
6. Editorial policy of foreign newspapers a cannot be controlled, as a result poses a greater danger of national security.
7. Presently small newspapers have been grapple a host of operating problems. The entry of foreign print media may very much affect adversely the small newspaper industry.

So the entry of foreign news agencies is a real threat to the small papers. These papers already have been facing problems like competition, low circulation, paltry advertisement revenue and TV and radio drained the newspaper industry's advertisement revenues.

8. Allowing the entry of foreign media implies foreigners claiming right of freedom of expression which is fundamental right guaranteed by the constitution of India to the Indian citizens only but not to the foreiners. Every country has its own laws and constitutions to protect their respective print media and right of freedom of expression, thus provisions of Article 19 would be thrown open to non-citizens. Thus entry of foreign media into India may have some legal implications. Article 19 of the Constitution stipulates that all citizens shall have the right to freedom of speech and expression. The provision of restriction of ownership of the press to citizens alone is correct one. Foreign corporations are not Indian citizens and hence have no fundamental right to force into our territory.
9. There is also an evident danger of foreign element taking advantage of a free entry to propagate terrorism, separatism, casteism and create social bitterness through publications. The anti-national element would exploit the advantages of press liberalisation to endanger the country.
10. Foreign print media are threat and would pose to nation's security and culture, national inetgrity, interest, tradition and native way of life. It amounts to cultural invasion.
11. Open door proposal allowing print media would adversely affect country's political and social through resulting foreign rule over Indian minds.
12. Foreign agencies publishing newspaper involves distribution of their news, only through the Indian meanss.
13. Foreign print media would definitely influence electorate and may endanger democracy.

14. Views are also there that foreign newspapers may lead to serious dent in the circulation and readership.
15. Indian newspaper and magazines are getting government advertisements, hence foreign media is a threat of the damocle's word.
16. It is quote possible to impose a restriction by foreign print media that the employees of the foreign-owned media should be foreigners.
17. The All India Newspaper Employees Federation, PTI Employees Union, National Union of Journalists, UNI Employees Federation and Media Watch Group, in the year 1994 express their opposition to the entry of foreign media on several grounds. There was a "Campaign against Entry of Foreign Media" (CARFORM) in 1994.

To Sum Up :

To summarise is foreign print media globalisation inevitable?

Is it necessary to globalise print media ?

Is global village homogenised ?

Are hybridised, synthesised and urbanised culture promote national interest ?

Globalisation of press or foreign media is not the same category as other economic sectors. Newspapers, through a part of national economic aspect, should not be considered like economic commodity, capital, technology etc. Because it is not an extension of economic policy, the press has social, cultural, national traditional values and commitments.

The conscious of social responsibility of the newspapers of a particular country should not be ignored. The media of the country ideally reflect the social and cultural values of the country, but foreign media do not. There is no doubt about the fact that the so called global society permits to know other cultures and civilization.

Foreign print media may be permitted to a very limited extent and in a restricted way to ventilate fair views under close monitoring. Parameters should be prescribed not causing harm to national integrity and friendly foreign relations.

The overwhelming majority of minus points submitted above indicate creation of an unfavourable environment that may likely be created with the foreign print media. But still it is not a conclusive opinion.

The entry on scientific, technical, educational and informative newspapers and journals can restrictively be permitted. Foreign publications should not be given blanket permission. Strict guidelines, code and standards can be prescribed. The screening procedure promotes quality publication and undesirable publications should be removed. Lower price and greater control over publications, ensuring majority Indian ownership by holding shares holding positions in the Board of Management and editors are some of the safeguarding measures.

Thus the issue is a sensitive. But invasion of foreign media poses a serious danger to the country's independence, sovereignty friendly relations, communal harmony.

13

Newspaper Industry

One Opinion : Electronic communications were killing print. That judgement has proved wrong or at least premature. True, the antenna of the media picked up tremors in the mid-1970s indicating that Americans' reading and writing skills were declining, and by concentrating public attention on alarming statistics and assertions of decline, the media moved the tremors up the Richter scale. Popular and expert opinion quickly blamed television as a major villain. Particularly as the apparent decline coincided with a drop in newspaper circulation. The analysts so explained the statistics as to raise doubts that the decline was real; experts disagreed about whether or not a problem in fact existed, and if it did, just how serious it was; and historians pointed out that concern about declining literacy had surfaced before and seemed cyclical in nature. Nevertheless, the message through the media was that indeed Johnny could not read or write, and schools and universities were put on notice to do something. Then the media picked up other tremors in society and moved on. Because it lacked dramatic visual appeal, the "story" of declining literacy lent itself more to examination by the print than the electronic media, so illustrating an important point. Although the media all perform the same functions, they cannot in every instance perform them equally well. To some extent their competition for audiences and advertisers is at one another's expense, but each possesses sufficiently unique attributes for supplementary and complementary roles to survive. This chapter, discusses a dynamic not a dying communications technology.

Mass Markets

The creation of mass markets, which only large and costly units could service efficiently, has led inevitably to a contraction of ownership in many cities and towns and thus to the development of newspaper chains. The high point in the number of newspapers published in the United States came in 1909, when there were 2600 daily publications. On this situation, magazine publisher Frank Munsey commented, "There is no business that cries out so loud for organization and combination as that of newspaper publishing. For one thing, the number of newspapers is at least 60 percent greater than we need."

Munsey dreamed of a national chain of 500 newspapers and tried to start it by buying newspapers in New York, Washington, Boston, Baltimore, and Philadelphia. Although his chain failed, he pioneered an accelerating trend in twentieth-century publishing.

In the first half of the twentieth century, more than 2000 new daily newspapers (including those changing from weekly to daily) were started. But, during the same period, 1947 daily newspapers suspended publication to become weeklies, 547 disappeared through merger or consolidation, and at least 302 local combinations took place. At the same time the number of newspaper chains increased from three, publishing 62 newspapers, to 70 publishing 386, with more than two-fifths of the daily and one-half of the Sunday circulation. In the 1950s there were scarcely more than 100 cities with competing daily newspapers. Of the 1500 cities with daily newspapers in 1977, only 2.5 percent-fewer than 40-had competing newspapers. By then the nation's 168 chains owned three-fifths of the nation's 1756 daily newspapers and controlled 71 percent of the circulation.

According to journalist historian Frank Mott, consolidation of newspapers is not a strictly recent tendency, it can be found in all periods. But since World War I, the skyrocketing cost of newspaper publication has been a strong influence in accelerating the tendency to consolidate.

Melville E. Stone established the Chicago Daily News in 1876 with a few thousand dollars capital; in 1925 it sold for $13 million. In 1963 two Omaha dailies were sold for $43 million, and in 1967 Newhouse Newspapers bought the Cleveland Plain Dealer for $53.4 million, Knight Newspapers paid $55 million for two Philadelphia papers in 1969. In 1976 Rupert Murdoch, the Australian press baron, paid, according to Folio magazine's estimate, $30 million for the New York Post at a time when all three New York dailies were losing circulation (between March 1974 and September 1976, the Times dropped from approximately 910,000 daily to 802,000, the Daily News from 2.12 million to 1.93 million, and the Post from 650,000 to 489,000).

In the typical American town in earlier days, more newspaper publishing ventures were attempted than the economy could support. Some newspapers-for example, those founded solely as voices of political parties or other interest groups-went out of business simply because they could not win general community support. Others were founded by people who went into the business apparently on the assumption that to make money it was only necessary to "buy newsprint white and sell it black." They soon discovered that, aside from the problems of editing a mass medium, such factors as rigid advertising and circulation rates made newspaper publishing a dubious enterprise at best. For the new entrant today the problems are even more formidable, particularly in metropolitan areas. Not only has population shifted increasingly to the suburbs, with businesses and service industries in pursuit, but inflation in the 1970s was forcing more and more families to stop subscribing to more than one newspaper.

Both in procuring their raw material and in marketing their products. Newspaper publishers exhibit the familiar behaviour of monopoly and oligopoly. As buyers they use the customary pressures for keeping down costs; as sellers they maintain rigid advertising and circulation rates, discriminate by rate differentials, and practice block selling of space in morning and evening newspapers in combination. The typical newspaper pays out for newsprint roughly one-third of its revenues, which is just about what it receives in circulation revenue. Practically all newsprint is sold in carload lots under long-term contracts, mostly to large publishers. Those who cannot afford carload lots get their newsprint from jobbers, brokers, and paper merchants at open market prices, which are sometimes higher by 10 percent or more than the carload rates.

Procuring syndicated features and wire services is no less difficult for the new entrant. The syndicated feature business is dominated by four major companies: AP news features, King Features, NEA Service, and United Features. Most franchises provide for exclusive territories. Furthermore, package selling enables large publishers to buy up rights to more features than they print. Oligopoly is similarly a chief trait of the two wire services.

The new newspaper is confronted in many markets by chain organization. Chains, especially of large newspapers, have certain special advantages: Notably, they make wider use of editorial and feature writers: it is easier for them to obtain new funds from the capital market; they engage in block merchandising of space to national advertisers, in centralized and large-scale research, and in bulk purchases of newsprint, ink, and equipment; they are better able to make maximum use of specialized technical and managerial services, and of electronic automation-central computers can serve all papers in the chain.

Despite these centralizing tendencies, American news institutions, and newspapers in particular, have been local rather than national because of "a peculiarity in American political organization and the prevailing pattern of family money spending." Ben Bagdikian has written:

> More governmental functions are left to the local level in the United States than in other developed countries. Schools, property taxes, land use, public health, large

> areas of business regulation, and many other political and social activities are controlled by locally elected and locally controlled bodies... These locally controlled policies have maximum immediate impact on family life, such as schooling for children, design and location of homes, routes of local highways, and rates of personal property taxes. Such decisions are made by a complicated but highly localized set of political bodies.

The United States has no national newspapers. The closest approximations are the Wall Street Journal, which in 1977 reached across the nation to 1.46 million people interested mainly in financial news, and the New York Times, one quarter of whose 854,000 daily subscribers in 1977 lived more than 100 miles from New York City. To a much lesser extent, the Washington Post also reached beyond the capital, but it did not compete seriously in national and international circulation with the times. In the late 1970s the Times was spending $35 million a year (the Post was spending $19 million) to support the world's largest full-time news staff-641 journalists (550 in New York, 40 in Washington, 19 scattered throughout the United States, and 32 abroad). There are fatter American newspapers than the Times (the average news hole-the space devoted to editorial words-of the Times in 1977 was 160 columns a day; the Washington Star printed 185 and the Chicago Tribune 218 columns a day), but they rely typically on wire service and syndicated material for much of their content. Almost everything in the Times is staff written.

These huge newspapers with an impact beyond their cities of publication form a tiny minority of American daily newspapers; only half a percent of all dailies have more than 500,000 circulation. Seventy percent of U.S. dailies have circulations of 25,000 or less; 53 percent are published in cities with populations less than 25,000. Although the New York Times has an influence in the United States and abroad out of all proportion to its size, the statistics in the tables below present a clearer perspective on the newspaper industry as a whole and vividly make Bagdikian's point about the localism of newspapers.

As Americans' disposable income has risen, retail stores and service enterprises have kept pace at the local level in competing for this income, typically by advertising through the local newspaper. In 1976 advertisers spent $33.6 billion in all media. Newspapers got $10.2 billion or 30 percent of that, 25.6 percent local, only 4.4 percent national. Because of family spending patterns, the population shift to the suburbs, and the mushrooming suburban shopping centers, a relatively new newspaper category has emerged: the shopper's guide or shopper or throwaway. A typical daily newspaper has a ratio of about 65 percent advertising content to 35 percent news and feature content. Shoppers, by contrast, contain 75 percent or more advertising content, and many are distributed free. And their numbers are growing. The U.S. Suburban Press, Inc., had 850 of these shoppers with a total circulation of 11.3 million in early 1976.

To curb shoppers' eating into their advertising revenues, established newspapers were supporting efforts by some states to exclude shoppers from the tax privileges enjoyed by "traditional" newspapers. In New Jersey state tax officials were struggling to come up with a satisfactory definition of "newspaper." The rise of the suburban press, whether as traditional newspaper or shopper, challenged the domination of major metropolitan newspapers, many of which began developing their own suburban or zone editions in the 1970s to compete for readers and advertisers.

The localism of newspapers and their efforts to attract and hold readers in a competitive market have made the newspaper in many respects a more direct descendant of the early magazine of the nineteenth century than is the contemporary magazine. The word "magazine" is derived from the French word magazine, 'meaning "storehouse," and early magazines were miscellanies of information and amusement. In its growing consumer orientation and emphasis on "news you can use," today's local newspaper is very similar. Readers of all ages can usually find something to interest them in the paper's coverage of local events and activities, in its local and syndicated features, comics, and games, and in its local retail ads and listing of local entertainment. Even the large metropolitan newspapers that concentrate on public affairs and appeal to a readership far beyond their cities of publication-the new York times, Washington Post, the Wall Street Journal, and the Christian Science Monitor-publish a miscellany of serious and entertaining content more diverse than that of a general-interest magazine.

In fact, it seemed in the late 1970s that newspapers had to publish more of such "soft" new and feature material to stave off circulation declines. By adding a section three days a week in 1976 and 1977—Living, a section on food and wine, on Wednesdays Home, on furniture, interior decorating, and gardening, on Thursdays, and Weekend, a guide to entertainment and the arts, on Fridays- the New York Times reversed its circulation decline, increasing circulation from a daily average of 821,000 in 1976 to 854,000 in 1977. Not only did more people buy the Times on the days with added sections-35,000 more than on unsupplemented days-more advertisers bought space. The Times sold more advertising in May 1977 than in any previous month in its history.

To some their local orientation offsets the standardization of American newspapers. Yet whatever character a publisher or editor or the community itself confers on a local newspaper, economy dictates a heavy reliance by almost all on wire and news services for national and international news and on syndicates for features, columns, and comics. Studies have long shown that the comics sections, and particularly the Sunday comics, are among the best-read sections in the paper. A study reported by N.W. Ayer and Company in 1976 found that more than 50 million copies of Sunday comics are distributed to American homes every week, where they are read by over 100 million people. And two organizations, Metro Sunday Comics and the Puck Group, supply over 76 percent of those copies.

Not only do these centralised sources of news and entertainment make for an essential similarity in newspaper content from place to place, but the newswriting techniques and formulas of the wire services-typically a summary lead paragraph followed by the facts in order or decreasing importance-have influenced reportorial style in such a way that even local stories read alike. The chemistry of the city council members and the nature of the issues they discuss may differ dramatically between Lompoc, California, and Brunswick, Maine, but the way in which the Lompoc Record and the Brunswick Times Record report them is unlikely to differ much. Researchers have argued, in fact, that because of professional norms concerning definitions of news and the inverted pyramid style of reporting, reporters ignore the colour, flavour, and very human disorder and tedium of city council discussion in favour of a concise, objective account of the decisions taken. The effect of this approach, the researchers argue, is to shore up the authority of local government by creating the impression that it is consistently acting decisively and rationally.

Even though the great majority of daily newspapers-approximately 85 percent-have circulations under 50,000, and may therefore appear small enough to serve as personal vehicles for strong-minded, colourful publishers who can stamp the newspaper with their own personalities, the forces of industrialization and urbanization accelerating after the Civil War virtually killed the dominance of flamboyant publishers like Bennett, Pulitzer, and Hearst whose paper were personal, idiosyncratic extensions of themselves. Most newspapers today are corporate and impersonal enterprises.

Examples of the colourful breed of the nineteenth century survive, of course. In New Hampshire, William Loeb, the publisher of the Manchester Union Leader, uses his statewide newspaper with vigorous partisanship against political candidates of whom he disapproves. Rupert Murdoch, the Australian publisher of the New York Post, seems a reincarnation of much of the best and worst of Pulitzer and hearst.

In Las Vegas, Herman M. Greenspun, publisher of the Las Vegas Sun, has carried an adventurous life into his paper. Editor & Publisher gives this account of the extraordinary derring-do of his fight for Israel's survival in 1948. He plundered a naval depot in Hawaii, and, posing as an agent for Generalissimo Chiang Kai-Shek, seized a yacht at gunpoint. He then filled a ship at Tampico

Bay with 6000 tons of contraband rifles, machine guns, howitzers, cannons, and tons of ammunition, and sailed to Israel. He was convicted in 1950 of violating the U.S. Neutrality Act and stripped of his civil rights. President John Kennedy pardoned him in 1961. Before becoming publisher of the Sun, Greenspun worked as publicity director for the Flamingo Casino, owned by hoodlum Bugsy Siegel, who was later gunned down. Since then Greenspun has campaigned against gangsters in Las Vegas, and as a result of his investigative journalism and his trenchant front-page column, "Where I Stand," has been hit with more than 100 lawsuits, so becoming the most sued publisher in the nation. He was one of the first publishers to attack Joseph McCarthy, the anti-Communist senator from Wisconsin in the early 1950s; he was the only newsman to testify before the Senate Watergate committee-he said he knew of a $100,000 campaign contribution to Richard Nixon from billionaire recluse Howard Hughes.

Newspaper publishing has other characters, but the generalization holds: Most newspapers are impersonal, corporate enterprises that reflect the middle-class values of their mainly middle-class owners. Not only does the scale of their enterprise distance many publishers from the daily operation of the newspaper, but the professionalization of journalists also sets publisher and reporter apart. The rise of journalism education and of organizations such as the newspaper Guild and the Society of Professional Journalists, Sigma Delta Chi, has to some extent institutionalized journalists' ethics and reinforced conventions such as objective reporting, adherence to which has given reporters a measure of independence from publishers' whims. The Underground Press Largely to protest middle-class values and accepted journalistic responsibilities and conventions and to express their protest in vivid, unrestrained language, an "underground" press flowered in the late 1960s and early 1970s, giving the lie fleetingly to the generalization that newspapers are impersonal, middle-class businesses. There were only four in 1965, but Robert Glessing counted approximately 3000 underground papers that had published at one time or another between 1965 and 1972.

Some underground papers built circulations in the tens of thousands, among them the highly successful Berkeley Barb. In 1969 wrangling between the owner.

Max Scherr, and his staff became public, revealing just how lucrative such an operation can be. It also revealed that, like the capitalists of the commercial press; some underground journalists are money-conscious. A large group of Scherr's helpers broke away and began to publish the Berkeley Tribe, but not before their negotiations to buy the Barb had reached figures in the hundreds of thousands.

It will not do to assign sweeping significance to the underground press. Ray Mungo, one of the founders of the Liberation News Service, which provided material for underground newspapers, has written:

> Lots of radicals will give you a very precise line about why their little newspaper or organization was formed and what needs it fulfills and most of that stuff is bullshit, you see-the point is they've got nothing to do, and the prospect of holding a straight job is so dreary that they join the "movement" and start hitting up people for money to live, on the premise that they're involved in critical social change blah blah blah. And it's really better that way, at least for some people, than finishing college and working at dump jobs for constipated corporations: at least it's not always boring... that's why we decided to start a news service-not because the proliferating underground and radical college press really needed a central information-gathering agency staffed by people they could trust (that was our hype), but because we had nothing else to do.

At the same time, it is important to recognize the real strengths of this new journalism. It provided a forum for ideas that were not considered, or not considered adequately, in conventional media. The undergrounders also provided a view of a different life style and afforded different and valuable perspectives.

What this new journalism proved was that a vast distance stretched between the conventional media and important segments of the public. There was a time when a newspaper or magazine served its own small public. The circulation was relatively slender, but editors spoke directly to the central interests of their readers, and they could usually count on reader loyalty. Anyone who cherished another point of view might attack, and a publication that posed a threat might be destroyed-the abolitionist papers, for example-but most people simply subscribed to publications that squared with their own prejudices and idiosyncrasies.

When the conventional media became large and few, however, and editors we're trying to attract mass audiences, separate voices could no longer be raised so readily in a free marketplace of ideas.

Many underground papers succeeded in building close relationships with their readers, at least in part because they revived the art of speaking to a relatively homogeneous audience. One important technique was to present news in heavily subjective prose: "A growing revolt against the selfish and reactionary American Medical Association came to a head here," began an article on Open City a Los a Angeles paper. "Objectivity is a farce." said Thorne Dreyer of Liberation news Service, Jeff Shero, former editor of The Rat, said, "We make our biases clear. That frees our writers to talk about their guts."

Strongest Challenge

Perhaps the strongest challenge to conventional journalism was this "gut reporting." The underground press had a marked distaste for the roots of journalism: the search for verifiable facts.

The underground press, like the revolutionary press of the eighteenth century, was a phenomenon of a period of protest and discontent. It faded for a variety of reasons: because the Vietnam War eventually ended; because the issues diminished in intensity, were resolved, or forgotten; because money and energy ran out; because the journalists turned 30. By contrast, the black press in the United States has struggled and survived by keeping one foot in conventional newspaper publishing and another in militancy and protest.

In 1976 the 325 black newspapers listed in Editor & Publisher International Year Book published mainly in metropolitan areas where black population concentrates, and competed with white metropolitan newspapers for readership and advertising. Only two of these black newspapers were dailies, the Atlanta Daily World and the Chicago Defender; a few published twice a week; most published weekly.

Their need for the advertising support of white-owned businesses and industries forced upon them a conservatism in editorial approach at a time when blacks and become increasingly militant, so creating a tension between publisher and readers. For example, John Sengstacke, publisher of the Chicago Defender, was delighted when Marshall Field and Company agreed to advertise in the defender. But marshall Field is not a store that many blacks can afford to patronize. Nor can Sengstacke afford to take too militant a stance on issues of concern to blacks if he wishes to retain the support of advertisers like Marshall Field. Sengstacke not only confronts this dilemma but must also compete for middle-class black readers, and also for black reporters, with the Chicago Sun-times and the Chicago Tribune. And he must compete for more militant black readers with Muhammad Speaks, published in Chicago by the Black Muslims, and with such other militant organs in Chicago as Black Truth, the Observer, and the Black Liberator.

The militant black organs fit comfortably into the tradition of the black press in this country. Historically it has been a press of protest, ever since John B. Russwurm and the Rev. Samuel Cornish started the nation's first black newspaper. Freedom's Journal, in 1827, to fight slavery. But today major black newspapers, such as the Defender, the Baltimore Afro-American, and the Pittsburgh Courier, which seek to survive in the commercial world by reflecting the interests mainly of middle-class blacks, tend to be more informational organs than organs of protest. And they have had to face the rising costs of the industry as a whole with little of the advertising support on which white newspapers have been able to count. Typically, therefore, these papers have had to scale down their enterprises. In 1945, the Pittsburgh Courier, with a circulation of 257,000, the Chicago Defender, with a circulation of 202,000, and the Baltimore Afro-American, with a circulation of 137, 000, were national weeklies. In the 1970s all three were local newspapers with much reduced circulations. In 1976 the Courier was circulating about 20,800 copies a week; the Afro-American, which published biweekly, was circulating 26,000 on Tuesdays and 28,000 on Saturdays; and the Defender, which became a daily in 1956, was circulating 20,000. Some consolidation and concentration in ownership has also occurred. For example, John Sengstacke bought the Courier chain in 1967, so acquiring 10 newspapers in nine states. By 1976 his chain had been reduced to five papers publishing in four states.

Although the number of black newspapers has expanded, the number of white newspapers has been remarkably constant for decadesdespitethe consolidation and mergers and decline in competition. The rise in educational and economic opportunities for blacks and their increasing militancy in securing those opportunities, often by starting newspapers to express their grievances, explains the expansion of the black press. But the black press in the mid-1970s was showing the same characteristic that explains the stability in numbers of the white press: an emphasis on localism. The major black national papers of the 1970s, Muhammad Speaks and the Black Panther, differed from the early national weeklies-they are organs of religious or political movements rather than of news and information. Most black newspapers, like most white papers, were directed at local communities. As white populations left the metropolitan areas, so contributing to the decline in competing dailies, suburban dailies replaced them to respond to the needs of suburban readers and advertisers.

Challenge of Broadcasting : Coverage of their immediate localities and in-depth, interpretive journalism became the major functions of newspapers after radio and television took over the function of reporting up-to-the-minute spot news. As newspapers lost advertising to radio in the 1930s, newspapers tried briefly to contain broadcast news competition. In 1933 the American Newspaper Publishers Association (ANPA) persuaded the press associations to suspend service to broadcasters. With the support of the radio networks, the Press Radio Bureau was formed in 1937 to edit the files of the press associations and to release news twice daily for no more than five minutes each. The news broadcasts could not be sponsored. But some radio stations refused to abide by the bureau's rules and a new press service, the Trans-Radio Service, was started to sell news directly to radio. By 1940 the ANPA capitulated; allowing the major wire services to sell news to radio and allowing radio to seek sponsors for news. Radio and television can get breaking news to their audiences almost instantly, and the time-consuming background, in-depth interpretive journalism of newspapers is heir adjustment to broadcasting's technological strengths. Because broadcast news is constrained by FCC regulations such as the fairness doctrine and because broadcasters are vulnerable to the government's licensing procedures, broadcast news is typically not as penetrating and controversial as print news.Broadcasters simply do not enjoy protection of the First Amendment equal to that enjoyed by newspapers. This is partly why newspapers rather than broadcasters tackled such controversial, complex, and largely non-visual stories as the Pentagon Papers and Watergate. In the American system of media economics, space is more elastic and less expensive than time. And because of the new electronic technologies in print journalism, particularly the integration of computer technologies into the editing process, newspapers in the 1970s were saving time in a way that enabled them to make more flexible and intelligent use of their space.

Newspapers, then, have survived the formidable competition of broadcasting and, to a much lesser extent, of magazines, by adjusting their functions and by retaining an independence from government and from direct advertising influence. Because many newspapers are local monopolies, advertisers tend to need newspapers more than newspapers need particular advertisers, although their mutual need is obviously great. How intensely readers feel they need newspapers is not really know, although the decline in daily circulation in the mid-1970s suggests that the sense of need was diminishing. Years of readership surveys have produced a profile of newspaper buyers that Ben Bagdikian summarized in 1971 as follows: "...the best educated; those in skilled professional, technical, managerial white-collar jobs; the wealthiest those who live in urban areas; those who are married; and people between the ages of thirty and fifty-four." But in a speech at the Allied Daily newspapers annual meeting in Seattle on May 15, 1975. Robert G. Marbut, president of Harte-Hanks Newspapers, Inc., reflected on these item's: daily newspaper circulation was declining; the ratio of daily newspaper circulation to the number of households had declined steadily over the past decade; and the dependence on newspapers by younger people-the ones 20-35 who are among the prime targets of advertisers-appeared to be declining. Marbut asked:

> How are these trends possible? Just the opposite should be true. As people become better educated and more affluent, they should be more prone to be loyal newspaper readers. And, since current trends indicate that we do have a larger number of better educated and more affluent people, why isn't the number of newspapers sold per household increasing rather than declining?

He warned the industry that unless each publisher produced "that unique package of news, opinion and other information designed for the specific needs of a particular market," someone else would do so. And he pointed to the growing number of hungry competitors:

> Just look at the number of other media chipping away at what newspapers used to consider safely within their franchise. Whether it be the television sales staff going after local advertisers like never before, or he blanket coverage shopper, or the direct mail penny sayer, or the preprint being delivered by a private delivery service, or the Government's setting up regional computerized job data banks, or in the future a computerized data bank connected to the home by bidirectional cable-all of these vehicles are supplying

> information to our markets-in what used to be our domain.

No profile of the typical newspaper buyer, then, no generalization about the newspaper's typical functions seems to fit precisely in the flux of the 1970s.

The modern magazine succeeded as a mass medium chiefly because of its original role as an adjunct of the marketing system. Like the newspaper, it was able, over the years, to appeal to an expanding range of tastes and interests. But, unlike other media, most magazines were designed for homogeneous audiences or special-interest groups. And, in contrast to the newspaper, their circulation was nationwide. Thus, although many magazines were directed to specialized audiences, magazines in general developed as a mass medium in the sense that they appealed to large numbers in a national market that cut across social, economic, and educational class lines.

Early in the twentieth century, some magazine publishers, notably those of pulps and digests, derived their income from a small unit profit on a high turnover of copies instead of from advertising. Still others relied on trade associations, fraternal organizations, and professional groups to make up any deficit. But with the rise of national advertising, the great majority-both in numbers and circulation-were bound closely to the marketing system. In effect, magazine publishing became fundamentally a matter of the publisher's deciding on a consumer group that advertisers wanted to reach, devising an editorial formula to attract and hold that group, and then selling advertisers access to it.

In terms of originating a market for the advertiser, the relationship of magazines generally to their audiences is quite different from that of other media. Some magazine publishers have first developed a publication and then let both readers and advertisers seek out the magazine. But the typical magazine follows a less risky strategy. It devises an editorial formula that can be counted on to attract a homogeneous and relatively small special-interest group; then it assembles advertisers who want to address that audience.

In Magazines of the Twentieth Century, Theodore Peterson notes four threats to magazine sin the first half of the twentieth century: the automobile, radio, movies, and television. Yet magazines have enjoyed virtually uninterrupted growth in numbers, circulation, and revenue since 1900. There were well over a thousand more magazines in the United States in the mid-1970s than in 1900; per-issue circulation rose over 98 million between 1950 and 1970, a gain of 44 percent; and advertising revenue tripled between 1950 and 1974, from $458.5 million to $1.5 billion. Peterson ascribes most of magazines' prosperity to population increase, more particularly to rising income levels and the expansion of the middle class, to the spread of popular education, and to the increase in leisure time. Typically magazines, like other print media, have been read by richer, better-educated Americans whose increase has sustained print against the competition of radio and television.

In the 1950s and 1960s, however, some of the major magazines did not merely rely on this group but challenged television on its own ground. They went for the mass audience, by direct mail campaigns and subscription offers at bargain rates. The massive circulations of such magazines as The Reader's Digest, the Saturday Evening Post, Life, and Look resulted Stung by television, these magazines lost sight of their real source of strength, the selective market. Now only the Digest survives in its original form, ranking second after TV Guide in total circulation in the United States.

Try as they might, the mass magazines could not adapt to change, could find no identity for themselves as other media displaced them. How Life, far and away the biggest revenue producer of all magazines before it died, tried tells us much about the structure and functions of the media in general and of the magazine industry in particular. Life's struggle shows that, despite opinion to the contrary, media structure and functions are not fixed but bend to the needs and wants of their constituencies.

Thirty-six years after its founding, Life, the last great mass-circulation, general-interest picture magazine, died in December 1972. because of its status as something of a national institution, Life's passing was mourned with more emotion then sense. Loyal readers and some staffers accused management of murder; Life could and should have been saved. So presumably could other mass magazines, such as Collier's, which died in 1956, the Saturday Evening Post, which died in 1969, and Look, which died in 1971. Chris Welles, a Life editor from 1965 to 1968, is more persuasive. He studied Life in its death throes in 1971, then conducted a postmortem in 1973, concluding: "The collapse of Life's profit-oriented *raison d'etre* derived from its increasing inability to fill the needs of its two essential constituencies-advertisers and readers."

Increasing affluence, education, and leisure time had fragmented the mass audience and enabled people to pursue a variety of interests to which hundreds of specialized magazines responded. Television satisfied mass tastes. And advertisers followed the audiences they wanted wherever they could be reached most effectively.

Henry Luce created Life in 1936 in the middle of the depression, "to see life: to see the world: to eyewitness great events," and to see them positively. Life was to combat the national gloom and to correct what Luce considered journalism's distorted priorities: "That evil makes big news and good makes little or no news." What particularly annoyed him was the press' interest in scandal. In a speech in September 1937, he said: if there is one fact about our society which is shouted daily to the people of America it is that rich folk get into trouble with chorines and gigolos, steal each other's wives and husbands, indulge in orgies, and are otherwise licentious.

On the relevant issue of whether the press has presented a fair picture to the public of an aspect of American life, the criticism should be turned around. For if there are a number of rich or solvent people who live reasonably decent lives, never get more than moderately drunk and are not sexual monsters-then that is the fact which the capitalist-controlled press has failed to establish.

With something of the awe of discovery, Luce argued that "the photograph ... turns out to be an extraordinary instrument for correcting that really inherent evil in journalism which is its unbalance between the good news and the bad." He explained how Life was using the camera as corrective:

> A few weeks ago Life published a picture essay on wheat-I mean wheat, growing and being happily harvested. The article had nothing to do with any frantic row in Congress over a farm bill, nothing to do with the horrors of drought and dying cattle. And it was the lead article and ran for nine pages. Now can you imagine and non-photographic magazine, intended to interest millions of readers, daring to devote its first nine pages to a descriptive contemplation of the fruitful and normal and quiet labours of farms and horses and harvesters and the wheat itself ripening beneath the sun? And yet it is precisely the kind of thing which Life is doing."

But no power of positive thinking could blind Life to the ugly realities of the 1960s and early 1970s. Its magnificent photographers produced some of the most searing and moving pictures of the Vietnam War, around which the discontent of the decade had gathered. Its reporters investigated the troubles prominent people get into. William Lambert reported on Supreme Court Justice Abe Fortas' agreement to accept a fee of $20,000 yearly for life from the Wolfson Foundation (Louis Wolfson was twice indicted for stock fraud). Fortas resigned in May 1969, the only justice ever to resign from the Supreme Court under pressure.

Curiously for a picture magazine, *Life* was in the vanguard of aggressive investigative reporting when it died. But Life's change in editorial formula did not impress advertisers, who in the 1970s could pursue the audience they wanted through the massive, undifferentiated reach of television and the concentrated, selective reach of specialized magazines. Because of this competition, Life's huge audience-it was said that in its prime 70 million adults read each issue of *Life-began* to fade away.

Life's mass circulation survived longer than that of its deceased rivals partly because it acquired a million and a half subscribers from the dying Saturday Evening Post. Circulation was sustained mainly by cheap subscription and low newsstand prices. A study not long before Life died estimated that the average Life reader paid only 12 cents for a magazine costing 41 cents to edit and print. Advertisers had to make up the remaining 70 percent of publishing costs at ad rates as high as $64,000 a colour page. Advertisers found that they could reach more people more cheaply on prime time television. In 1971 the advertising cost per thousand persons reached by Life was about $7.71; by television, about $3.60. Advertisers questioned Life's identity and argued that people no longer cared enough for Life to pay a reasonable share of the costs. Advertisers withdrew. Between 1966 and 1972 Life's advertising revenues dropped from $170-to $91-million. Its only consistently dependable advertisers were cigarette and liquor manufacturers, who were banned from advertising on television. Publishing costs meanwhile were soaring. Paper prices were expected to double within five years, and postal rates were expected to rise 142 percent within the same period. Life tried for a more affluent, educated audience by allowing its circulation to drop by attrition from 81/2 to 51/2 million between 1970 and 1972, by charging higher subscription rates, and by experimenting with different editorial formulas such as an emphasis on investigative reporting. Readers still drifted away. News-stand sales averaged only 184,000 an issue for the first six months of 1972, a 20 percent drop from 1971 and lower than the sales of Weight Watchers. In its last five years life lost $35 million: another $30 million loss was projected for1973 and1974. Confronting that, and fading reader and advertiser interest. *Life* elected euthanasia. Perhaps more imaginative and sharply focused editorial formulas could have saved Life, but it is doubtful that *Life* could have survived as a mass magazine. As advertisers were quick to see, the times were out of joint for that medium.

Today American magazines reflect virtually every shade of thought and opinion, virtually every interest, of their readers. They cover everything from hot rodding, coin collecting, yachting, hunting and fishing, and preparing to be a bride to gourmet dining and calorie counting. Despite the fierce competition and the uncertainties, magazine publishing on a small scale is perhaps the communication most accessible to the new investor. What counts most is the idea. If the entrepreneur has a fresh idea for a magazine, there are likely to be persons willing to finance it. If the magazine can be sustained while it seeks acceptance by readers and advertisers, there is always some change that it will achieve a modest success. And there is a remote change that it will wind up in the company of giants.

The ease of entry into the magazine industry, in contrast to the formidable obstacles encountered in newspaper publishing, broadcasting, and motion pictures, explains why the industry today is dotted with relatively small units, small staffs, and modest offices with little equipment. Magazine publishers ordinarily do not invest in presses and equipment, but instead let out their printing on contract. A publisher who does not wish to compete out their printing on contract. A publisher who does not wish to compete with large-circulation leaders can still launch a successful magazine on a million dollars or so-a comparatively small sum for starting a national medium. Some that began as regional publications started with far less. Jann Wenner began as regional publications started with far less. Jann Wenner began Rolling Stone as a rock music magazine with less than $20,000 and aimed it at San Francisco. Bay Area readers. Then he expanded to national distribution, diversifying content to include top New York writers Truman Capote, Tom Wolfe, and Norman Mailer. In 1977 Wenner, then only 30 years old, moved Rolling Stone to New York. Its circulation was up to 450,000; Wenner wanted it up to a million by 1980.

Factors that make it easy for one publisher to enter the industry also make it easy for competitors to enter. Successful magazines invariably breed imitators, for publishers cannot hide their formulas for success, forced as they are by the nature of publishing to exhibit their best ideas in public.

What Hugh Hefner chose to exhibit in public in Playboy soon stimulated imitators, most formidably Bob Guccione's Penthouse. Hefner had attracted readers with his centerfolds of nude women, the blemishes and too intimate parts of their voluptuous bodies discreetly air brushed. Guccione disdained touching up his photographs and successfully challenged Playboy with candid frontal nudity. For decades DeWitt Wallace had been trying through his Reader's Digest to keep America at moral attention: Hefner and Guccione claimed to be liberating America from its sexual taboos. Whatever the validity of their claim, their magazines reflected the sexual permissiveness of the 1970s.

Both their contents and their distributional methods violated normal publishing conventions. Most magazines rely heavily on advertising: typically about 60 percent of a magazine's contents is advertising, 40 percent is editorial. Playboy and Penthouse virtually reversed the ratio, charging the reader the entire cost of the magazine. Advertising, therefore, was almost pure profit. Their distributional costs were lower than those of most major magazines because they relied more on news-stand sales than on subscriptions, which involve solicitations and distribution of sales through the increasingly expensive postal system.

In the mid-1970s Penthouse, which claimed a worldwide circulation of 5.3 million, was selling over 90 percent of its copies at news-stands. Note that the vast bulk of Time's circulation sells via subscription, although occasional striking covers may well increase sales dramatically. Playboy took malicious pleasure in July 1976 in pointing out that Time was not above using nudity (Playboy mentioned Time's putting the entertainer Chain in a see-through dress on the cover of a best-selling issue) to sell magazines even though in a cover story. "The Porno Plague," in April 1976. Time had criticized Playboy "and its far crasser imitators" for the practice. In a period of escalating postal rates. Time's reliance on subscriptions for approximately 95 percent of its circulation was a crippling expense. In October 1975, therefore, Time began an experiment in three cities whereby subscribers received their Time from a newspaper carrier rather than a mail carrier. Delivery by carriers of cooperating newspapers was expected to be considerably cheaper than postal delivery.

The Competition

Competition by imitation is usually a Darwinian process. The fittest survive. Black publisher John H. Johnson has made a success of limitation because he has not competed with his models. He modeled Black World, titled Negro digest until 1970, on The Reader's Digest Jet, a news weekly, copied the format of the Cowles magazine Quick. Tan copied the true confession magazines. In 1945 Johnson launched Ebony as a monthly and sensational version of Life. He toned down the sensationalism in the 1950s, and Ebony became a magazine for middle class blacks. In the militant 1960s Ebony abandoned its earlier cautiousness and tackled black grievances. An entire issue in 1965, for example, was devoted to "The White Problem in America." Johnson explains that "Ebony's goal is to reflect the attitudes and opinions of our readership as well as to lead. We don't go too far ahead, but we're always pushing for more."

Because newspapers cater mainly to a heterogeneous local community and television mainly to the national undifferentiated mass, the magazine has become the vehicle of the aspirations or ideologies of special-interest groups, one of the means by which they push for more. For decades men dominated the publishing of women's magazines, so reinforcing, it was charged, stereotypes of women as mothers and homemakers. In 1973 journalist Pamela Howard described the professional goals this way: "Ten years ago, I dreamed about becoming editor-in-chief of a woman's magazine. Accordingly, I went to work at one of the largest in the country, only to find that all the Katharine Hepburn roles were filled by short men."

A man, Cyrun Curtis, founded the Ladies' Home Journal in 1883. Although his wife, Louisa Knapp, edited it for six years, it was editor Edward Bok who took the magazine's circulation over a million in 1903. Bok, it was said, had no affection for women, but succeeded with his readers by emphasizing the concept of service for women. And not only for women, apparently. During World War I the Journal ranked third among magazines most demanded by soldiers. Despite their emphasis on serving women, however, magazines like the Journal and McCall's have not led the women's movement as they have led women's magazines in circulation, Helen Gurley Brown gave new direction to women's magazines when she became editor of the Hearst Corporation's

Cosmopolitan and dealt candidly with the non-housewifely aspirations and sexuality of women, particularly young single women.

Essence, founded for black women in May 1970, was torn in its first two years by internal strife, caused, some said, by the fact that it was run by men. Initially intended strictly as a fashion and beauty magazine, it had to convince potential advertisers that black women had sufficient buying power to make them a worthwhile market. Advertisers had also to be educated to Essence's requirement that ads in no way demean black women. Moreover, Essence requires that all ads show a black woman, Marcia Gillespie, who started as managing editor in November 1970, became Essence's fourth editor-in-chief in May 1971 and began to change the magazine. "I had wanted to combat the negative imagery which for centuries had been foisted on Blacks," she said. "Forever, it seems, we Blacks have heard how we are stupid, lazy shiftless, unable to build family units.... I didn't want little Black girls growing up as I had thinking only white women were beautiful. I wanted then, through Essence to see and to feel what Black women really are-incredibly vital people who have been boxed intellectually, creatively and emotionally." Marcia Gillespie's approach has been immensely successful. Circulation has grown from 75.000 in 1970 to 550.000 in 1977; between 1970 and 1976 advertising revenue rose from $208,000 to $3.8 million.

When Gloria Steinem and Elizabeth Forsling Harris decided in 1971 to publish his magazine, they were determined to keep women in control. Steinem was to be editor and president. Harris publisher and chairwoman of the board. His was a deliberate protest against the conventional women's magazines (while working at the Ladies' home Journal, Steinem was handed a story by an editor and told, "Pretend you're a women and read this"). For too long, Steinem declared, women have been "sanitized, deodorized, slicked up, and fixed up" in magazines. According to Harris, the purpose was to "communicate the commonality of feeling among women around the country." Pamela Howard described the magazine as "a forum for women who are exploring new ways of living."

Women sports, founded by tennis star Billie Jean King, promoted and celebrated one of these new ways, a career as a female athlete. In the great variety of women's magazines, a shared purpose has united them, symbolized in July 1976 by a meeting of 30 women's magazines to discuss how best to ensure passage of the Equal Rights Amendment to the Constitution.

These women's magazines are comparatively new special-interest magazines of narrow focus. Many of their individual concerns have been forthrightly discussed, advocated, or condemned for years in such journals of opinion, comment, and controversy as Ramparts, The Nation, national Review, new Leader, The New Republic, and Progressive. Their emphasis is on ideas rather than on reportage, and their positions are rarely neutral.

Most of the journals since the turn of the century have been organs of liberal thought, although a few, such as the National Review, founded in 1955, have spoken for conservatism. In their agitation for political reform and social justice, the magazines have often been far ahead of popular thinking. For that reason and others, their way has always been difficult; their circulations have been counted in the thousands instead of in the millions of the general interest magazines, their advertising volume has been lean or non-existent, and their financial position has ever been precarious. Yet they seem to have wielded an influence all out of proportion to their circulations, for they have aimed at opinion leaders instead of the great mass audience. Frank P. Walsh once remarked that he had written an article about railroads for the Nation in the days when its circulation was about 27,000 and a series on the same subject for the Hearst newspapers when their total circulation was around 10 million. No one ever commented on the newspaper series, he said, but as soon as the Nation article appeared, his phone jangled with calls from persons of importance. Charles Beard has credited the journals of opinion with contributing to such reforms as women's suffrage, old-age pensions, social security legislation, wages-and-hours laws, public housing, and public ownership of hydroelectric sites.

Despite the magazine industry's response via specialized magazines to the political beliefs, social concerns, and leisure activities and hobbies of an audience with increasingly diverse interests, a role for the general interest magazine survived in the mid-1970s. One bold test of this notion was Time Inc.'s launching of People magazine in February 1974. Conventional wisdom was that Life died in 1972 partly because television had killed the relevance and appeal of the still photograph, at least in news.

The *National Geographic* was still a haven for lovers and practitioners of photography, but it was not concerned with the timeliness of its contents. Rather it captured in magnificent colour what relatively unexplored and exotic peoples and places remained in the world, or it glamorized the familiar. Somewhat like The Reader's Digest, the geographic contrived a timelessness for each issue. It was not a publication read on the run and discarded. Bookshelves around the world groan under the weight of back issues of the Geographic.

Photojournalism, in fact, has struggled for its less than a century of existence to overcome journalism's bias toward print. It was not until the 1880s that the halftone photoengraving process was perfected, not until the 1890s that the halftone photoengraving process was perfected, not until the 1890s that a way was developed to run off photographs on a rotary press, making it possible to print photographs in newspapers and mass magazines. Unfortunately, these developments coincided with the yellow journalism of Pulitzer and Hearst, who used photographs unscrupulously and sensationally. Then in the 1920s the tabloids outdid Pulitzer and Hearst, selecting, retouching, and faking pictures for maximum sensational impact. Long after it was technologically possible to use photographs, therefore, many newspapers shield away from them or used them sparingly. When the Associated Press managing.

Editors Association decided in 1935 to devote its next session to photography, many editors protested, arguing that photography would lower the dignity of the American press, that photography should not encroach on print.

The damage that yellow journalism inflicted from the 1890's through the 1920s on the respectability and perceived value of photojournalism and graphics cannot be overestimated. By reinforcing the arrogance of print, yellow journalism set back intelligent analysis of what information is best communicated verbally, what visually, and of how words and pictures can be used most effectively to enhance each other's shared purpose-to communicate. In this respect, the advertising industry, typically scorned by journalists, has been light years ahead in its imaginative use of photography, graphics, colour, and design to communicate its messages. Magazines have long had to compete for readers' attention with the colour and allure of advertisements beside their articles and have been much more visually innovative than newspapers. It was about the time that newspaper editors in the APME were deciding to dignify photojournalism by assigning a session to the topic that Henry Luce discovered the positive power of the camera and Life was born. And Life's photography did much to make photojournalism respectable for newspapers. So when Life died and television was seen as an accessory before the fact, many concluded that the day of the general-interest picture magazine was dead.

Yet People is basically a picture magazine; some have described it as television in print. It runs about 15,000 words an issue; Time runs three times/that many. Despite requiems for the picture magazine, People was paying its way within 20 months of its launching in 1974, a remarkable achievement in contemporary publishing. Photojournalists have criticized the magazine as a prostitution of Life, as an exploitation of the form rather than an extension of it, and some have sought their professional future in newspapers rather than in magazines. People offered a flashy, quick look and read into the lives of celebrities. Gossip? No more than a high-class fan magazine? "We do not urn gossip," says Managing Editor Richard B. Stolley. "Everything is checked for accuracy. Instead of concentrating on the issue, we look at the personalities behind them. Our policy is to tell you new things about personalities you already know. We also include unknown people doing things we think are exceptional." People's Washington correspondent Clare Crawford reported in late 1975: "The Fords love this magazine. The President has told me that he hopes we don't mess it up' with pictures of blood vessels and hearts, the way they did with Life. And that's the key to People's success. Nobody from Presidents on down can resist reading about other people."

Superficially this marriage of people and pictures has characterized New York magazine, launched by Clay Felker in 1968. In fact, New York is a mix of serious journalism and lively, imaginative graphics which has had considerably more than local impact on publishing. Early on it became a vehicle for the "new journalism" of writers like Tom Wolfe, Jimmy Breslin, and Gail Sheehy, who were applying the literary techniques of the short story and novel-dramatic scene, dialogue, interior monologue-to the presentation of thoroughly researched journalism. Their writing styles, which reflected much greater sensitivity to the visual sense, to all the senses, than just-the-facts-ma'am objective reporting, and the magazine's bright, provocative graphics gave a pace and excitement to new York that other magazines soon imitated. Milton Glaser, New York's design director, said, "the magazine is not designed to look beautiful, but to convey a sense of energy, compression, density, information. We want it to be fast-paced like the city, easily accessible, undemanding. We want people to get in and out of it very easily."

In almost every respect, then, it was the antithesis of the staid, dignified New Yorker, which has never been concerned to hurry its readers through the magazine. Rather. The New Yorker communicates an aura of decorous quiet, of leather upholstery and muted paneling, of civilized, reflective conversation by the elegantly styled and coiffed people in the ads it carries. Tradition weighs heavily on The New Yorker, which cherishes the character given it by its founder Harold Ross and by writers James Thurber and E. B. White.

New York, by contrast, has been as mercurial as its founder Clay Felker and as the times it has reflected. In the early 1970s critics condemned its articles as poorly researched, sensational, vulgar, superficial, and trendy. Newsweek dismissed the magazine as "a tedious collection of pop trivia." As Watergate spread gloom in the nation and New York City's bankruptcy depressed the inhabitants, the magazine's breeziness was almost unseemly. Investigative journalism was in vogue, and, although still graphically colorful and irreverent, New York became a more conservative, solidly researched magazine-until the Australian, Rupert Murdoch, bought it in January 1977. Murdoch, who then owned 88 newspapers, 11 magazines, and some television properties in Australia, England, and the United States, is known for a "blood, guts, and girls" formula, and New York admirers were concerned that the magazine would succumb to Murdoch's earthy sensationalism.

Before Murdoch's takeover, New York seemed to be going through a process Clay Felker had described soon after he started New York:

> There appears to be an almost inexorable life-cycle of American magazines that follows the patterns of humans: a clamorous youth eager to be noticed; vigorous, productive middle-age marked by an easy-to-define editorial line; and a long slow decline, in which efforts at revival are sporadic and tragically doomed."

In the post-Vietnam and-Watergate trauma of the mid-1970s, national nostalgia had revived a pale version of the Saturday Evening Post. Life was publishing special issues such as "the Year in Pictures" and was talking of a comeback. Some magazines came and went with the public's whims and fads. Many kept pace with society's elemental concerns, and, despite the inexorable life-cycle Felker describes, survived.

We have glanced at only a selection of the diverse range whose covers blaze from news-stands and supermarket racks. As a whole, magazines more than any other medium reflect the pluralism of American society and the multifarious interests, serious and trivial, perennial and passing, that affluence and leisure enable it to indulge.

Like other communications industries, book publishing is a business seeking profit. Like the news media, however, it acknowledges certain responsibilities to the cultural life of the nation: to support and promote scholarship and literature, to influence and elevate taste, to teach and delight. And these responsibilities may transcend, perhaps limit, profit. To some extent, it is easier for the book publishing industry than for the news media to meet its responsibilities. Unlike newspapers, magazines, and broadcast programs, books are not subsidized by advertisers. The news media must please two constituencies-audiences and advertisers. Book publishers must please only one-readers.

In the United States, however, books are not as popular with the mass of Americans as the products of the other media of communication. In 1975 book publishing industry sales amounted to $3.8 billion, $1.5 billion of which, or 40 percent, was spent on educational materials for schools and colleges. But the buying of educational materials is not usually discretionary. In fact, such a minority of Americans chooses to buy books that, strictly speaking, book publishing is not a mass industry. A national best seller may sell between 2 and 3 million copies, which may be read by twice that number of persons. The New York Daily News sells almost 2 million copies daily to New Yorkers; Time magazine sells more than 4 million copies a week; Family Circle sells more than 9 million a month; The Reader's Digest more than 18 million a month; and readership for each of these publications is probably three times circulation. A reasonably popular network television show can expect an audience of between 20 and 30 million on a single night. Even the exception, a best seller, then, cannot rival the reach of the other media. The average hardbound trade book may sell no more than 10,000 copies, the average mass market paperback no more than 100,000.

"Mass market" is a misnomer. Although literacy is almost universal in the United States, the American masses do not yet read books. It was the implication of Marshall McLuhan's pronouncements in the mid-1960s that they never would because the advent of the electronic media had signaled the death of print. In fact, the 1960s were boom years for book publishing. From 1963 to 1969, industry sales rose 59 percent. So far from killing print, the electronic media seem instead to have stimulated reading.

Book sales slowed in the 1970s, but retained solid growth. Between 1971 and 1975, years of recession and retrenchment in the American economy, book sales rose 30.8 percent. Hard times particularly affected education, the source of much of the demand for books. Enrollments in schools and colleges declined or leveled off, and taxpayers and their elected representatives at the local, state, and federal levels cut school and college appropriations.

Moreover book publishing was especially vulnerable to the increasing use in schools, colleges, and libraries of the Xerox and other copying machines. Until 1976 U.S. copyright law had been virtually unchanged since 1909, long before the invention of the automatic copier. For years copyright bills to protect the rights of authors were mired in complexity and controversy in Congress. The bill that finally passed in 1976 still permitted some copying for educational purposes without compensation to authors.

Book publishing managed the recession of the 1970s relatively well largely because the industry was a part during the boom years of the 1960s of the multimedia merger and consolidation. RCA bought Alfred Knopf, Pantheon Books, and Random House. CBS bought W.B. Saunders and Holt. Rinehart and Winston, itself created by mergers. Time Inc., bought Little, brown; ITT bought Bobbs-Merrill and Howard Sams; and the Times Mirror Company, publisher of the Los Angeles times, bought a number of book publishing enterprises.

John P. Dessauer comments that these mergers and consolidations ... made resources available without which the industry could probably not have capitalized on its opportunities and fulfilled its obligations to educational and consumer audience alike. They brought new management and new business acumen to the field which had been seriously lacking and which, in many instances resulted for the first time in orderly budgeting, forecasting, planning, and fiscal arrangements.

But, Dessauer adds, the mergers and consolidations "also placed the power of ultimate decision and policy making in the hands of people unfamiliar with books, their peculiarities, and their markets."

The R. R. Bowker Company, which keeps statistic son the book publishing industry, lists 12,000 book outlets of all kinds in the united States. Of these ...6700... handle new books; 900 are department store book departments: 2900 are college bookstores: 7300 handle paperbacks: 1700 carry law, medical, technical, and scientific titles; 4000 sell religious books: 3000 handle juveniles: 1300 are rare book dealers; and 1000 are secondhand dealers.

The book industry refers to these retail outlets as "traditional trade stores," some of which sell books exclusively, others of which sell them only as a sideline. In addition, there are more than 90,000 mass market outlets-news-stands, drugstores, and supermarkets. From early in this century, books have also been sold directly to the reader, by mail order and by book clubs. The first book clubs, the Book-of-the-Month Club and the Literary Guild, founded in the 1920s, appealed to people who could not easily get to a bookstore or who wanted advice on the latest books, and offered them free books and considerable savings on those the club selected. With the increase in affluence and leisure, the book clubs-like the magazine industry-have become increasingly specialized, catering now to the special interests of readership groups: the American Garden Guild Book Club, Antiques Book Club, Detective Book Club, the Movie Book Club, and the Nostalgia Book Club, among others.

Magazine publishers have been the leaders in mail order publishing, an enterprise they began in the 1950s. Time Inc., The Reader's Digest, Newsweek, and Playboy, which are some of the largest organizations involved, prepare and publish their own books and try to sell them, for the most part, to the subscribers to their magazines. From this variety of publishing sources and through this variety of distribution methods, an ever-larger number of books are published each year competing for the attention of a comparatively small number of Americans interested in buying books.

Typically the direct forms of advertising in which publishers engage-in polishers' catalogues and in ads in the important trade publications of the industry, Publishers Weekly and Library

Journal-have nothing like the impact on potential readers as the "free" advertising that books receive in the review columns of newspapers and magazines. The most influential of these include the New York Review of Books, Saturday Review. Time, Newsweek, Harper's, and the Atlantic Monthly. The most influential of these include the New York Review of Books, Saturday Review. Time, Newsweek, Harper's, and the Atlantic Monthly. The most important review medium is unquestionably the New York Times Book Review. But all of these combined, and the other newspapers and magazines that review books, cannot review more than a fraction of the books published each year. With all the space it tries to give book reviews, the New York Times Book Review criticizes and comments on less than 3000 books a year. Moreover, the reach of these publications is limited to a relatively small number of people, who tend to be wealthier and better educated than the average. None of these review media is as effective, therefore, as the brief appearance an author may be lucky enough to secure on a network talk show such as Johnny Carson's "Tonight" show on NBC."

Book publishing has "used" the other media of communication to secure sales in more dramatic ways. The growth of the paperback industry has enabled publishers to rush to press with the news in book form. Bantam was one of the first to experiment with "instant publishing" when it published the Report of the Warren Commission on the Assassination of President Kennedy in book form 80 hours after the official government commission report was released to the public in September 1964. (Normally a book takes about six months from completion of the manuscript to publication date.) So successful was its first attempt-the book was an instant best seller, selling over a million copies within weeks-that Bantam published 56 "instant books," or 'extras" as the company calls them, in the next 10 years.

In the 1970s, then, the oldest of the American media, like the other print media, had adjusted to the popularity of the electronic media. It has yielded much of its earlier concentration on fictional entertainment to the movies and television. During the first the first paperback revolution in publishing, in the 1840s and 1850s, and on through the enormous success of the sensational "dime novel' of the 1870s and 1880s to the romantic historical and family novels of the early 1900s, fiction dominated book publishing. The trend toward nonfiction, began after World War I and has accelerated since. In 1960, 16 percent of the new books or new editions published were fiction; in 1974, less than 9 percent were fiction.

Much of the non-fiction exploited sensation and trivia in the news, but the public's taste for these ephemera subsidized the book industry's commitment to the less profitable or unprofitable publication of what the 19th century poet and critic Matthew Arnold called "the best that is known and thought in the world."

Newspaper circulation was recovering in the late 1970s; by proliferating ever more specialized publications, the magazine industry sustained overall circulation; and although the boom in book sales of the 1960s leveled off in the 1970s, the book industry managed modest growth. Print survived the doom prophesied for it partly because owners of print media were alarmed enough to invest heavily in audience research, partly because new technologies enabled quicker, more flexible responses to what the public wanted. Print survived mainly, one suspects, because the written word gives information and ideas, fact and fiction, a life that the electronic media with all their dazzling visual appeal cannot supplant. Significantly, the passion and energy of the generation of the 1960s, the first generation to be dominated since birth by television and one excited by McLuhan's probes, took concrete though not always coherent form in print, in the underground press.

14

Relevance of Print Media

In the modern context, newspapers cannot compete with radio or TV in being first and fast with news. They can, however, serve independently and as supplementary to these media by giving more balanced account of news alongwith backgrounds, better interpretative, investigated and thorough reporting and coverage, wider variety of reading material and shades of opinions in their columns. Magazines deal more with opinion interpretation, incisiveness and colour. Noticed or read by the elite and policy makers, leaders of parties and professions, as also by workers, farmers, students and housewives, they can influence public opinion and more so the policy makers. Today, the press is not merely observing and reporting but asking, pursuing, investigating, doubting, demanding and sometimes even biting. It is far more vigilant and rancorous about fundamental and civil rights, corruption, economic exploitation and social abuses. Modern newspapers illuminate the mind through their cartoons, illustrations, graphics, features and human interest writings.They highlight or underline particular events by their headlines, leads, cutlines and column boxes. Their searching interviews, columnist writings and editorials furnish better comprehension of complicated events and affairs. Reader columns in newspapers tie in readers and provide noticeable columns of public grievances. There are also engagement columns,notices,fitting advertisements, etc. for those who need them. Notwithstanding occasional bias and slants in reporting and writing, their concentrated urban approach and obsession with political and sensational news, professionally competent and disciplined dailies and magazines command comparatively better respect, credibility and acceptability than any other media. Even grassroots media, community papers and other small professional or specialised periodicals are dear to readers,thoughfor different reasons. Thus, newspapers today occupy a prestigious position in the galaxy of media with their roles varying from the 4th Estate to the 5th Estate, from an informer to a critic, from a narrator to a commentator, from an investigator to an analyst, from a mentor to a teaser, from a peace preacher to violence or racialism baiter.

In developing countries the press has a special role to play as a social monitor, a constructive critic, the stimulator of debates on public issues and a medium of feedback while balancing the wheel of the Governmental structure. A great social vitaliser and the right arm of liberty, it is also a big enemy of tyrants and an exposer of public corruption. The media is also an interpreter of public events and a professional forum for investigative and interpretative journalism. It acts as a watchdog of a sleeping democracy and a public university for the masses. "A people without reliable newspapers," said Harold Laski, "is sooner or later a people without the basis for freedom."

The Background

In India, Independence constituted a turning point in the history of the Indian Press. It brought to a close the era of journalism as a mission and the media was left free to become a business or an industry. Refashioning the Press was part of the larger enterprise of refashioning society. The partition of the country made the Muslim League-dominated newspapers to quit or lapse. Consequently the Urdu and Bengali press suffered the most. Some of the important Urdu papers from Lahore sought to find a new home in Delhi, Amritsar and Jalandhar. The Anglo-Saxon group of papers lost their punch, homogeniety and *raison d'etre* as a group. Comparing the Indian press then with the contemporary press in the West, there was no national newspaper in India which could play the role of an activist or act as the voice of the nation. There was not a single daily in the country with a circulation of even one lakh. The Times of India printed 94748 copies, the Hindu 69748, the Statesman 65032 and the Hindustan Times 48141 copies. The circulation of these big papers was in fact a pittance of the circulation of some foreign newspapers of the time: Le Petit journal selling more than a million copies per issue since 1886; in 1900 the daily Mail, London crossed the seven figure mark; in 1979, the Japanese Yomiuri Shimbun sold over 13 million copies per day in a nation of about 110 million. In Britain with a population of about 55 million the Sun sold four million copies a day. The position of Indian language dailies was still lower. *Swadesamitran* with 39509 copies was considered a topnotch language daily; then followed *Sakal* (27262), *Mathrubhumi* (25736) and *Andhra Patrika* (23086). There were no worthwhile dailies in several states and languages. The capacity of newspapers, therefore, to influence public opinion for good for bad was of a limited nature.

Another feature of the Indian press was its concentration. Our of a total of 330 dailies, five owners controlled 29 papers and 31.2 per cent of circulation, while 15 owners controlled 54 newspapers and 50.1 per cent of the circulation. The Telugu daily Andhra Patrika, selling 23086 copies accounted for more than 50 per cent of the circulation in its language area. The diffusion rate which is an index of media growth was 7 per thousand.

The circumstances after the partition were alarmingly unsettling, but despite handicaps the Press in general increasingly turned its attention to the numerous constructive tasks ahead. The news started being presented and interpreted from that angle. Gradually newspapers strove for improved professional techniques and conveniences. Important or big newspapers began to enlist the services of special correspondents and seek more facilities of various kinds. Feature writings got impetus. Some eminent journalists like M. V. Kamath, Khushwant Singh, Kuldip Nayar, Dom Moraes, Arun Shourie, B. G. Verghese, A. G. Noorani, Shoba Kilachand, Abu Abraham, etc., achieved distinction by writing their sparkling by-lined columns in big English newspapers and magazines. The language newspapers too inducted equally famous personalities. In fact, some newspapers became popular because of these columns.

Most papers also followed the technique of writing behind-the-scene stories based on current affairs. That made newspapers more readable and in turn attracted more readers. Starting from R. K. Karanjia and Baburao Patel and passing on to Khushwant Singh, M J. Akbar, Ashwini Sarin, Neera Chaudhary, Pritish Nandy, Aroon Purie, Chaitanya Kelbag and Vikram Vohra emerged enterprising people journalism, which talked about not only political shenanigans and scoops but also focussed on prominent personalities, their life-styles, fads and habits. Couched in chatty, masala style, these writings made newspapers readable and provocative.

Journalists like Khushwant Singh gave a package of religion, sex and politics including jokes and made-up stories, which made some magazines and newspapers more poplar and caused an increase in their sale. M. J. Akbar's redressing of the Telegraph and Pritish Nandy's revamping of The Illustrated Weekly of India as a feature magazine, are other promotional devices to give a new look to publications and boost their circulation.

Journalistic ranks have expanded and management has shown signs of improvements. The result of these developments was a rise in circulation. As for the various language press, the increase in circulation was a cumulative result of the increase in formal education, rise in purchasing power caused by growing industrialisation, trade and commerce, the information explosion caused by the spurt of new planned programmes, acrimonious politics and class, caste and communal clashes, expansion of communications and transport facilities, the awakening caused by general elections, mass media and advertising expansion. Consequently the circulation of some dailies and weeklies touched record levels.

Quantitatively the press grew enormously both in terms of dailies and periodicals and their circulation (average number of copies sold or distributed free per publishing day). The number of all newspapers-covering any printed or cyclostyled periodical publication like dailies, weeklies and other periodicals-rose from 4769 and 1952 to 19937 in 1982, with a few periods of steep ascents like in 1970, 1979 and 1981 when there was a rise both in terms of number and circulation. Since the sixties the number of dailies quadrupled from a modest 330 to 1334 and periodicals of all categories and periodicity also expanded four times from 4439 to 18603. The circulation of all reporting newspapers depicts the same scale of having rocketed from over 1052000 to 50094000-more than five times, and of dailies from 2.5 millions in 1947 to 14.84 millions in 1982, indicating a six-fold expansion. The spurt in the circulation of periodicals during the last three decades was more pronounced and rose from 8 million to over 35 million-nearly four and a half times. This phenomenal expansion in number and circulation of periodicals is popularly known as the periodical or magazine explosion.

This quantitative stride has some important implications. The first is that now newspapers and periodicals are published by more States and Union Territories than in the sixties. Blanks where no newspaper is published are only Arunachal Pradesh and Lakshadweep and thin areas are Nagaland, Andaman and Nicobar, Goa, Daman and Diu, Mizoram, Pondicherry, Meghalaya, Tripura, Manipur and Himachal Pradesh. So even today, at one end of Press development are heavyweight States and Union Territories like Maharashtra, West Bengal, Uttar Pradesh, Kerala, Delhi and Tamil Nadu where a large number of newspapers with sizable circulation originate; at the other end are blank or thin areas in this respect. Similarly there is a wide variation yet in the circulation of dailies per thousand population (an important criteria to judge whether a place is below or above Unesco's minimum norm of 100 copies per thousand or population). The range among the States differs from 44.14 copies in Kerala and 24.71 in Maharashtra to 3.62 copies in Nagaland, 2.72 copies in Sikkim and 1.95 copies in Assam. Among Union Territories the scale moves from 116.22 in Chandigarh and 48.36 in Delhi to 0.95 in Mizoram and 0.01 in Dadra and Nagar Haveli.

The second important feature of this growth pattern is a revelation of much faster rate of development in languages than in English. In fact a silent revolution has been taking place in the course of which the two century old dominance of the Press in English has been overcome by the Indian language Press in terms of both number and circulation. And it is not merely that the total circulation of all Hindi Newspapers including dailies has surpassed that of English newspapers, but the number and circulation of language newspapers as a whole has gone up. Also, in areas outside metropolitan cities, language newspapers have generally eclipsed every other English newspaper issued from these areas. The rate of growth of newspapers in Malayalam, Bengali, Kannada, Punjabi and Telugu is conspicuously high. In comparison, however, the share of Tamil, Urdu, Marathi and Gujarati in the total circulation chart has recorded a downward trend.

It is interesting to note that the circulation of some Indian language newspapers has reached spectacular proportions. The Anand Bazar Patrika in Bengali with a circulation of 416514 copies retains the pride of place as the largest circulated single daily in 1981 followed by another Bengali daily, Jugantar with a circulation of 314018 copies. Among periodicals Malayala Manorama, a Malayalam weekly from Kottayam, has the largest circulation.

Notable Trend

Another notable trend in the Indian press is towards localism. Purely local interest newspapers appear to be gaining ground at the expense of regional or national dailies. Pune affords a significant example. Three local Marathi dailies Sakat, Kesari, and

Tarun Bharat not only compete with two big dailies originating from Bombay but command around 90 per cent of the total circulation of the five dailies in Pune. Similarly the dominance of the English daily Tribune of chandigarh has not been surpassed by prestigious national English dailies coming in from Delhi.

Newspapers in India continue to be largely an urban phenomenon. Even in that respect there is a concentration inter se. Over 30 per cent of the newspapers are located in the four metropolitan cities. State capitals account for nearly 17 per cent. Other big cities with a population of over one lakh contain 30 per cent of the total. There are eighteen cities which account for 50 per cent of the total number of newspapers in the country. Only a handful of rural newspapers exist (which devote 40 per cent of their contents for rural areas). Dailies are completely urban. But the analysis of publication of newspapers bring out one significant point that more newspapers are published from cities and towns other than metropolitan cities and state capitals. The reason is that except English papers which are largely concentrated in the four metropolitan cities, Hindi papers are published mainly from medium towns (with a population of one lakh and more) while the press in Assamese, Bengali, Kannada and Tamil are mostly concentrated in the State capital towns.

Location may be a matter of convenience or the question of availability of printing facilities. But circulation pattern is a better norm of judging how far medium serves the rural people. Dailies coming from big cities claim more than nineteenths of the total circulation of dailies in the country. The Press Commission's study of 11 dailies (4 big, 5 medium and 2 small) reveals that rural circulation of these papers varied from 9.75 to 21.96 per cent in the case of nine papers and in the case of Dinamani of Madras and Yugadharma of Jaipur, Nagpur and Jabalpur it stood at 63.56 per cent and 57.45 per cent respectively. The average rural circulation of these papers was 22.28 per cent.

In 1981, the number of newspapers stood at 19144. A sample of the reporting newspapers to the RNI shows that while the circulation of 453 newspapers owned by joint stock companies was more than 19.6 million (that is nearly 38.4 per cent), nearly 65 per cent of the newspapers are owned by individuals, but their share in the total circulation is only 36.2 per cent.

The way a press actually functions is influenced largely by the news values which prevail among journalists. And that is reflected in the gatekeeping function of the practioners, including various forms of information or knowledge control or the selection and highlighting of news stories and their projection, headlining, backgrounding and interpretation.

Joseph Pulitzer, publisher of the St. Louis Post-Despatch and the New York World once instructed his staff to look for news stories that are original, distinctive, dramatic, romantic, thrilling, unique, curious, quaint, humorous, odd and apt-to-be talked about. To these may be added newness, the prominence of persons or places concerned, the proximity of the event to the place of publication, the human interest involved and timeliness. These constitute some of the attributes of good newscasting according to Western standards. The Second Press Commission of India finds that most of the commercial newspapers in India do not pursue these guidelines. Rather they imitate the cheap, though currently known as popular journalism of the West by highlighting news about petty politics, politicians and their pourings, flooding their news holes with stories of crimes, violence and aberrations and displaying creaking headlines and sensuous illustrations and ads. Equally questionable is the sense of "human interest" which often find reflection in the reporting of foreign news and photographs, foreign serials or syndicated features. The desi (local) contents are hardly flattering. These comments seem to be rather harsh, but it is very much our journalism today.

The Commission maintains that objection is not against reporting dirty politics, sensational events or crime and tension which in any way form a part of news flow. Rather it is to the preoccupation with them to such an extent that the readers are not supplied the information and discussion they need to discharge their responsibility to society, or to make judicious decisions or exercise wisely their franchise right.

The disproportionate picture of coverage in the Indian press is revealed by another study of the Second Press Commission. According to this study, Assamese dailies devoted the maximum of edited space-37 per cent-to political items and news regarding conflicts and tension, perhaps because of the controversy in the State on the issue of foreign nationals. Tamil, Punjabi, Hindi, Oriya and Telugu , dailies also devoted a large amount of space ranging from 41.6 to 31.6 to such items. These items occupied 23.7 per cent of the space in English dailies, the least for any daily.

Items devoted to economic development and , Government matters occupied 40.5 per cent space in Oriya dailies which was the maximum for any language. Hindi dailies devoted 29.0 per cent and English dailies 36.5 per cent space to such items. Assamese dailies devoted the least-19.6 per cent-space to such news.

In Sindhi dailies, news items on unrest, law and order and courts occupied 21.2 per cent of the space. Hindi dailies gave 1735 per cent and English dailies English dailies devoted the maximum 9.9 per cent space to sports, while Hindi dailies gave 6.0 per cent. Sindhi newspapers had the least amount-1.00 per cent-of space given to such items.

Gujarati dailies had the maximum 22.5 per cent-space devoted to items on entertainment and culture. The percentage was 18.4 for Hindi and 6.4 for English dailies. The least space 5.8 per cent given to such items was in Oriya dailies.

Items of interest to woman and on social and human interest matters occupied 13.4 per cent of the space in Sindhi dailies. Hindi dailies gave 5.6 per cent and English dailies 4.1 per cent space to such items. The least space-3.0 per cent-give to such items was in Assamese dailies.

According to a random survey conducted by PR unit of the Council of Scientific and Industrial Research (CSIR) the space devoted to science news in Indian newspapers varies from .63 to 10.65 per cent of the total news content. The Hindu, Economic Times and Financial Express were found to be leading in the coverage of science news.

These analyses depict the need of a serious attempt on the part of the reader and professionally oriented newspapers to give deeper thought to the problem of giving a balanced coverage and adoption of healthier professional norms in selecting and projecting news in their columns.

Perhaps more distressing is the coverage of human interest stories culled out from western newspapers. That only shows the trend and mentality even of our best gatekeepers of newscasting. The Press Commission has quoted the selection of the following news stories and photographs by five leading English newspapers published in Delhi as illustrations of this unedifying trend, "(i) a 22-cm story of 2nd December 1980 (AP report from Leeds, U.K.) under the headline "Girl escapes attack by "ripper"'; (ii) 3-column photograph of 3rd December, 1980, showing two policemen on their night patrol talking to a young woman out alone on a Leeds Street near where the mass murderer, known as the Yorkshire Ripper, claimed his 13th victim; (iii) whole of the first page of the weekly section of a newspaper of 14th June, 1981 devoted to the first instalment of "The Yorkshire Ripper Story'; (iv) a 16-cm story (AP report from Los Angeles) on 25th June, 1981 under the headline 'Rapist on parole held again'; and (v) front-page 9-cm story (UNI report from Nairobi) on 6th November, 1981 about a Kenyan African who had 40 wives and wanted more."

This perversity is at its worst in film magazines in India and elsewhere in the Third World, continued the Commission's report. How morbidly these magazines pack their pages with rumours, gossips and speculative and unseemy exposures of the private lives of film stars, instead of dilating on professional aspects of the media or carrying critical articles of film appreciation.

Newscasting or reporting about development or rural affairs is no better. There too the trend is in giving more importance to what is wrong than what is right, to conflicts rather than to resolving them, to airing grievances than to getting redressals. It is no wonder then that the maximum output of the press in development or rural reporting consists of a miscellaneous succession of stories and images which have no relation to the actual lives of rural people or even to poor and weaker sections in urban areas. And what happens in such situations is that generally simple science, relevant technology, activating success and human interest stories or field based reports, which are the heart of development reporting, go by default.

Apart from this low rating of proper news values even techniques and quality of development reporting, except in a few newspapers and magazines, is poor, says the Commission, Readers hardly get a feeling of participation in the reported events, programmes or social change. Again, interpretative or in-depth journalism is as a low ebb yet.

According to the Commission, all investigative reporting is no development reporting, but the latter is essentially investigative. Apart from it one may add that it should also be interpretative, educative, expository and promotional in nature. It has also to be venturesome and innovating-professional qualities born out of commitment to public interest, fundamental duties and regard for the public weal. The actual news values displayed by professional gatekeepers or reporters in the bulk of newspapers today is however wide off these marks. According to a Magsaysay Award winner, India's editors or reporters even don't read public documents properly. Some of them plagiarize, add a few words of their own to it and call it a scoop. Even if they read a newspaper file, they call themselves investigative journalists. Most editors have competent staff, but they don't use it to good account.

There is need, therefore, to give news values a different orientation in the interest of higher professionalism, social health and national development, argues the Press Commission. It urges the organisations of publishers, editors and journalists to evaluate, on a continuing basis, the concept and contents of healthy news culture in the light of changing socio-political ethos. It reinforces Hutchins Commission's observation that journalists today should not regard only events as news, but also social and economic processes. Many activities of utmost social consequences lie below the surface of what are conventionally regarded as reportable incidents. In the Indian context these could be: Induction of new farming technology or participatory management in factories, adoption of new sources of energy like solar or gobar (cow dung) gas, introduction of new designs of low-cost housing, etc.

The Press Commission further holds that if conflict is news but not resolution of conflict, if the unusual and the bizarre is news rather than the normal, if news is what happened just a while ago (even if the event was not significant) and not a significant happening of a week or a month earlier which has only now come to light, the portrayal or reality in the press is bound to be distorted. Added to this aberration is often the slanting or hoisting of news done on the dictates of the personal or business interests of owners and pressure groups.

The former Prime Minister, Mrs. Indira Gandhi, in her theme address at Namedia in December 1983 also adverted to this unhealthy news sense displayed by our newspapers. She said that many journalists consider it smart to initiate the popular Western definition of bad news being good news and are bored by constructive and developmental activity. In this connection she cited a recent survey by the Press Council which showed that only two per cent newspaper space was devoted to social issues. Is this what really interests readers? she asked. Are they content to remain ignorant of what is happening in various spheres, of what deepens their understanding, what helps them discharge their duty as well-informed citizens? she added.

To rectify this aberration, what is actually required is the sharpening of news sense and social sensitiveness among media practitioners. They should also develop the ability to interpret events and trends in the context of various disciplines and cultural milieu of the region.

Should journalists alone be the gatekeepers of news? Should the desk personnel or reporters be allowed to have a free hand in selecting, interpreting, shaping, displaying, timing, withholding or repeating news, or should be consumers of news also be permitted to have a say in the matter? The Press Commission has preferred to follow the existing practice of leaving the discretion in these matters to journalists, government information officials and media managers. The commission also wants editors to have the final say in the acceptance or rejection of advertisements especially those which border on or cross the line between decency and obscenity or those which promote the notion of women as sex objects and run contrary to the social or news value of their newspapers.

The practice in the West however varies. In free marketing democracies like Japan, USA, West Germany and France, newspaper publishers seek to follow the 'serve and sell' policy of giving the bulk of news and editorial matter according to the ascertained demands, tastes, needs and feedbacks of readers. In some countries like Japan even incentives are offered to make housewives buy a particular brand of paper. On the other hand, in socialist countries or authoritarian states, the party guardians or autocratic rulers and their agents act as the censors of reading material, determining what will go and what will not.

As mentioned earlier, freedom of the press is not merely a professional right that is inherent in journalists or publishers. Ideally these interests have to be reconciled: those of the publishers, readers and society. Feedback surveys or ballots, readers' columns, opinion polls, interviews and direct contacts with readers, policy makers and public representatives can bridge the gap partly. Suggestion and public opinion columns, panel discussions, direct mail ballots and coupons, publisher's letters, professional seminars and magazines as also the ombudsmanship of the Press Council can further fill in the void.

In the absence of regular readership and public feedback mechanism or other safeguards, however, the claim of journalists to be sole censors or arbiters appears to be presumptuous. When newspapers are controlled by big business or are influenced by vested interests or pressures, they run the risk, says the Commission, of becoming vehicles of expression of these internal and external influences. It is not, however, difficult as research and comparative studies bear out, to remove the dichotomy and gulf by delinking and diffusing ownership and control and by adopting a package of readership feedback mechanism and research, public representative consultation process and norms, codes and guidelines for gatekeeping evolved by the professional bodies. Some of these suggestions have been recommended by the commission itself. What one may conclude is that by taking some of these measures newspapers can become people's universities and development activists without compromising their professional standards, social responsibilities and communication role as free public informers, educators and custodians of public interest. And perhaps in this direction lies the future development of journalism in India.

As described earlier there has been an increase in the number and circulation of periodicals since 1970. Today we see glossy and attractively produced Magazines which can compete with any of their Western counterparts in excellence. The gross circulation of any one of these periodicals, however, has not yet touched a seven figure-a phenomenon common among many advanced countries. Nor have any of these magazines come anywhere near even a; single multi-editioned magazine like the Reader's Digest which publishes over 31 million copies in 17 languages.

In the group of Indian periodicals which appeared in 1981, monthlies constituted the largest ingredient followed by weeklies, fortnightlies, quarterlies and annuals. In terms of circulation also monthlies had an edge over others.

Maximum Number

The maximum number of periodicals are brought out in Hindi followed by English, Bengali and Urdu. In terms of circulation too Hindi periodicals maintain the top position (27.6 per cent). Then come English periodicals (20.6 per cent) and Tamil (10.9 per cent). Among the Indian languages Malayalam has the maximum circulation of weeklies as well as of other periodicals per 1000 of the linguistic population (1979 figures). Kashmiri comes at the bottom with hardly any circulation. Fifty-seven periodicals have a circulation of one lakh or more copies (1980). Five of them have a circulation exceeding 3 lakhs. The two top have circulation exceeding 5.5 lakhs.

The Registrar of Newspapers Report categorises, the journals into 21 groups according to the contents. The Second Planning Commission Report however, divides them into ten categories : (1) News and current affairs journals: (2) opinion journals; (3) farm journals; (4) economic and financial journals; (5) science journals; (6) literary and cultural magazines; (7) women journals; (8) children journals; (9) sports journals; and (10) film journals. According to the Commission's calculation, news and current affairs journals constitute the largest group. The Illustrated Weekly of India, India Today and Link are the mast bearers of this group. A feature of the growth of such periodicals in recent years has been the emergence of investigative reporting in some of these journals and also a marked increase in circulation of such journals since 1977. Some top journalists, however, consider this type of investigative reporting, at least in a few of these journals as muck raking or gutter reporting; but a few better reports have proved to be earth shaking or stunning revelations. Qualitatively the coverage in India Today, Gentleman, the Illustrated Weekly of India, Sunday, Probe, Celebrity, Imprint, Sunday Observer, etc. is commendably supported by interpretative graphics and illustrations.

Literary and cultural magazines constitute the second largest group. The bulk of these magazines particularly those with a large circulation, however, follow a formula of mixed contents in order to appeal to different tastes and thereby attract more readers. Kumudam, a Tamil weekly, is a leading illustration of this group.

Opinion journals are distinct from news magazines as also from journals of entertainment for leisure time reading. They are generally imbued with social concern and a sense of purpose. Seminar and Mainstream are illustrations of this category.

Covering nearly three-fourths of the country's rural population there are only 345 farm journals (1979 figures). Shetkari and Gramsevak belong to this group. The number of copies of farm journals per 1000 rural literate population is only 1.5 per cent, a discouragingly low figure. Some weaknesses of these journals are that they use heavy terminologies in explaining technical information and they do not engage experts to write or report for them. It is probably because they cannot afford it.

Hindu Survey of Indian Industry, Business World, Business India and Udyog represent the economic and financial category of journals. The number of these journals is not sizable in the aggregate, though some of them are fast sellers. Their number, however, had taken an upward trend since 1952 and so also their circulation.

The growth of science journals to which belongs also a better seller like Science Today was evidently noticeable during the eighties but not significantly or adequately enough. Although the number rose from almost scratch and so also the circulation of these journals, their development is not as much as it should be according to its need. To popularise science and technology and inculcate scientific temper among the people is an imperative need. But the existing journals in this category cannot perform this task satisfactorily. This misgiving was also expressed by the Press Commission.

The number of women journals is still small despite an increase during the eighties. *Vanitha,* a Malayalam monthly from Kottayam has the highest circulation in this group. One dimension which distinguishes these journals from their Western counterparts is what a Press Commission Study points out that these journals consistently seek to direct women's energies into a narrow channel and to define their concerns, preoccupations and aspirations within an arbitrarily imposed feminine framework. The covers of these magazines generally feature a brightly dressed woman, baring some parts of her body. Apart from these aspects, these journals depict women's mental faculties and behaviour in a way as if they can fit only into a male-dominated social relationship. The study says that readers get an impression that the outside world belongs to men and that the issues which arise there do not affect woman except indirectly through the men related to them. The trend, however, is now changing for the better.

Despite some increase in the number of children's journals, their position in the market is very thin. The position of Indrajal Comics in this group is the highest. Most magazines in this section only provide entertainment in the for of light reading. Some also carry informative articles including those on current and sports events, but the number of such articles in an issue is not more than two or three. One regrettable trend noticed by the Press Commission in children's magazines is an effort to depict sex and violence in a bid to increase circulation. Instead of resorting to originality and creativity, which can help to sell the magazines also, their sponsors are trying to lean on cheap circulation gimmicks.

Sports journals had a low rate of expansion of circulation upto 1975, but thereafter they started showing progress. Sports World today crosses five figures. Qualitatively they do not reflect the latest trends in sports journalism.

Film journals indicated an increase in number since the sixties, but professionally and circulation-wise their record does not show much improvement. Only Filmfare an English fortnightly from Bombay, touches a respectable figure. A study for the Press Commission says that the bane of many film journals is the lack of professional standards. Many of these journals resort to gossip and scandal about alleged peccadillos of film stars. It is an interesting finding that many articles in such magazines are written by PR men in the pay of film producers of staff and therefore attacks on some film stars are deliberate or -tendentious.

As an activist in the all round development of Indian society, development journalism can be a faithful ally of the whole process. This brand of journalism is, however, not merely economic or financial journalism. Neither is it a government mouthpiece. It doesn't imply polishing up press releases issued by the PR Departments. It is a positive, forward looking, field based, two way participatory and development promotional reporting and writing. It is pragmatic, result and action oriented and barefoot type of journalism. To this end, it has to be bold and venturesome investigative or expository reporting involving issues, problems and exercises of social significance or public interest. But the perspective is not to write merely what is wrong, but also what can be the right thing and how it can be brought about. It should probe into the reasons for success or failures at different places under different conditions of various development programmes. Development Agency's National Adult Education or National Rural Employment programmes, Marginal Farmers and Agricultural labours Project, etc. affect the lives of common people such as small farmers. It is indeed a sad reflection that newspapers in India have not adequately taken up this type of dynamic journalism or reporting. It has not undertaken initiative in reviewing or reporting in depth development activities nor reporting incisively about socio-economic programmes or about the green and white revolutions that are taking place in rural or remote areas. The Press Commission draws attention particularly to one defect in this area of development reporting. It finds that many newspapers today depend heavily on official hand-outs or briefings and not on field work or direct observation preferably participant observation. Instead of venture-some reporting in so far as it is oriented to social and economic issues like the exploitation of Harijans, tribalsor contract labour the trading in human flesh or delays and corruption in public administration, they feel contended in loading their stories with big and small statistics. They fail to help the readers know how the beneficiaries feel or react about the claims and achievements of different development programmes.

The Commission points out yet another omission in development reporting. This relates to the praiseworthy performance of non-official agencies and workers in fields like education, leprosy relief, etc. Indeed it is a poor reflection on the professional standards of newspapers that they do not take initiative in India in reviewing such activities. Rather they themselves become aware of them after some non-officials have been honoured with international or national awards. Surely, the free press in developing countries should be more socially conscious and enterprising than what our press actually is. Also, there is a need for the big and small media to operate as change agents, watch-dogs or gatekeepers in the process of socio-economic development taking place in various parts of the country. At the moment only a few language newspapers especially in Oriya, Telugu, Marathi, Malayalam, Bengali and Hindi are devoting an increasing proportion of space to development coverage like that of health, family welfare, industry, science and technology, agriculture, education and public utilities. This conclusion is based on a study entitled "Percentage of front page space devoted to different themes in daily newspapers." Another study of the Commission reveals yet another healthy trend among some language newspapers (Bengali, Kannada and Malayalam dailies) besides English which were reporting regularly on development topics and socio-economic issues. Topics covered in such reports include the condition of tea garden labourers, problems of drought and irrigation, dowry deaths, ill-treatment of women, plight of undertrial prisoners, living conditions of slum dwellers, and the like. This is a welcome development which needs to be emulated and encouraged also in other newspapers which have set their heart on serving rural people. This task, however, will warrant social aptitude and barefoot qualities on the part of reporters and communicators and their ability to understand, interpret and report on socio-economic issues in terms of the problems, needs, experience and language frameworks of rural readers.

Liberty of Press

Press freedom provides the oxygen in a climate of a healthy democracy. It is a matter of common experience that the press can do well and perform its professional work smoothly if it operates in the open and competitive information market and does not itself throttle or vitiate the process of collecting, selecting and presenting the news objectively and truthfully. The Press commission had therefore underscored that it is only on this type of free press that people can largely depend for the primary data of their political thinking. It is because of the freedom both from black laws or menacing pressures from without and the irresponsible journalism from within that the Fourth Estate can function as a watch-dog, ombudsman, constructive critic, public investigator and expositor, philosopher, guide and even an entertainer of the society.

Press freedom is conceded by the constitution, but not as a separate entity or a special privilege. It is included in the individuals' right to freedom of speech and expression. The government, however, has resented the licentiousness shown by a few newspapers in always criticising the ruling party and only harping upon what is wrong about things. All our governments have preferred press freedom to be linked with social and fundamental responsibilities and the obligation to report objectively. Taking into consideration the constraints of the Indian model of democracy and socialism and the objectives laid in the Preamble of the Constitution or its Directive Principles of the State Policy, the second Press Commission has advocated that the Press should be neither an adversary nor an ally of the Government, but a constructive critic. To be a mindless adversary or an unquestioning ally would be to abdicate judgement, states the report of the Press Commission. It further stresses that journalism is a public utility service and not merely an industry. Whereas a doctor may cause harm only to a few dozen or at the most a few score patients during the full span of his carreer, a dishonest or unprofessional journalist can poison the minds of hundreds of thousands or millions of his fellowmen. It is true that journalism has to be a viable business if it is to be free from want and patronage, but a special plea for its fundamental duty and its responsibility to the society and readers is not far stretched. The Press Commission has therefore urged that in the changed circumstances today, the protection of the freedom of the issuer of news alone is not enough; the freedom of the consumer (readers and public) must also be protected.

The press is a great social asset, for it has to serve the entire community of varying minds with its raw material for thought, as also to act as a watch-dog by exercising its role to warn and curb forces of repression, corruption and divisiveness.

It is possible to have a free but responsible press and good, responsive and democratic government at the same time. In fact, the freedom of the press is the mother of all other freedoms. This freedom can be used to create a brave new world or to bring about universal catastrophe. It is imperative for the society and government to protect journalists and assure them conditions for working unhindered or undertake unrestrictedly investigative reporting strictly for professional purposes. 'More journalists are killed or kidnapped, victimised or persecuted than members of any other profession,' says Sean MacBride, Chairman of the International Commission for the Study of Communication Problems. They certainly need protection and perhaps a special status,' he adds. In India these suggestions need special consideration for instances abound when journalists were murdered or manhandled by terrorists, agents of politicians or infuriated mobs or were sacked by their proprietors at the instance of political barons or some other wire-pullers.

Press freedom is very fragile. It can be weighed from two sides; (1) the external and internal pressures, and (2) draconian or vexatious laws. The press has to be protected both ways.

The pressures could be six-fold: (1) physical attacks on the editor or the offices of the newspaper or its employees by the aggrieved or angry mobs, (2) obstructions posed in the expression of political opinions not to the liking of trade unions and newspaper employees, (3) interference in the editorial autonomy by proprietors with a view to protecting their own business interests, (4) pressures from advertisers (5) interference by the functionaries of the government through selective and politically motivated exercise of powers under the law and through extra legal action, and (6) inducements or favours sought by the journalists themselves. To give protection to the press in these respects the Press Commission and many other authorities have advocated the expansion of the jurisdiction of the Press Council to be able to look into these complaints. The legal areas in which press freedom is sought to be augmented comprise immunity regarding disclosure of sources of information, defamation, contempt of legislatures and courts and regarding a few limitations ordained by the Press and Registration of Books Act 1867, Post and Telegraph Act, Industries (Development and Regulation Act) 1951, etc. To this end, the second Press Commission has suggested certain amendments in the existing press laws to expand reasonably the scope of press freedom and at the same time underscored the need to protect the right to privacy of the individual and prevent newspapers from indulgence in free style of character assassination.

Beside the promotion of products and services, advertising has a great role in sustaining the newspaper industry and free press. Press advertising as a factor of newspaper economy is therefore taken very seriously by newspaper managements of modern times. Any restrictions imposed on advertising space or expenditure or newsprint supply would naturally evoke resentment among big and medium papers.

Till the second half of the sixties the advertisers and big advertising agencies in India depended primarily on dailies for extensive advertising. Thereafter a clear cut differentiation began to emerge that while daily newspapers should be used primarily for advertising capital goods, employment and trade notices and for institutional campaigns and periodicals should be employed for sustained advertising of consumer goods. In fact the sudden increase in advertisement revenue after the sixties enabled leading Indian periodicals to improve their production standards and editorial content, thereby attracting a wider readership. Even for the bulk of other periodicals, income from advertisements became the mainstay of their economy.

Value of Advertisement

Today advertisements occupy a substantial proportion of space in newspapers. It is, however, only the big general interest magazines, and comparatively the English dailies attached to newspaper chains, and combines of large business houses who usurp the lion's share in the cake of advertising revenue. A trend to rectify this imbalance has been sought by the government by pursuing a liberal policy of giving special rates of government advertisements to language news papers besides augmenting their newsprint supply and granting them rebate from excise duties, etc. But still the big and medium dailies and periodicals, not withstanding competition from radio TV commercials, continue to have edge.

Notwithstanding the maximum of 40:60 space allotment suggested for advertisements by the first Press Commission, the space given to advertising has been actually increasing in big newspapers. According to data given in the annual reports of the Press Register there was no paper in 1965 which gave 60 per cent or more space to advertisements and there were only 10 papers which devoted 50 to 59 per cent space to advertisements. In 1981, three big and medium and 37 small papers started devoting 75 per cent or more space to advertisements. And 5 big 25 medium and 112 small papers used between 50 and 74 per cent of their space for advertisements. The percentage of space devoted to advertisements was generally more in the case of dailies that periodicals. However, the average space devoted to advertisements was found to be 39 per cent in the case of dailies 27 per cent in the case of weeklies and 31 per cent in the case of monthlies. According to ORG survey, 77 per cent of the total advertising revenue income and 51.8 per cent of the space was accounted for by big newspapers with a circulation of 50, 000 and above. This, a small chunk of big newspapers have an economic or competitive edge over the bulk of small and medium newspapers in the country. On an average the share of advertising revenue to the total income was merely 52 per cent in the case of big papers and a little over 26 per cent in the case of medium papers. The bigger dailies, particularly the big English dailies were usurping a disproportionately larger chunk of advertisement revenue in 1981 and therefore were in a position to offer more pages on the same selling price. Even from the point of view of the resale price, the big papers provided a benefit to the customers.

The second press Commission therefore felt that the prescription of a price-page schedule with fixed news to advertising ratio is absolutely necessary for the existing newspapers. In view of the need to help small and medium newspapers overcome disadvantage of lower advertisement incomes and smaller number of pages the Press Commission recommended a specific ratio of 60 per cent for big papers. A bold and fair suggestion, but its validity is a matter of speculation.

Good Production

In India as has been already seen, good production did not brother the pioneer journalist in the past. Photo journalism and colour reproduction were at their embryonic stage. The opinion advocacy or adversary Journalism of those days with low print orders did not lend themselves to competitive or marketing urges in terms of variety or innovativeness in design or production. Things, however, started changing for the better during the 1950s and 1960s. The vocation became a business of industry and subjected to: marketing and advertising pressures for better looks and attractive layouts and typography. The challenge of utilising resources optimally, effective economies in costs and ensuring speedier delivery schedules, motivated the owners to resort to modern printing technology for their papers. By this time the Indian printing scene was also exposed to the new trends in the West where two types of technological revolutions were sweeping the scene. Web offset and electronic printing technologies involving photo composition or computer controlled teletype setting or electronic typewriters were replacing the conventional hot metal linotype and monotype composing processes. For a' multilingual developing country like India these two technologies suited immensely, though they were costly. Among the obvious advantages of these technologies to Indian publishing in languages are the superior and consistent quality of letter image, elimination of the use of scarce material such as lead and the unlocking of capital invested in lead type faces.

During the last two decades, the big chain English newspaper publishers or language newspapers bringing out multi-editions and affected by competition have been gradually reeling towards sophisticated and modern technologies of various shades. So is the trend with some of the class A and class B printing houses where big magazines and medium newspapers are being printed as job work. For instance, three giants among the Malayalam press Malayala Manorama, Mathrubhumi and Kerals Kaumudi are in competition to get into the faster and the latest printing processes. Of these three big Malayalam papers Kerala Kaumudi was the first to install the transmission link, a process by which composed matter can be sent column by column within two transmission points, thus enabling the resident editor to choose matter of local importance in his edition. This is an improvement on the facsimile transmission method employed by the Hindu which results in a comparatively more rigid similarity between all editions of the paper. Another high technology gadget that distinguishes Kaumudi is the tele-photo by which any major event occuring anywhere in the world can be splashed within a few hours in this paper.

There are today many language newspapers especially in Urdu, Hindi, Gujarati, Marathi and Telugu which have resorted to one or the other of the modern technologies. This is enabling them to offer colour printing as also modern layout and typographical designs to their advertising clients and readers-a significant landmark in language journalism.

The Hindu, was the first newspaper in India to install the latest computer technology both for printing and type setting processes. Instead of hot metal composing on stereo plates, a feature common to most of the other big dailies, typesetting in this paper is done by a typesetter working on one of the 24 video display units in an airconditioned office. The type text is stored in one of the two computers and on editorial command, a lasercamp photo typesetter produces bromides of the text and advertisement copies which are set and designed into complete pages, according to layout plans. Each page is then photographed by an automatic computerised camera to obtain a negative. This is then printed by contact on to a thin polymer plate under high intensity lights. After etching, which takes only minutes, the plate is ready for printing the headquarter's edition. The images of these of these pages are then sent at the rate of seven minuted a page by facsimile transmission to Bangalore, Hyderabad, Coimbatore and Madurai for simultaneous printing of regional editions. Recently the Indian Express, telegraph and Aaj installed computerised photo typesetting systems.

The Illustrated weekly of India an allied magazine of the Bennett Coleman and Co. now uses electronic technology in colour separation and automatic processing of film negatives as also adopts a sophisticated printing process of in-depth colour printing known as photogravure.

The Weekly's photogravure machine has nine units and it can print an 80-page at the rate of 90000 copies per hour. It can also control paper tension and colour alignment. Folding and stitching is done automatically.

Another illustration of the latest technology-based printing press was the opening of a new unit called Mayar printers at Okhla Industrial estate where the new electronic dot generating colour scanner, the process camera, film and plate processors and photo typesetting units have been installed. This plant is fully computerised.

Apart from these sophisticated presses, according to the Press Registrar's Report of 1981. 366 dailies have their own publishing arrangements. Also 398 dailies have their own composing arrangements. In these units however the printing technologies used are predominantly relief, stereo plate flat-bed, lithography and offset and for composing mono, lino, inter type and hand composition systems with a sprinkling of photo composition. To help modernise the printing industry the government has assured all possible help. In the existing situation, there seems to be three options open for must of the newspaper publishers: (1) to continue with the old technology, (2) to obtain secondhand reconditioned equipment or to resort to the manufacture of such machines locally, or (3) to take a leap into the new technology. At the 21st All India printers Conference, eminent overseas speakers advised Indian Printers not to hesitate in making up their minds in favour of adopting the new technology for it is like a moving train. The longer one takes to make up his mind, the harder it is to jump in later on.

The old technologies, however, cannot be discarded like the village cart. Some experts have suggested that India should continue to have an appropriate mix of old and new processes in such a manner that the adoption of the new technology by existing processes may allow them to survive initially for such period as they would choose to replace the old technology altogether. The Press Commission has left it to each publisher to decide what technology would suit its requirements best. Newspapers, particularly those which want to grow, should have an open mind and a progressive outlook while selecting proper technology. It has further recommended that the proposed newspaper development Commission should special attention to the development of printing and other technologies suitable for the Indian press, especially for Indian language and small and medium newspapers. The Press Commission own preference was how ever for new electronics technology which has a clear advantage so far as composition in Indian script is considered. To meet the immediate requirement of small and medium newspapers it suggested that these units should be allowed to important, rebuild or recondition machines available abroad.

Till the time new production technologies sweep printing scene in the country, the well produced Hindu, Malayala Manorama, Times of India, India Today, Gentleman and Illustrated Weekly of India will coexist with hundreds of shabbily produced small papers, though liable to serve useful function at the grassroots level.

The Indian media scene presents a picture of congested basti with an overcrowding of small newspapers. In a total number of 1914 units, only 17$ belong to the category of big newspapers and the rest to the category of small papers. Although small newspapers have increased in number their share the total circulation has declined markedly during the last quarter century. In the daily press, the big paper have a share of 54.3 and medium 25.4 per cent of the circulation. In a country like India where three quarters of the people live in small towns and villages, mofussil newspapers, invariably small ones with circulation ranging from a few hundreds to 15000, have distinct role to play in the process democratizing communication than big newspaper. Their functioning is however handicapped, their circulation in the rural areas is circumscribed, their economy is depressed and the their impact is reduced. People who have experience of publishing large and small daily newspapers testify that small newspapers can still grow more if they make themselves useful the local community by conveying information of local relevance and interest and seek to bag rural advertisements, rather than compete with the state capital or metropolitan newspapers ineffectively. Eve at the present stage of development in our country newspaper serving one or more districts with common cultural and economic features likely to be successful. The reassuring examples of community newspapers the USA and critical newspapers in the UK are appropriate. The development of such newspapers will reduce the disparity between India's large rural population as compared to the small circulation and readership of newspapers in rural areas. Even if it is conceded that newspaper readership per copy is higher in rural papers, the rural reach of the Indian press is so limited that it should call for concern and attention, says the Press Commission. In this connection, extension of educational opportunities for children and illiterate adults and gainful employment for the youth, women and rural people is very necessary.

No Links

The soul of a people is in the press. But the press at times in the hands of a few financial magnates who may murder its soul by corruption or narrowness of commercial interests. The question has often been raised in India as to how the economic independence of the press can be preserved from crippling and subservience to commercial and financial interests of the controlling groups. In this connection the second press Commission feels that newspapers controlled by the big business are liable to become vehicles of expression of the ideologies of their owners. To curb this trend, the

Commission has suggested the delinking of the press. To this end the Commission recommended a law should be enacted preventing, in phased from, a person carrying on the business of publishing a newspaper to have any direct or indirect interest beyond ten per cent in any other kind of business. Similarly it wanted that any other business person from outside having a business in excess of ten per cent elsewhere should not have permission to dominate any publishing concern. Other remedies suggested to obviated interference or nomination of unprofessional proprietors are the prescription of price-cum-page schedule and fixing of news to advertising space ratio of 40 to 60 in big papers.

This proposal of delinking has drawn the heaviest fire from four dissenters in the press Commission, who have characterised these recommendations as discriminatory and detrimental to the economics of big newspaper publishing. Whatever be the legal or professional implications of these proposals and that certainly needs to be further probed into there is no doubt that the media at small places should be allowed to play their role effectively. The proprietors of big papers should not be permitted either to injures healthy journalism at the grassroots level or poison the functional autonomy of working journalists.

An equitable, balanced, multilateral and evenly distributed spread of information is a vital condition for the growth of a well informed citizen. It can have meaning only if the system at all levels reflects and smoothly transmits news dealing with the life and problems of people.

India today has four main news agencies and a number of other non-wire news and feature agencies. The four main agencies are Press trust of India , United news of India, Samachar Bharati and Hindustan Samachar. The first two supply news in English and the other two operate through the media of Hindi and other Indian languages.

PTI started operating in 1949 after taking over Reuter's business in India as well as the interest of the Associated press of India. It is the biggest Indian news agency, employing a 1300-

strong editorial and technical staff. Its news service is carried over a teleprinter network of over 60,000 kilometres in length. More than 200 newspapers in the country subscribe to PTI service, besides AIR, Doordarshan, Central and State Governments, commercial establishments, universities and public institutions. PTI has arrangement with Reuters Agence France press of France the united Press International of USA and some other technical news agencies. PTI has also its own correspondents at selected places abroad.

The UNI started its operation in 1961. Within a decade it had spread its teleprinter network over 25000 kilometres. At present, UNI has 50 branch offices and a network of 50000 kilometres of leased teleprinter lines. It gets its reports from correspondents as also from half a dozen foreign news agencies AP, DPA, ANSA, Tass and few others. The agency has also launched a weekly background Service, Agricultural Service, Economic News service to cater to the special needs of newspapers, periodicals and other subscribers.

Hindustan samachar and Samachar bharati mainly serve the language press. The former, India's first multilingual agency, was started in 1948. It became a workers cooperative in 1957. A second Indian language agency, Samachar bharati, came into existence in 1967. In 1970 the agency became almost a public sector company when five state governments bought more than 50 per cent of its shares.

The small agencies provide news of local interest and significance. Specialised agencies in photographs, cartoons and other visuals seek to enrich reporting and make newspaper contents more attractive and interesting, more explanatory and understandable. India's news agencies need to be streamlined and their efforts need to be directed towards rural areas and the needs of small newspapers operating in mofussil areas. At present our news agencies are hardly equipped to report social and economic changes taking places in the countryside. The press Commission has therefore laid stress on the starting of small news agencies especially in languages. These would offer two way news and comments in different perspectives. The commission also desires the emergence of more agencies specialising in photographs, cartography and other visuals. It envisages the scope for pooling and federating systems for ensuring a countrywide dissemination of the more significant stories of success and failures in rural areas. The other need it has stated is to evolve teleprinters in various languages.

Among the non-wire news-feature agencies which have made a mark are Indian news and feature Alliance, public Opinion Trends which specialises in dissemination pertaining to neighbouring countries, the cartographic News Service and Pan Asian newspaper alliance, a photo agency, Some other non-wire agencies provide news and analysis in specific perspectives.

Since 1976 the non-aligned countries representatives have taken note of the persistent and serious disparities and imbalance in the global information situation and its adverse effects on non-aligned countries. Dependence on big international agencies made these agencies the arbiters of world reality for; developing countries. This accounted for much of the biased reporting in the Western media about developing countries. There was hardly any news; about developing countries unless it be of disaster or: disturbances coups, murders or sex. The stupendous tasks of development or changes being brought out in villages and towns found no mention. Some of the Western media even used reporting as an adjunct to project the foreign policies of their countries; and in certain cases even for acting as cover for intelligence agencies.

Information ministers of the non-aligned countries who met at new Delhi between 8-13 July 1976 therefore stressed the need to liberate their information and mass media from the colonial legacy and expressed their collective determination to rectify this situation. To give practical shape to this the Non-Aligned News Agencies pool was set up on 13 July 1976. The basic philosophy of the New pool, as stated by Shri H. K.L. Bhagat at a three-day international Seminar on improving News Pool held on 25-27 April 1984 in New Delhi, was the right of each country to participate in the global process of communication on an equitable and just basis.

It is a system of news exchange based on professional cooperation, equality, coordination and collective- self reliance among the 87 Pool partners. This pool transmits more than 60000 words around the world each day. India is currently having direct communication links with Belgrade, Djakarta, Bahrain, Havana, Colombo, Hanoi and Kuala Lumpur through satellite and with Dhaka and Islamabad through terrestrial link. The Press trust of India operates the non-aligned news agencies pool from India. The working of this Pool has however raised some misgivings. Critics of the pool allege that no thought has been given to ensure internal democratisation, objectivity and credibility. The government control can lead to controlled versions of news. The supporters of the pool on the other hand argue that it is not an inward looking closed circuit system of information. The objective is to supplement and not to supplant the existing translational news agencies. The setting up of the Non -aligned news Agencies Pool is only an attempt at greater flow of developmental news among the non-aligned countries. To this end, the creation of a full-fledged Third World news agency to disseminate the non aligned point of view on a global scale was suggested at the Namedia meet held in New Delhi between 9 and 12 December 1983. The conference also asked non-aligned nations to do much more than what they have done so far to increase the flow of information among their own people and among non-aligned countries by reducing tariffs and developing news agencies. They also urged professionalists to intensify their endeavours to widen and strengthen the base of free and balanced flow of communication and evolve commonly acceptable norms to improve the news pools credibility and utility.

15

Publication of Newspaper

One of the great advantages of democracy is that it provides for peaceful voluntary adjustment of disputes through negotiation as an alternative to their settlement by force or fiat. Democracy has accordingly been described as institutionalised peaceful settlement of disputes, making provision for ballots instead of bullets and for counting of heads instead of cracking them Peaceful settlement of controversies being an essential ingredient of democracy, it would follow that *bandhs,* agitations and street demonstrations have not much relevance in a true democracy. As things, however, are, we find that they have become a permanent feature of our public life. Not only that, they create problems of law and order and consume at good part of the time of our law enforcement agencies.

Democracy is a delicate form of government which rests for its successful functioning on conditions which are rather precarious but all the same vital. It postulates that despite difference son matters of detail, emphasis and degree, there should be a broad consensus on major national issues like the fundamental structure of society and form of government. Where, however, the differences and animosities between the winning party and the losing party reach such a point that the losing party entertains apprehensions about its political and physical survival, there arises real danger to democracy. Likewise, democratic structure faces a serious threat when the party defeated at the polls does not reconcile itself to the verdict of the electorate and refuses peaceably to lose.

In either event there arises a grave risk of constitutional barriers being brushed aside. It, therefore, becomes imperative in a living democracy that the victors and the vanquished at the polls should both abide by the rules of the game. Democracy can indeed work properly upon the assumption that the minority will accept the rule of the majority and will not take matters to the streets and the majority in turn will not rule too oppressively and pay due attention to the view of the minority even though it ultimately does not accept it. In other words, both the majority and the minority have rights as well as obligations.

The Tolerance

Tolerance of criticism and dissent is the most essential attribute of democracy. In fact democracy is so conceived that criticism of the ruling party, instead of being a weapon of destruction, becomes an instrument of better government. Despite that ideological basis of democratic polity, we find that there is increasing allergy to criticism and every attempt is made to hush it. Democracy postulates an open society. It rests upon accountability of those in power for their doings and conduct to the public. This is possible only if there is no attempt to put an official cloak of secrecy on the acts of those in power, and to whittle down freedom of information. As things are, there persists a strong impression that an official cloak of secrecy is being used to cover the lapses, bunglings and even misconduct of those in power. This is most unfortunate. Undoubtedly a country can have some national secrets. There can also be no doubt that in certain spheres of government, we have to maintain secrecy. It would, however, be wrong to extend the cloak of secrecy to cover and hide the lapses of those in power. The best safeguard for protection of legitimate official secrets is the credibility of those in power. Secrecy can be maintained, if credibility is preserved.

Excessive adulation amounting almost to deification of the individual in power is another danger, which we have to guard against, for inevitably it degenerates into a personality cult which, whatever its relevance in dictatorship, is the antithesis of democracy. Democracy postulates that the nation is greater than the party, and the party is greater than the individual. Excessive adulation of the individual paves the way to dictatorship and an authoritarian regime. We must beware of warning that no nation can be grateful at the cost of its honour in the same way as no man can be grateful at the cost of his honour, and no woman can be grateful at the cost of her chastity.

Democracy and liberty are twin sisters. In fact the trinity of democracy, liberty and the rule of law is the presiding deity of all liberal societies. Certain basic rights and civil liberties are an essential part of democracy. We have indeed enshrined them in Part III of the Constitution under the head

"Fundamental Rights". We legitimately take pride that our Constitution provides for them. It has, however, to be realised that rights postulate corresponding obligations. Awareness of obligations is the *sine qua non* of all progress.

Democracy makes some assumptions about the capacity of the people, and it presumes the presence of certain material and intellectual conditions favourable to the exercise of that capacity. Where large sections of the population have perpetually to think of the means of bare subsistence, they would not have much interest in political issues. For starving people, as also for people in dire poverty, discussion of general political issues and democratic values is often teasing dilettantism and a luxurious exercise. The danger of money power having sway in such an atmosphere and of polluting the purity of the electoral process is also immense. For the ultimate success, long life and durability of the democratic process, it is essential that the economic conditions of the people should be improved. Economic betterment of the bulk of the population, in the ultimate analysis, is the factor upon which the reality of democracy depends. A few cases of affluence and luxury in a vast desert of poverty and privation constitute dangerous irritants for the health and even survival of democracy. When a sense of class exploitation reaches deep into the masses of the population, democratic institutions are put to severe strain.

Democracy postulates adherence to the norms of democratic behaviour. Recent happenings in legislative chambers with rowdy scenes, physical assaults and even grossly indecent behaviour will not go with the democratic temper. Another disturbing feature is that individuals and their lapses and weaknesses, rather than policies, consume most of the time of the legislatures in India. It has to be emphasised in this context that the nation has to spend a huge amount for every minute during which the legislature is in session. Disruptions of the legislative session, because of unparliamentary behaviour and conduct, result in an unnecessary drain and undue strain on the public exchequer. Still another disturbing feature is that the debating skill and reasoned arguments are at a discount, while lung practice, theatrical gimmicks and intemperate language are being increasingly looked upon as hallmarks of success.

Democracy also contemplates that the forum for testing whether the leader of the party in power enjoys the confidence and support of the majority of legislators should be the floor of the legislature itself. It would be wholly wrong for the constitutional head of the State, as has been done by some Governors, to usurp that function and make himself the arbiter in the matter. He can assume this role only in the contingency of the head of the government declining to test his majority support on the floor of the legislature at an early date. This apart, any attempt by the constitutional head to do so would be an unwarranted encroachment on the power and function of the legislature.

The State was also ordained by the Directive Principles to regard the raising of the level of nutrition and the standard of living of the people and the improvement of public health, as among its primary duties. The fact that in certain areas of the country the people have still to walk for miles together to procure drinking water, and that because of lack of proper nourishment and want of adequate medical facilities, we come across sunken cheeks and lustreless eyes is a sad reflection on that solemn pledge.

One of our failures lies in the insufficient attention paid to improving the living conditions of people in rural areas. As long as there is a big disparity in living standards of people in rural and urban areas, this exodus from rural to urban areas is bound to continue. Such an exodus can only be checked, if we provide gainful employment to people in rural areas throughout the year.

The Directive Principles enjoined upon the State a duty within the limits of its economic capacity and development to make effective provision for securing the right to work. As against that we find that there has been a sharp increase in the number of unemployed since the coming into force of the Constitution. The tragedy is that amongst those unemployed, we have a large number of engineers, technicians and others possessing technical qualifications.

It is also necessary to strike a note of caution against any tendency to allow ideological affinity for socialism being used as a masquerade for diversion of State funds to public sector undertaking yielding no profit and causing a financial drain. Large-scale nationalisation must justify itself in economic terms and the long-term interests of the public. By no means can it avoid the rigour of financial discipline and demands of accountability.

Material and Documents

Newspaper means any material or document other than a book on which the words are written or printed. A paper printed daily or weekly. According to the Press and Registration of Books Act, 1867, newspaper means any printed periodical work containing public news or comments on public news. A newspaper is classified into three categories such as big newspaper, medium newspaper and small newspaper. According to explanation given for the purpose of clause (b) Section 5 of the Press Council Act, 1978, a newspaper shall be deemed to be:

(1) *Big newspaper*, if the total circulation of all its editions exceeds 50,000 copies for each issue;

(2) *Medium newspaper,* if the total circulation of all its editions exceeds 15,000 copies but does not exceed 50,000 copies for each issue;

(3) *Small newspaper,* if the total circulation of all its editions does not exceed 15,000 copies for each issue.

Newsletter : A newsletter is a publication in letter-size format usually issued periodically. It is a sheet containing news issued to members of a group or organisation.

For instance, a newsletter from the cricket association, the consumer association etc.

Editor : In the press the word editor is frequently used. The editor is a person who edits a newspaper. He prepares a manuscript or newspaper for publication. According to the Press and Registration of Books Act, 1867, the editor means the person who controls the selection of the matter published in a newspaper. Accordingly paper news, *i.e.,* any document including a newspaper other than a book. It further provided that book includes every volume, part or division of a volume and pamphlet in any language and every sheet of music, map, chart or plan separately printed.

Editorial : The matter or news in a newspaper written by an editor or belonging to editors. The editorial is a leading article in a newspaper. It consists of comment on the news, and opinion expressed by the news organisation.

Edition : Newspapers containing the same matter; printed during one press run. In other words, the number of copies of a newspaper printed at a time.

Publication : Publication means:

(a) in the case of a literary, dramatic, musical or artistic work, the issue of copies of the work to the public in sufficient quantities;

(b) in the case of a cinematograph film, the sale or hire or offer for sale or hire of the film or copies thereof to the public;

(c) in the case of a record, the issue of records to the public in sufficient quantities;

but does not, except as otherwise expressly provided in the Copyright Act, include :

(i) in the case of literary, dramatic or musical work, the issue of any records recording such work;

(ii) in the case of a work of sculpture or an architectural work of art, the issue of photographs and engravings of such work. (Section 3 of the Copyright Act, 1957).

Publication of Newspaper : Publication of newspapers should be strictly in accordance with the rules laid down for the purpose. Section 5 of the Press and Registration of Books Act, 1867, lays down rules concerning publication of newspapers. The relevant rules under this section as to publication of newspapers are as under :

(1) Without prejudice to the provisions of section 3, every copy of every such newspaper shall contain the names of the owner and editor thereof printed clearly on such copy and also the date of its publication.

(2) The printer and the publisher of every such newspaper shall appear in person or by agent authorised in this behalf in accordance with rules made before a District, Presidency or Sub-Divisional Magistrate within whose local jurisdiction such newspaper shall be printed or published, and shall make and subscribe, in duplicate, the following declaration:

"I. A.B., declare that I am the printer (or publisher or printer and publisher) of the newspaper entitled... and to be printed or published, or to be printed and published, as the case may be at..."

And the last blank in this form of declaration shall be filled up with a true and precise account of the premises where the printing or publication is conducted.

(a) Every declaration under rule (2) shall specify the title of the newspaper, the language in which it is to be published and the periodicity of its publication and shall contain such other particulars as may be prescribed.

(b) Where the printer or publisher of a newspaper making a declaration under rule 2 is not the owner thereof, the declaration shall specify the name of the owner and shall also be accompained by an authority in writing from the owner authorising such person to make and subscribe such declaration.

(c) A declaration in respect of a newspaper made under rule (2) and authenticated under section 6 shall be necessary before the newspaper can be published.

(d) Where the title of any newspaper or its language or the periodicity of its publication is changed, the declaration shall cease to have effect and a new declaration shall be necessary before the publication of the newspaper can be continued.

(e) As often as the ownership of a newspaper is changed, a new declaration shall be necessary.

(3) As often as the place of printing of publication is changed, a new declaration shall be necessary:

Provided that where the change is for a period not exceeding thirty days and the place of printing or publication after the change is within the local jurisdiction of the Magistrate referred to in rule (2), no new declaration shall be necessary if :

(a) a statement relating to the change is furnished to the said Magistrate within twenty-four hours thereof; and

(b) the printer or publisher or the printer and publisher of the newspaper continues to be the same.

(4) As often as the printer or the publisher who shall have made such declaration as is aforesaid shall leave India for a period exceeding ninety days or where such printer or publisher is by infirmity or otherwise rendered incapable of carrying out his duties for a period exceeding ninety

days in circumstances not involving the vacation of his appointment, a new declaration shall be necessary.

(5) Every declaration made in respect of newspaper shall be void, where the newspaper does not commence publication:

(a) Within six weeks of the authentication of the declaration, in the case of a newspaper to be published once a week or oftener;

(b) Within three months of the authentication of the declaration, in the case of any other newspaper; and

(c) In every such case, a new declaration shall be necessary before the newspaper can be published.

(6) Where, in any period of three months, any daily, tri-weekly, biweekly, weekly or fortnightly newspaper publishes issues the number of which is less than half of what should have been published in accordance with the declaration made in respect thereof, the declaration shall cease to have effect and a new declaration shall be necessary before the publication of the newspaper can be continued.

(7) Where any other newspaper has ceased publication for a period exceeding twelve months, every declaration made in respect thereof shall cease to have effect, and a new declaration shall be necessary before the newspaper can be republished.

(8) Every existing declaration in respect of a newspaper shall be cancelled by the Magistrate before whom a new declaration is made and subscribed in respect of the same.

Provided that no person who does not ordinarily reside in India, or who has not attained majority in accordance with the provisions of the Indian Majority Act, 1875, or of the law to which he is subject in respect of the attainment of majority, shall be permitted to make the declaration prescribed by this section, nor shall any such person edit a newspaper.

(d) prescribing the manner in which a Register may be maintained and the particulars which it may contain;

(e) prescribing the particulars which an annual statement to be furnished by the publisher of a newspaper to the Press Registrar may contain;

(f) prescribing the form and manner in which an annual statement or any returns, statistics or other information may be furnished to the Press Registrar;

(g) prescribing the fees for furnishing copies extracts from the Registrar and the manner in which such copies may be furnished;

(h) prescribing the manner in which a certificate of registration may be issued in respect of a newspaper; (i) prescribing the form in which, and the time within which, annual reports may be prepared by the Press Registrar and forwarded to the Central Government.

Every rule made under this section shall be laid as soon as may be after it is made before each House of Parliament while it is in session for a total period of thirty days which may be comprised in one session or in two or more successive sessions, and if, before the expiry of the session immediately following the session or the successive sessions aforesaid both Houses agree in making any modification in the rule or both Houses agree that the rule should not be made, the rule shall thereafter have effect only in such modified form or be of no effect, as the case may be; so, however, that any such modification or annulment shall be without prejudice to the validity of anything previously done under that rule.

The Registration : The Press and Registration of Books Act, 1867 (Act 25 of 1867) has been enacted in India for the regulation of printing presses and newspapers for the preservation of office of books and newspapers printed in India and for the Registration of such books and newspapers. The press laws enquiry committee which was set up by the Government to enquire into the press laws made certain recommendations in 1948 for amending the

Press andRegistration of Books Act, 1867. Subsequently the Press and Registration of Books (Amendment) Bill 1952 was introduced in Parliament and the amending Act 55 of 1955 came into force and amending Act 26 of 1960.

Right and Responsibility

"A free press is responsible to its readers and to them alone. It cannot be either the slave or the lackey of Government."

"One of the best tests of professionalism is the ability to present objectively a story about someone or some event with which the writer or newspaper is in strong agreement."

No country can make law abridging the freedom of speech, or of the press.

(1) Bill of Rights derives what is to be perhaps the most basic ethical tenet of journalism. The press is independent of government.

(2) The Founding Fathers of the then infant Indian nation were suspicious of the tendency of Government, even the best-intentioned government, to become tyrannical at times. Governments are composed of human beings, and human beings can and do commit wrongs. Thus the authors of our Constitution envisaged the press as a kind of social critic with a role apart and distinct from that of government.

Journalists are as patriotic as the next person in pursuing a national interest, and nothing in our bill of rights says that newspapers and government cannot cooperate on occasion. But the clear intent of the founder was that the press and government should not be in bed together. They are natural adversaries with different functions and each must respect the role of the other. Sometimes a free press can be a distinct annoyance and embarrassment to a particular government, but that is one of the prices of liberty. A free press is responsible to its readers and to them alone. It cannot be either the slave or the lackey of Government.

(3) Independence is at the heart of any statement of ethical principles respecting the conduct of the press. A

> newspaper's proprietor may choose to ally it with a particular political party or interest, but journals in our country are trying to be politically independent as well as independent of Government. This means not that they refrain from endorsing an individual party or candidate, but that they owe no prior allegiance and make the endorsement as an exercise of their independence. The decision is voluntary on the part of the proprietors and editors.

From this it follows that an independent press must cherish that role by resisting pressures of all kinds— from local as well as national governments, from special interest groups in the community, from powerful individuals, from advertisers. This is a noble standard that is sometimes more difficult to follow in a small, community than in a large one. It may be relatively easy for a large and well financed newspaper to risk the displeasure of a particular interest group or advertisers; but for a small paper, where the support of such an advertiser or interest has a direct bearing on management's ability to meet the payaroll, it takes courage to resist pressure. Some papers exhibit more courage than others, but respect for the principles is one of the responsibilities the press owes its special constitutional role. Refusal to be intimated by any source ought to be a badge of the journalist's profession.

From this also follows the point that the newspaper and its staff should exemplify independence in their own actions. Not only should they be independent in fact, but, as the British Say of justice, they must be seen to be independent. A newspaper that rewards its friends with an unwarranted puff story of fawning editorials will not long be respected. A newspaper whose reporters also are on the payroll of a special interest or accept free trips or lavish gifts will find it hard to be convincing in its criticisms of corruption or other ethical practices in government.

Occasionally newspapers attempt to justify the acceptance of gifts or services. A conscientious reporter will hardly be corrupted, so the argument goes, by a free meal or ticket to a sports event or the theatre. Perhaps not, but appearances are important. Newspapers ought to pay their own way.

Admittedly, in small communities, journalists sometimes may encounter problems in maintaining a completely independent role. There are pressures to participate in volunteer services or in clubs and business associations or even in local government. Conflicts of interest may arise frequently. Journalists cannot expect to be monks walled apart from the community. But neither can they serve two masters with opposing interests. A conscientious editor or reporter will at least be aware of the conflicts and keep his professional responsibilities foremost in mind. Not surprisingly, the independent journalist may find himself in a lonely position with few or no close friends in the community where he works. Sometimes his best friends inevitably must be other journalists. But that is one of the prices he must pay for the career and challenge he has chosen.

What special responsibilities does the press incur in return for the protected status its freedom enjoys ? None that is explicitly spelled out. A newspaper has the right to be captious or partisan or untruthful or bigoted or whatever else its conscience allows it to be. And, although newspapers are answerable to the laws of treason, sedition and libel, still within a very large compass they set their own responsibilities. The idea behind this is that from the clash of opinions and ideas presented by a freepress, ultimately something resembling truth emerges. "Though all the winds of doctrine were let loose to play upon the earth", wrote John Milton in his *Aeropagitica,* "so Truth be in the field, we do injuriously be licensing and prohibiting to misdoubt her strength. Let her and Falsehood grapple; who ever know Truth to the worse in a free and open encounter"?

That may be impressive as a philosophical doctrine, but you and I know that things do not always work that way in practice. Truth does not always emerge unless someone digs it out; and there is no single patented version of what constitutes truth. In a community where only one newspaper services —and this is increasingly the pattern in the United States — a reader may not encounter differing opinions unless the newspaper chooses to present them. Radio and television are not always an effective substitute.

But this is not such a calamity as it once would have seemed, for the reason that there is more and more sense of professionalism among our journalists. This means recognition of the importance of fair and balanced reporting in which opinions that may differ from those of the writer, or the newspaper, or a government official, are nevertheless accurately portrayed. In fact, one of the best tests of professionalism, is the ability to present objectively a story about someone or some event with which the writer or newspapers is in strong disagreement.

A good newspaper does not deliberately separate its own opinions from the objective presentation of facts. News stories and analysis are presented on the news pages, with the regions and sources identified wherever possible. The newspaper's own opinions are presented on the editorial page, which also may carry signed columns from syndicated writers or staff members of the newspaper itself.

Indian newspapers today are beginning to recognise the responsibility to open their letters' columns and opposite-editorial pages to views of every perception. Many newspapers receive far more letters than they can publish and, therefore, must choose what they regard as a fair representation; editing for libel, decency and germaneness. Some newspapers .are the employee's ombudsmen, whose duty is to be a sort of public advocate in listening to complaints, offering remedies and appraising the performance of the paper. Most newspapers also recognise the responsibility to correct errors promptly, often in a box that appears in the same place in each issue.

Of course a newspaper may endorse the highest standards of ethical behaviour and still have its reputation sullied by the behaviour of its staff members. Arrogance and contempt for the rights of others are one of the surest ways to bring this about. Newspapers need to guard very carefully against undue intrusions on the privacy of persons about whom they are reporting. A photograph of a person jumping off a building or plunging into a fire may be dramatic, but editors ought to debate long and hard over whether they are violating someone's rights or dignity by publishing it. Does the publication serve a defensible purpose, one that will be understood by readers ? Or is it using an indignity to pander to curiosity ?

Reporters enjoy no special rights beyond those of other citizens. They must be forcible in pursuing facts. Indeed, one of the most important functions of a free press is to serve as a watchdog. But its staff members have no dispensation to be rude or discourteous. Television has many sins of its own, but one thing it purveys very quickly to viewers is whether reporters at a news conference are behaving arrogantly or with unnecessary brusqueness. Some, lamentably, seem to have become actors who view their function as making the news, not merely reporting it.

Apart from idiosyncratic behaviour, newspapers may also be affected by a phenomenon that I call "prizemanship"—the presentation of a story either on the part of the reporter or by a broader decision of newspaper management in a fashion calculated to win one of the prizes now offered to newspapers or individual journalists. A few years ago *The Washington Post* won a Pulitzer Prize for a story about an eight-year narcotics addict. Subsequent investigation by others led to an acknowledgement by the reporter, that she had made up the story in order to illustrate a situation. She resigned, and the newspaper returned the prize in embarrassment. I have no doubt that there are other similar fictional stories unidentified. Even if you don't invent "facts" it is relatively easy to present them in such a way as to make a dramatic impression upon prize judges.

Prizes are not bad, but the best ones are those that are conferred by the action of outsiders without the knowledge or participation of the individual journalist or newspaper. Conscientious journalists and newspapers must resist the temptation to display or doctor the story in such a way as to advance a purpose not directly related to the news.

There is one further precept in my own code of journalistic conduct—beyond independence, non-involvement, objectivity, fairness and willingness to correct errors. That is a recognition of our own fallibility. Journalists have no special mandate from God, and a little humility on our part is much in order. The truth sometimes has many sides. No one has a monopoly on it. Even in the dedicated pursuit of truth, error is frequent and innocent persons may suffer. A cardinal journalistic sin, in my view, is that journalists may tend to take themselves too seriously and have an inflated view of their own importance. Therefore, I should like to see posted above the desk of every member of the press the advice Oliver Cromwell gave the General Assembly of the Church of Scotland in 1650 : "I beseech you, in the bowels of Christ, think it possible you may be mistaken."

Press Council : The role of the Press in a democracy is that of a watchdog for the interests of the people. But if this powerful watchdog is not reasonably restrained or disciplined, it might run berserk to bite the people, whom it is supposed to serve. Barring occasional lapses, well-established newspapers in India have generally maintained standards of professional rectitude even in the face of coercive and corruptive influences. However, unfortunately, there is a section of the Press, known as Yellow Journalism, which frequently indulges in smut and slime games, smear campaigns, scurrilous, sensational, baseless and graceless writings. The abuse of this Press freedom by a few delinquents tends to undermine the credibility and confidence of the Press, as a whole, in the public mind. The problem is how to curb or deal with this evil ? Should it be controlled from without, or by law through a governmental agency or other external mechanism with a plentitude of punitive powers, derived from a plethora of restrictive legislation ? It so, would not such external control involving excessive interference by the government or its agencies, in effect, negate the freedom itself ? Another factor which has to be taken into consideration is that the range and terrain of moral restrictions on the freedom of the Press are not always co-terminus with those prescribed by law. Indeed, the range of ethics in its application to particular cases, is often wider than that of law. The observance of the professional ethics, therefore, is the subjective duty of the Press itself. In the performance of this ethical duty, it is imperative that the Press should be inspired by the consciousness that abuse of this freedom, even if not legally punishable, tarnishes the fair name of the Press, and, therefore, deserves to be censured by fellow journalists.

Views of the Mahatma

The whole problem, with its parameters and a key to its solution was pithily put in a nutshell by Mahatma Gandhi— who was an eminent journalist in his own right—in these words: "The sole aim of journalism should be service. The newspaper Press is a great power, but just as unchained torrent of waste submerges the whole countryside and devastates crops, even so an uncontrolled pen serves but to destroy. If the control is from without, it proves more poisonous than want of control. It can be profitable only when exercised from within."

The first British Royal Commission on the Press (1949) also felt that the best way, consistent with the freedom of the press, or maintaining a proper relationship between the press and society, was self-regulation by the press itself. This is the basis of the concept of a Press Council.

The first Press Council or Court of Honour was set up in Sweden, in 1916. It is a voluntary body composed of the representatives of the press. There is also an Ombudsman of the press who is generally a professional judge. All complaints against the press are first screened by him, and if they are found worth inquiry, are forwarded to the Press Council for consideration. By 1980, there were 50 Press and Media Councils in the various countries of the world. A few of them, including the Press Councils of India, Italy and Turkey have been set up under statutes.

Press Council of India : Council Act, 1965, was enacted, and under it, the first Press Council was set up in 1966. The Act was, however, repealed in 1975 during the Emergency, and the Press Council was abolished. The Act was re-enacted substantially on the same terms, in 1978, and the Press Council was re-established under it, in 1979. The Council is a body corporate having perpetual succession and a common seal and shall by the said name sue and be sued.

Objectives of the Press Council : The twin objects of the Press Council of India are embodied in the Press Council Act, 1978. Section 13 of the Act of 1978 states that the objects of the Press Council are to preserve the freedom of the press and to maintain and improve the standards of newspapers and the news agencies in India.

(1) The Council shall consist of a chairman and twenty-eight other members.

(2) The Chairman shall be a person nominated by a Committee consisting of the Chairman of the Council of States (Rajya Sabha), the Speaker of the House of the People (Lok Sabha) and a person elected by the members of the Council under sub-section (6) and the nomination so made shall take effect from the date on which it is notified by the Central Government in the Official Gazette.

(3) Of the other members:

(a) Thirteen shall be nominated in accordance with such procedure as may be prescribed from among the working journalists, of whom six shall be editors of newspapers and the remaining seven shall be working journalists other than editors, so, however, that the number of such editors and working journalists other than editors in relation to newspapers published in Indian languages shall be not less than three and four respectively;

(b) six shall be nominated in accordance with such procedure as may be prescribed from among persons who own or carry on the business of management of newspapers, so, however, that there shall be two representatives from each of the categories of big newspapers, medium newspapers and small newspapers;

(c) one shall be nominated in accordance with such procedures as may be prescribed from among persons who manage news agencies;

(d) there shall be persons having special knowledge or practical experience in education and science, law, and literature and culture of whom respectively one shall be nominated by the University Grants Commission, one by the Bar Council of India and one by the Sahitya Academy;

(e) five shall be members of Parliament of whom three shall be nominated by the Speaker from among the members of the House of the People (Lok Sabha) and two shall be nominated by the Chairman of the Council of the States (Rajya Sabha) from among its members; Provided that no working journalist who owns, or carries on the business of management of any newspaper shall be eligible for nomination under clause (a); Provided further that the nominations under clause (a), and clause (b) shall be so made that among the persons nominated there is not more than one person interested in any newspaper or group of newspapers under the same control or management.

(4) Before making any nomination under clause (a), clause (b) or clause (c) of sub-section (3), the Central Government in the case of the first Council and the retiring Chairman of the previous Council in the case of any subsequent Council shall, in the prescribed manner, invite panels of names comprising twice the number of members to be nominated from such associations of persons of the categories referred to in the said clause (a), clause (b) or clause (c) as may be notified in this behalf by the Central Government in the case of the first Council and by the Council itself in the case of subsequent Councils;

Provided that where there is no association of persons of the category referred to in the said clause (c), the panels of name's shall be invited from such news agencies as may be notified as aforesaid.

(5) The Central Government shall notify the names of persons nominated as members under sub-section.

(a) In the Official Gazette and every such nomination shall take effect from the date on which it is notified.

(b) The members of the Council notified under sub-section (5) shall elect from among themselves in accordance with such procedure as may be prescribed, a person to be a member of the committee referred to in sub-section (2) and a meeting of the members of the Council for the purpose of such election shall be presided over by a person chosen from among themselves. (Section 5 of the Press Council Act 1978).

Term of Office

(1) Save as otherwise provided in this Section 6 the Chairman and other members shall hold office for a period of three years; Provided that the Chairman shall continue to hold such office until the Council is reconstituted in accordance with the provision of Section 5 or for a period of six months whichever is earlier.

(2) Where a person nominated as a member under clause (a), clause (b) or clause (c) of sub-section (3) of Section 5, is censured under the provisions of sub-section (1) of Section 14, he shall cease to be a member of the Council.

(3) The term of office of a member nominated under clause (e) of sub-section (3) of Section 5 shall come to an end as soon as he ceases to be a member of the House from which he was nominated.

(4) A member shall be deemed to have vacated his seat if he is absent without excuse, sufficient in the opinion of the Council, from three consecutive meetings of the Council.

(5) The Chairman may resign his office by giving notice in writing to the Central Government, and any other member may resign his office by giving notice in writing to the Chairman, and upon such resignation being accepted by the Central Government, or as the case may be, the Chairman or the member shall be deemed to have vacated his office.

(6) Any vacancy arising under sub-section (2), sub-section (3), sub-section (4) or sub-section (5) or otherwise shall be filled, as soon as may be, nomination in the same manner in which the member vacating office was nominated and the member so nominated shall hold office for the remaining period in which the member in whose place he is nominated would have held office.

(7) A retiring member shall be eligible for re-nomination for not more than one term. (Section 6 of the Press Council Act, 1978).

Functions of the Council : The Council may, in furtherance of its objects, perform the following functions, namely:

(a) to help newspapers and news agencies to maintain their independence;

(b) to build up a code of conduct for newspapers, news agencies and journalists in accordance with high professional standards;

(c) to ensure on the part of newspapers, news agencies and journalists, the maintenance of high standards of public taste and foster a due sense of both the rights and responsibilities of citizenship;

(d) to encourage the growth of a sense of responsibility among all those engaged in the profession of journalism;

(e) to keep under review any development likely to restrict the supply and dissemination of news of public interest and importance;

(f) to keep under review cases of assistance received by any newspaper or news agency in India from any foreign source including such cases as are referred to it by the Central Government or are brought to its notice by any individual, association of persons or any other organisation;

Provided that nothing in this clause shall preclude the Central Government from dealing with any case of assistance received by a newspaper or news agency in India from any foreign source in any other manner it thinks fit;

(g) to undertake studies of foreign newspapers, including those brought out by any embassy or other representative in India of a foreign state, their circulation and impact.

Explanation—For the purposes of this clause, the expression "foreign State" has the meaning assigned to it in Section 87 A of the Code of Civil Procedure, 1908;

(h) to promote a proper functional relationship among all classes of persons engaged in the production or publication of newspapers or in news agencies;

Provided that nothing in this clause shall be deemed to confer on the council any functions in regard to dispute to which the Industrial Disputes Act, 1947, applies;

(i) to concern itself with developments such as concentration of or other aspects of ownership of newspaper and news agencies which may affect the independence of the press;

(j) to undertake such studies as may be entrusted to the Council and to express its opinion in regard to any matter referred to it by the Central Government;

(k) to do such other acts as may be incidental or conducive to the discharge of the above function.

This apart, the Act also confers an advisory role on the Council which can undertake studies and express its opinion in regard to any Bill, Legislation, Law or other matter touching the Press and convey its opinion to the Government or the persons concerned.

The Council is entitled to entertain and deal with complaints against the Press or by the Press. Ordinarily, it takes cognizance on a complaint filed by the person aggrieved. But it has authority to take congnizance *suo moto* also. The complaint is first processed by the Council's secretariat, and if the Chairman is of the opinion that a particular complaint does not disclose sufficient grounds for conducting an inquiry, the Council may not take cognizance of it. If the Chairman finds that there are sufficient grounds for holding an inquiry, a show-cause notice is issued to the respondent—whether he be the editor or publisher of the newspaper, or the Government or its agency. If the subject matter of the complaint is sub judice in a court of law, the Council ceases to have jurisdiction to hold an inquiry into the matter.

Inquiry Committees : The complaints, after initial processing by the Secretariat, are entrusted to either of the two Inquiry Committees of the Council. Representatives of the parties are also heard. Lawyers engaged by the parties are also allowed to act on behalf of their clients. The hearings before the Inquiry Committees and the Council are open to the public; the decisions are taken, after the public have withdrawn from the meeting room. The decisions of the Inquiry Committee are in the form of recommendations, which are not announced unless approved, with or without modification, by the Council. The decisions of the Council are published in its Quarterly Review and Annual Reports.

The Powers : The Press Council of India is vested with certain powers of a Civil Court. Section 15 of the Press Council Act, 1978, gives the council the same powers throughout India as are vested in a Civil Court while trying a suit under the Code of Civil Procedure, 1908. The general powers of the Council under the section are:

(1) For the purpose of performing its functions or holding any enquiry under the Press Council Act, 1978, the council shall have the same powers throughout India as are vested in a Civil Court while trying a suit under the Code of Civil Procedure, 1908, in respect of the following matters, namely:

(a) summoning and enforcing the attendance of persons and examining them on oath;

(b) requiring the discovery and inspection of documents;

(c) receiving evidence on affidavits;

(d) requisitioning any public records or copies thereof from any court or office;

(e) issuing commissions for the examination of witnesses or documents; and

(f) any other matter, which may be prescribed.

(2) Nothing in sub-section (1) shall be deemed to compel any newspaper, news agency, editor or journalist to disclose the source of any news or information published by that newspaper or received or reported by that news agency, editor or journalist.

(3) Every inquiry held by the Council shall be deemed to be a judicial proceeding within the meaning of sections 193 and 228 of the Indian Penal Code.

(4) The Council may, if it considers it necessary for the purpose of carrying out its objects or for the performance of any of its functions under this Act make such observations, as it may think fit, in any of its decisions or reports, respecting the conduct of any authority, including Government.

Censure Power: The powers and procedure of the Press Council are exercisable not only in respect of enquiries against the newspapers as studied under the functions of the council but also in respect of enquiries held at the "instance of the newspapers against the Government or against any other person. AIR: 1975 Delhi 79(82); 1974 Rajadhani LR 632. The power to censure is given under section 14 of the Press Council Act, 1978. Accordingly:

(1) Where, on receipt of a complaint made to it or otherwise, the council has reason to believe that a newspaper or news agency has offended against the standards of journalistic ethics or public taste or that an editor or a working journalist has committed any professional misconduct, the Council may, after giving the newspaper,

or news agency, the editor or journalist concerned an opportunity of being heard, hold an inquiry in such manner as may be prescribed by regulations made under the Press Council Act, 1978 and, if it is satisfied that it is necessary so to do, it may, for reasons to be recorded in writing, warn, admonish or censure the newspaper, the news agency, the editor or the journalist or disapprove the conduct of the editor or the journalist, as the case may be:

Provided that the council may not take cognizance of a complaint if, in the opinion of the chairman, there is no sufficient ground for holding an inquiry.

(2) If the council is of the opinion that it is necessary or expedient in the public interest so to do, it may require any newspaper to publish therein in such manner as the council thinks fit, any particulars,relating to any inquiry under this section against a newspaper or news agency, an editor or a journalist working therein, including the name of such newspaper, news agency, editor or journalist.

(3) Nothing in sub-section (1) shall be deemed to empower the council to hold an inquiry into any matter in respect of which any proceeding is pending in a court of law.

(4) The decision of the council under sub-section (1) or sub-section (2), as the case may be, shall be final and shall not be questioned in any court of law.

Regulations : The council is empowered to make regulations, with the prior approval of the Central Government. The Regulations may be for:

(a) Regulating the meetings of the council or any committee and the procedure for conducting the business.

(b) Specifying the terms and conditions of services of the employees appointed by the council.

(c) Regulating the manner of holding any enquiry under the Press Council Act, 1978.

(d) Delegating to the Chairman or the Secretary of the Council any of its powers.

(e) Any other matter for which provision may be made by regulation.

The Central Government shall cause every regulation made under the Press Council Act to be laid, as soon as may be after it is made, before each House of Parliament, while it is in session, for a total period of thirty days which may be comprised in one session or in two or more successive sessions, and if, before the expiry of the session immediately following the session or successive sessions aforesaid, both Houses agree in making any modification in the regulation or both Houses agree that the regulation should not be made, the regulation shall thereafter have effect only in such modified form or be of no effect, as the case may be; so, however, that any modification or annulment shall be without prejudice to the validity of anything previously done under that regulation.

The Central Government is empowered to make rules to carry out the purposes of the council. The Government makes rules consulting the council. Section 25 of the Press Council Act, 1978, gives power to the Central Government in particular, and without prejudice to the generality of the foregoing powers, such rules may provide for all or any of the following matters, namely:

(a) the procedure for nomination of member of the council;

(b) the manner in which panels of names may be invited;

(c) the procedure for election of a member of the committee;

(d) the allowances or fees to be paid to the members of the council for attending the meetings of the council, and other conditions of services of such members;

(e) the appointment of the Secretary and other employees of the council;

(f) the matters referred to in clause (f) of under paragraph of Civil Court Powers referred to above;

(g) the rates at which fees may be levied by the council;

(h) the forms in which, and the time within which the budget and annual report are to be prepared by the council;

(i) the manner in which the accounts of the council are to be maintained and audited.

Every rule made under this section shall be laid, as soon as may be after it is made, before each House of Parliament, while it is in session, for a total period of thirty days which may be comprised in one session or in two or more successive sessions, and if, before the expiry of the session immediately following the session or the successive sessions aforesaid, both Houses agree in making any modification in the rule or both Houses agree that the rule should not be made, the rule shall thereafter have effect only in such modified form or be of no effect, as the case may be; so, however, that any such modification or annulment shall be without prejudice to the validity of anything previously done under that rule.

Code of Conduct

"The question, whether or not, the Council should formulate code of conduct for journalists, has repeatedly cropped up. But, on each occasion, successive Press Councils, after due consideration of the question and its implications have consistently taken the view that it is neither feasible nor desirable or necessary to formulate a comprehensive rigid code of this kind. Because of their elusive nature these moral principles cannot be imprisoned in the strait jacket of rigid definition or formulas; nor do these notions of right or wrong, good or bad prevailing in the society at large, remain immutable or statics for ever. Forces unleashed by rapid social and technological changes are having an inexorable impact on the tastes and attitudes of the people and their expectations from the Press. This makes the problem more complex. These ethical norms are not absolute. They have relativity not only to other dynamic social factors involving a multitude of imponderables but also to the subject-matter, the situation, the facts and the circumstances of each case. For all these reasons, the Indian Press Council Act advisedly leaves it to the Council to "build up" this ethical code over a period of time on case-by-case basis.

The precedents set by the Council through adjudications apart the Act affords great latitude to the Council to improve upon the standards of journalism, through innovation or by articulating general guidelines for this purpose even without reference to specific case pending before it. Such broad guidelines have been articulated by the Council with respect to certain matters including coverage of communication disputes by the Press.

International Principles : Ten International Principles of Professional Ethics in Journalism formulated by the International and Regional Organization of Professional Journalists are:

1. People's RIGHT TO TRUE INFORMATION
2. The journalist's DEDICATION TO OBJECTIVE AND REALITY
3. The journalist's SOCIAL RESPONSIBILITY
4. The journalist's PROFESSIONAL INTEGRITY
5. Public ACCESS AND PARTICIPATION
6. Respect of PRIVACY AND HUMAN DIGNITY
7. Respect for PUBLIC INTEREST
8. Respect of UNIVERSAL VALUES AND DIVERSITY OF CULTURES
9. Elimination of WAR and other great EVILS CONFRONTING HUMANITY
10. Promotion of a NEW WORLD INFORMATION AND COMMUNICATION ORDER

Adaptation : Adaptation in relation to a literary work means any abridgement of the work. Adaptation under the Copyright Act, 1957 means:

(i) in relation to a dramatic work, the conversion of the work into a non-dramatic work;

(ii) in relation to a literary work or an artistic work, the conversion of the work into a dramatic work by way of performance in public or otherwise;

(iii) in relation to a literary or dramatic work; any abridgement of the work or any version of the work in which the story or action is conveyed, wholly or mainly by means of pictures in a form suitable for reproduction in a book, or in a newspaper, magazine or similar periodical; and

(iv) in relation to a musical work, any arrangement or transcription of the work. (Section 2 of the Copyright Act, 1957).

Meaning of Copyright : For the purpose of the Copyright Act, 1957, copyright means the exclusive right, by virtue of and subject to the provisions:

(a) in the case of a literary, dramatic or musical work, to do and authorise the doing of any of the following acts, namely:

(i) to reproduce the work in any material form;

(ii) to publish the work;

(iii) to perform the work in public;

(iv) to produce, reproduce, perform or publish any translation of the work;

(v) to make any cinematograph film or a record in respect of the work;

(vi) to communicate the work by radio-diffusion or to communicate to the public by a loudspeaker or any other similar instrument the radio diffusion of the work;

(vii) to make any adaptation of the work;

(viii) to do in relation to a translation or an adaptation of the work any of the acts specified in relation to the work in clauses (i) to (vi);

(b) in the case of an artistic work, to do or authorise the doing of any of the following acts, namely:

(i) to reproduce the work in any material form;

(ii) to publish the work;

(iii) to include the work in any cinematograph film;

(iv) to make any adaptation of the work;

(v) to do in relation to an adaptation of the work any of the acts specified in relation to the work in clauses (i) to (iii);

(c) in the case of a cinematograph film, to do or authorise the doing of any of the following acts, namely:

(i) to make a copy of the film;

(ii) to cause the film, in so far as it consists of visual images, to be seen in public and, in so far as it consists of sounds, to be heard in public;

(iii) to make any record embodying the recording in any part of the sound track associated with the film by utilising such sound track:

(iv) to communicate the film by radio-diffusion;

(d) in the case of a record, to do or authorise the doing of any of the following acts by utilising the record, namely:

(i) to make any other record embodying the same recording;

(ii) to cause the recording embodied in the record to be heard in public;

(iii) to communicate the recording embodied in the record by radio-diffusion.

Any reference in subsection (1) to the doing of any act in relation to work for a translation or an adaptation thereof shall include a reference to the doing of that act in relation to a substantial part thereof. (Section 14 of the Copyright Act, 1957).

Period of Copyright

Literary, Dramatic etc.: Copyright shall subsist in any literary, dramatic, musical or artistic work other than a photograph published within the life time of the author until 50 years from the beginning of the calendar year next following the year in which the author dies. (Section 22).

Anonymous and Pseudonymous Works : A copyright shall subsist until 50 years from the beginning of the calendar year next following the year in which the work is published in the case of literary, dramatic, musical or artistic work other than a photograph. (Section 23).

Posthumous Work : Term of copyright in case of posthumous work is also fixed. Copyright exists in the case of literary, dramatic or musical work or an engraving in which copyright subsist at the date of the death of the author or in the case of any such work of joint authorship are immediately before the date of the death of the author who dies last, but which or any adaptation of which has not been published before that date. In these cases copyright shall subsist until 50 years from the beginning of the calendar next following the year in which the work is first published or where an adaptation of the work is published in any earlier year. (Section 24).

Photographs : The term of copyright in photographs shall subsist until 50 years from the beginning of the calendar year next following the year in which the photograph is published. (Section 25).

Cinematograph Films : The period for which copyright shall subsist in the case of cinematograph films until 50 years from the beginning of calendar year next following the year in which the film is published. (Section 26).

Records : Copyright shall subsist in the case of a record for a period of 50 years from the beginning of the calendar year next following the year in which the record is published. (Section 27).

Government Works : Where Government is the first owner of the copyright, copyright Shall subsist until 50 years from the beginning of the calendar year next following the year in which the work is first published. (Section 28).

Works of International Organisations : Copyright shall subsist in the case of a work of an international organisation until 50 years from the beginning of the calendar year next following the year in which the work is first published. (Section 29).

Offences : Chapter XIII of the Copyright Act describes various offences and penalties. Sections 63-70 of the Act provide for offences. The following are the various offences :

Infringement of Copyright : Infringement of copyright or other rights conferred by the Copyright Act is an offence. It shall be punishable with imprisonment which may extend to one year or with fine or with both. Any person who knowingly infringes or abets the infringement of:

(a) The copyright in a work; or

(b) Any other right conferred by the Act. (Section 63)

Seizure of Infringed Copies : The police is empowered to seize infringing copies. Where a Magistrate takes cognizance of any offence of infringement of copyright in any work, it shall be lawful for any police officer not below the rank of sub-inspector to seize all copies wherever found without any warrant from the Magistrate. All the copies so seized shall be produced before Magistrate. If any person having an interest in any copies of a work seized may make an application to the Magistrate within fifteen days of such seizure for such copies to restore him. The Magistrate after hearing the applicant and the complainant and after making such further inquiry he may make such order as he deems fit. (Section 64).

Plates for Making Infringing Copies : The Act also imposes penalty by way of punishment with imprisonment which may extend to one year or with fine or with both. The offence attracts penalty if any person who knowingly makes or has in his possession any plate for the purpose of making infringing copies of any work in which copyright subsists. (Section 65).

Disposal of Copies : There is a provision for disposal of infringing copies or plates for the purpose of making infringing copies. The court may order that all copies of work or all plates in the possession of the offender to be delivered up to the owner of the copyright. This is whether the alleged offender is convicted or not. (Section 66).

False Entries in Register : An offence of making false entries in the register or producing or rendering false entries attracts penalty. The offender shall be punishable with imprisonment which may extend to one year or with fine or with both, if any person who :

(a) makes or causes to be made a false entry in the Register of Copyrights kept under this Act; or

(b) makes or causes to be made a writing falsely purporting to be a copy of any entry in such register; or

(c) produces or tenders or causes to be produced or tendered as evidence any such entry or writing knowing the same to be false. (Section 67).

Making False Statements : The Act imposes a penalty for making false statements for the purpose of deceiving or influencing any authority or officer. Any person who :

(a) with a view to deceiving any authority or officer in the execution of the provisions of the Act; or

(b) with a view to procuring or influencing the doing or omission of anything in relation to the Act, 1957, or any matter thereunder, makes a false statement or representation knowing the same to be false shall be punishable with imprisonment which may extend to one year or with fine or with both. (Section 68).

Offences by Companies : Where an offence has been committed by a company every person who is incharge and responsible to the company for the conduct of the business the person and the company shall be deemed to be guilty of such offence. He is not liable if he proves that the offence was committed without his knowledge or he exercised due diligence to prevent the commission of such offence. Where it is proved that the offence was committed with the consent or connivance or is attributable to any negligence on the part of any director, manager, secretary or other officer of the company, they shall be deemed to be guilty of that offence and shall be liable to be proceeded and punished. (Section 69).

Cognizance of Offences : Only Presidency Magistrate or a Magistrate of the first class shall try any offence under the Copyright Act, 1957. (Section 70).

Appels : A separate chapter is provided for appeals. Sections 71-73 of the Act deals with appeals against orders and procedure. Section 71 permits appeal against certain orders of the Magistrate under Sub-section (2) of Section 64 or Section 66. Sub-section (2) of Section 64 deals with the order of the Magistrate regarding against the application for infringing copies to be restored to him. Section 66 deals about disposal of infringing copies or plates for the purpose of making infringing copies. Under these sections any person aggrieved by the order may go on appeal within thirty days of the order. The appellate court may direct the execution of the order be stayed pending disposal of the appeal. (Section 71).

Section 72 deals with appeals against the orders of the Registrar of Copyrights and the Copyright Board. The aggrieved person may go on appeal to the Copyright Board against the final decision or order of the Registrar of the Copyrights within three months from the date of the order. Similarly, any aggrieved person may go on appeal to the High Court against the final decision or order of the Copyright Board within three months.

There shall be no appeal against a decision of the Copyright Board in respect of certain disputes to be decided by the Copyright Board alone. The High Court makes rules as to the procedure to be followed in respect of appeals.

Infringing Copy

(i) in relation to a literary, dramatic, musical or artistic work, a reproduction thereof otherwise than in the form of a cinematograph film;

(ii) in relation to a cinematograph film a copy of the film or a record embodying the recording in any part of the sound track associated with the film;

(iii) in relation to record, any such record embodying the same recording: and

(iv) in relation to a programme in which a broadcast reproduction right subsists, a record recording the programme, if such reproduction, copy or record is made or imprinted in contravention of the provisions of this Act. [Section 2(m) of the Copyright Act, 1957].

The following are the circumstances as to when copyright in a work shall be deemed to be infringed:

(a) When any person, without a licence granted by the owner of the copyright or the Registrar of Copyrights under the Copyright Act or in contravention of the conditions of a licence so granted or of any condition imposed by a competent authority under the Copyright Act :

   (i) does anything, the exclusive right to do which is by this Act conferred upon the owner of the copy right or

   (ii) permits for profit any place to be used for the performance of the work in public where such performance constitutes an infringement of the copyright in the work unless he was not aware and has no reasonable ground for believing that such performance would be in infringement of copyright, or

(b) When any person :

   (i) makes for sale or hire, or sells or lets for hire, or by way of trade displays or offers for sale or hire, or

   (ii) distributes either for the purpose of trade or to such an extent as to affect prejudicially the owner of the copyright, or

   (iii) by way of trade exhibits in public, or

(iv) imports (except for the private and domestic use of the importer) into India.

any infringing copies of the work.

Explanation : For the purposes of this section, the reproduction of a literary, dramatic, musical or artistic work in the form of a cinematograph film shall be deemed to be an "infringing copy".

Broadcast reproduction right

(1) Where any programme is broadcast by radio diffusion by the Government or any other broadcasting authority, a special right to be known as "broadcast reproduction right" shall subsist in such programme.

(2) The Government or other broadcasting authority. as the case may be. shall be the owner of the broadcast reproduction right and such right shall subsist until twenty-five years from the beginning of the calendar year next follow ing the year in which the programme is first broadcast.

(3) During the continuance of a broadcast reproduction right in relation to any programme, any person who,

(a) without the licence of the owner of the right:

(i) rebroadcasts the programme in question or any substantial part thereof; or

(ii) cause the programme in question or any substantial part thereof to

be heard in public; or

(b) without the licence of the owner of the right to utilise the broadcast for the purpose of making a record recording the programme in question or any substantial part thereof, makes any such record, shall be deemed to infringe that broadcast reproduction right.

16

The Censorship

All citizens of India have a fundamental right as indicated by the fundamental law of the land, *i.e.*. Article 19 (1) of the Constitution of India, called as *"Right to Freedom of Speech and Expression"*. It is to be noted that Freedom of the Press is not expressly mentioned in Part III of the Constitution of India, which declares a right to freedom of speech and expression, one of the rights to be fundamental. Article 19(1) (a) of the Constitution of India concerns *Freedom of Speech and Expression,* but does not specially mention *Freedom of the Press.* But Freedom of Speech and Expression covers and includes *Freedom of the Press.* The said Article is so wide in scope that Freedom of the Press is included in Freedom of Speech and Expression.

The Scope : The judicial decisions on the ambit of freedom of the press help us to know the scope of freedom of the press. In Express Newspapers Private Limited Vs. Union of India, it was held that the right of freedom of press includes the right of free propagation and free circulation without any previous restraint on publication. Similarly in Romesh Thappar Vs. State of Madras: Freedom of circulation is essential to the effective exercise of the freedom of press. Indeed without circulation a publication would be of little value. Jamison Vs. State of Texas : Freedom of press is not confined to newspapers and periodicals but includes pamphlets, leaflets, handbills and every sort of public matter affording a vehicle of information and opinion.

Not Absolute Freedom : The freedom of speech and expression is not absolute and unlimited, at all times and under all circumstances. It was held that the right does not include the abuse of the power of tongue or pen, any more than freedom of other action includes an injurious use of one's occupation, business or property.

It does not give immunity to every possible use of language. Unrestricted Freedom of Speech and Expression which is wholly free from restraint would amount to uncontrolled licence which would tend to lead to disorder and anarchy and it would be hazardous to ignore the vital importance of our social interest in public order and security of the state.

The Restrictions : The Constitution of India permits to impose reasonable restrictions on the right to freedom of speech and expression. Article 19 (1) (a) gives the right to freedom of speech and expression. Following it Article 19 (2) of the Constitution has been added to impose reasonable restrictions on the exercise of the right to freedom of speech and expression given in Article 19(1) (a). Article 19 (2) reads that: Nothing in sub-clause (a) of clause (1) shall affect the operation of any existing law, or prevent the state from making any law, in so far as such law imposes reasonable restrictions on the exercise of the right conferred by the said sub-clause in the interests of the sovereignty and integrity of India, the security of the state, friendly relations with foreign states, public order, decency or morality, or in relation to contempt of court, defamation or incitement to an offence.

The Proclamation : The President of India is empowered under Article 352 (1) of the Constitution of India towards proclamation of emergency in the country. In exercise of the powers conferred by clause (1) of Article 352 of the Constitution, the President of India by proclamation may declare an emergency. If the President is satisfied that a grave emergency exists whereby the security of India or of any part of the territory thereof is threatened, whether by war or external aggression or internal disturbance, he may by proclamation make a declaration for emergency.

Suspension of Article 19 during Emergency : There is a provision in the Constitution under Article 358 for suspension of provisions of Article 19 during emergencies. While a proclamation of Emergency is in operation, nothing in Article 19 shall restrict the power of the State as defined in Part III to make any law or to make any executive action which the State would but for the provisions contained in that part be competent to make or to take, by any law so made shall, to the extent of the incompetency, cease to have effect as soon as the proclamation ceases to operate, except as respects things done or omitted to be done before the law so ceases to have effect.

Suspension of Enforcement : Similarly another stipulation is towards suspension of the enforcement of the rights conferred by the Constitution during emergencies. Where a proclamation of Emergency is in operation, the President may by order declare that the right to move any court for the enforcement of such of the rights conferred by Part III as may be mentioned in the order and all proceedings pending in any court for the enforcement of the rights so mentioned shall remain suspended for the period during which the proclamation is in force or for such shorter period as may be specified in the order [Article 359(1)].

Power to Impose Censorship : The Central Government is empowered by the Defence and Internal Security of India Act, 1971 [Act 2 of 1971], by notification in the Official Gazette to make rules as appear to it necessary or expedient for securing the defence of India and civil defence, the internal security, public safety, the maintenance of public order and the efficient conduct of military opeartions or for maintaining supplies and services essential to the life of the community. Accordingly the Defence and Internal Security of India Rules, 1971 have been formulated. Therefore, Rule 48 gives power to impose censorship. The relevant provisions are as follows :

(1) The Central Government or the State Government may for the purpose of securing the defence of India and Civil defence, the public safety, the maintenance of public order or the efficient conduct of military operations, by order addressed to a printer, publisher, or editor, or to printers, publishers and editors generally:

(a) require that all matters, or any matter relating to a particular subject or class of subjects, shall, before being published in any document or class of documents, be submitted for scrutiny to an authority specified in the order;

(a1) direct that any matter required to be submitted for scrutiny to the authority aforesaid shall not be published in any document or class of documents except with the permission, in writing, of such authority and, where such authority deems it necessary to impose any conditions or restrictions in granting such permission, except in accordance with such conditions and restrictions (including conditions as to making of any modifications, whether by way of additions, omissions or otherwise in the matter) as such authority may impose;

(b) prohibit or regulate the making or publishing of any document or class of documents, or of any matter relating to a particular subject or class of subjects or the use of any press;

(1A) where an order under sub-rule (1) has been made, no person shall circulate or cause to be circulated copies of any document published or made in contravention of the order or any extract or translation therof;

(1B) where the Government making an order under sub-rule (1) considers it necessary to specify in such order more than one authority for the purposes of that order, it may specify in such order that one of such authorities shall be the principal authority and that other authorities shall in the discharge of their functions in pursuance of the order, follow such principles of guidelines as the principal authority or any such officer of that Government as may be authorised in this behalf by the principal authority may, from time to time, require to be followed in this behalf.

(2) If any person contravenes any order made under sub-rule (1), then,without prejudice to any other proceedings which may be taken against such person, the Government making the order may declare to be forfeited to Government every copy of any document published or made in contravention of such order and any press used in the making of such document.

(3) If any person contravenes any provision of sub-rule (1A) or any order made under this rule, he shall be punishable with imprisonment for a term which may extend to five years, or with fine or with both.

Censor : The word censor on press means an official examination of material before publication. As a result of censor power a part of material or any contents of the material may be removed which though good in the public interest, or which may offend people or expedient for securing the defence of India and civil defence, the internal security, public safety, the maintenance of public order etc. The chief censor or other authorised officer may examine the materials and remove any information in part or whole which the authorities do not wish to be made known to the public and may classify such material as "not for publication". In view of the provisions of the censorship order materials for publication should be submitted to the censor authority.

Press Censorship : In exercise of powers conferred by clause (1) of Article 352 of the Constitution of India, the President of India, on June 26, 1975, by proclamation declared that a grave emergency exists whereby the security of India is threatened by internal disturbances. On the same day a Censorship order was issued under Rule 48 (1) of the Defence of India Rules 1971. Section 3 of the Defence of India Act 1971 empowered the Government to frame Rule 48. The censorship order was issued by the Central Government on June 26, 1975, in exercise of powers conferred upon it.

The censorship order was thrice amended. First time by the Central Government by order No. SO. 316 (E) dated July 6, 1975, and the second time by the Central Government by order No. SO. 431 (E) dated August 12, 1975, and the third time by the Central Government by order No. SO. 73 (E) dated February 2, 1976. The censorship order is as follows :

Censorship Order : The censorship order was passed by the Central Government under Rule 48 (1) of the Defence of India Rules, 1971. The following is the text of the Central Censorship Order, Ministry of Home Affairs :

> Whereas the Central Government is of opinion that for the purpose of securing the defence of India and civil defence, the public safety and maintenance of public order, it is necessary so to do;

Now, therefore, in exercise of the powers conferred by Sub-rule (1) of Rule 48 of the Defence of India Rules, 1971, the Central Government hereby makes the following order, namely:

(1) That no news, comments, rumours or other report, relating to:

(a) any contravention or alleged or purported contravention of any of the provisions of Part III, rules 31 and 33 of Part IV, Rules 37, 38, 39, 43, 46, 47, 48, 50, 51, and 52 of Part V, Part VIII and Part IX of the said Rules including orders made thereunder,or

(b) any action taken in relation to such contravention, or

(c) any action taken under the provisions of the Maintenance of Internal Security Act, 1971 (26 of 1971), or

(d) the proclamation of Emergency made by the President on the 25th day of June, 1975 under Article 352 of the Constitution, or

(e) the order made by the President on the 27th day of June, 1975 under Article 359 of the Constitution, or

(f) any action taken under the provisions of the Defence of India Act, 1971, (42 of 1971) or under the provisions of that Act as amended by the Defence of India (Amendment) Act, 1975 (32 of 1975) or under the rules or orders made thereunder, or

(g) any 'prejudicial report' as defined in clause 7 of Rule 36 of the Defence and Internal Security of India Rules, 1971,

(h) the proclamation, in relation to the State of Tamil Nadu, issued on the 31st day of January, 1976, under Article 356 of the Constitution, by the President,

(i) the proclamation, in relation to the State of Gujarat, issued on the 12th day of March, 1976, under Article 356 of the Constitution, by the President, shall be published in any newspaper, periodical or other document unless such news, comments, rumour or other report has been submitted for scrutiny to an authorised officer and the publication thereof is authorised in writing by such officer

(2) That no such publication shall be made except in accordance with such conditions or restrictions as such officer may impose.

Explanation: In this order authorised officer means the Chief Censor to the Government of India Additional Chief Censor to the Government of India. Director, Public Relations, or Deputy Principal Information Officer in the Press Information Bureau of the Government of India at New Delhi or a Director of Information or a Director of Public Relations of a State Government or Union Territory Administration or such other officers as may be authorised in this behalf by the Central Government or the State Government or the Administration of a Union Territory.

(3) That the Chief Censor to the Government of India referred to in the Explanation above, shall be the principal authority and all the other authorities referred to in that explanation shall, in the discharge of their functions in pursuance of this order, follow such principles or guidelines as the said Chief Censor or any officer of the Central Government authorised in this behalf by the said Chief Censor may, from time to time, require to be followed in this behalf.

This order is hereby addressed to all printers, publishers and editors.

Chief Censor : Under Central Censorship order certain matters were required to be submitted for scrutiny to the authorised Government Officer prior to their publications. The authorised officer means the Chief Censor to the Government of India, Additional Chief Censor to the Government of India, Director, Public Relations or Deputy Principal Information Officer in the Press Information Bureau of the Government of India, or Director of Information or a Director of Public Relations of a State Government or Union Territory administration or such other officer. The Chief Censor is the principal authority and all other authorities have to discharge their functions and follow such principles or guidelines of the Chief Censor.

The Censorship order stated that no such publication shall be made except in accordance with such conditions and restrictions as the officer may impose.

There were 3 wars which India faced since independence, first in 1962, the Chinese invasion, second in 1965, the Pakistan war and third in 1971, again a Pakistan war. There were proclamations of emergency issued on 26th October, 1962, and on 3rd December, 1971. Though there was external aggression there was no pre-censorship of the press on any of the three war situations. Therefore, 26th June, 1975, has been considered as an important milestone in Indian history because for the first time a censorship order was passed by the Central Government under Rule 48 (1) of the Defence of India Rules, 1971.

The printer, publisher or an editor must submit all matters or any matter relating to a particular subject for scrutiny to the specified authority. Rule 48 (1) and other clauses enable the Government to scrutinise materials. The government has wide and blanket powers.

Censorship Guidelines : On 5th August, 1975, guidelines were issued for the press by the Chief Censor. The following are the guidelines:

(1) The purpose of censorship is to guide and advise the press to guard against publication of unauthorised, irresponsible or demoralising news items, reports, conjectures or rumours. To this end, these guidelines are intended to enlist the voluntary cooperation of all sections of the press in maintaining an atmosphere conducive to the maintenance of public order, stability and economic growth in the country.

(2) Censorship covers any news report, comment, statement, visual representation, film photograph, picture and cartoon.

(3) Censorship applies to the publication of news, comments or reports relating to the proceedings in Parliament, any Legislative Assembly or a Court of Law.

 (b) Courts of Law:

  (i) The name of the judges and the counsels may be mentioned.

  (ii) The operative part of the order of the Court may be published but in appropriate language.

  (iii) Nothing should be published which infringes Censorship.

(4) The following should be kept in view in publishing news, comments or reports:

 (e) Nothing which is sought to be published should relate to agitations and violent incidents.

(f) Quotations, if torn out of context and intended to mislead or convey a distorted or wrong impression, should not be published.

(g) There should be no indication in the published material that it has been censored.

(h) No reference should be made to the places of detention and the names of the political personalities detained.

(i) Nothing should be published which is likely to:

   (a) affect India's relations with foreign countries;

   (b) denigrate the institutions of the Prime Minister, President, Government and Judges of Supreme Court and High Court;

   (c) threaten internal security and economic stability;

   (d) cause disaffection among the members of the armed forces or public servants;

   (e) undermine the public confidence in the national credit or in any Government loan;

(5) Quotations from AIR broadcasts, news agency reports and statements officially released by Government are permissible provided that such quotations give a true account of what has been stated and nothing is taken out of relevant context or distorted in any manner.

(6) In case of any doubt about the advisability or otherwise or publishing any news, report or comment, the Chief Censor should be consulted.

The Guidelines : The third proclamation of emergency took place in the year 1975. On 26th June, 1975, guidelines for the press in the present emergency, 1975,were issued. The guidelines for the press are given below:

> Declaration of national emergency to meet the threat to the security and stability of India by internal disturbances will point to the need for extreme caution and circumspection in the handling and surveying of

news and comments. The press requires to be advised to guard against publication of unauthorised, irresponsible or demoralising news items, conjectures and rumours and yet the press should be enabled to fulfil its obligation to the public. One of the most powerful aids to the Government and the people in an emergency is the press. In the manner in which information is printed, published and disseminated, there can be an accretion of enormous strength to those who are posing a threat to internal security.

In an emergency declared to meet an internal threat, the concern of the Government is mainly with the misguided and subversive elements within the country which by their acts may try to prejudice the peace and stability of the nation. In a democratic country in which citizens are fully conscious of their duties and responsibilities to the nation, the aim of the Government is not so much to rely in every case on the wide and extraordinary powers conferred on it, but as far as may be to enlist the voluntary cooperation of all sections of the population in maintaining an atmosphere conducive to the fulfilment of the primary task of ridding the nation of the causes of emergency.

General Guidance

(1) Where news is plainly dangerous, newspapers will assist the chief press adviser by suppressing it themselves. Where doubts exist, a reference may and should be made to the nearest press adviser.

(2) Where matter has been submitted for examination before publication, the advice of the press adviser should be followed.

(3) When guidance is being given advising against the publication of news or comments relating to a particular matter, no mention of or reference to that matter should be made without obtaining fresh clearance. Moderation should always be observed and all sensationalism

avoided. This should be observed particularly in illustration of posters and headlines.

(4) No publicity to be given to rumours.

(5) When any document or photograph is officially issued, care must be taken to retain the sense of the accompanying caption or description.

(6) No reproduction of objectionable matter already published in any Indian or foreign newspaper.

(7) No unauthorised news or advertisement or illustration to be published in regard to vital means of communication.

(8) Nothing to be published about arrangements relating to the protection of transport or communications, supply and distribution of essential commodities etc.

(9) Nothing to be published which is likely to cause disaffection among the members of the armed forces or public servants.

(10) Nothing to be published which is likely to bring into hatred or contempt or to excite disaffection towards the Government established by law in India.

(11) Nothing to be published which is likely to promote a feeling of enmity and hatred between different classes of persons in India.

(12) Nothing to be published which is likely to cause or produce or to instigate or incite, directly or indirectly, the cessation or slowing down of work in any place.

(13) Nothing to be published which is likely to undermine the public confidence in the national credit or in any Government loan.

(14) Nothing to be published to encourage or incite any person or class of persons to refuse or defer payment of taxes.

(15) Nothing to be published which is likely to instigate the use of criminal force against public servants.

(16) A prejudicial report means any report, statement or visible report, whether true or false, which, or the publication of which is or is an incitement to the commission of any of the prejudicial acts mentioned above.

General Guidelines

The press is advised to keep the following main points in view while filing messages, news, stories and comments etc.

(1) Any attempt to subvert the functioning of democratic institutions;

(2) Any attempt to compel members to resign;

(3) Anything relating to agitations and violent incidents;

(4) Any attempt to incite the armed forces and police;

(5) Any attempt promoting disintegration and communal passions endangering the unity of the country;

(6) Report containing false allegations against leaders;

(7) Any attempt at denigrating the institution of the Prime Minister;

(8) Any attempt endangering law and order to disturb normal functioning;

(9) Any attempt to threaten internal stability, production and prospects of economic improvement.

Working Journalists and other Newspaper Employees

(Conditions of Service) and Miscellaneous Provisions

ACT, 1955 (ACT 45 OF 1955)

The Act has been passed to regulate certain conditions of service of Working Journalists and other persons employed in the newspaper establishments.

Definitions (Section 2)

(a) *Board :* 'Board' means (i) in relation to working journalists, the Wage Board constituted under Section 9; and (ii) in relation to non-journalist newspaper employees, the Wage Board under Section 13C.

(b) *Newspaper* : 'Newspaper' means any printed periodical work containing public news or comments on public news and includes such other class of printed periodical work as may, from time to time, be notified in this behalf by the Central Government in the official gazette.

(c) *Newspaper Establishment* : 'Newspaper establishment' means an establishment under the control of any person or body of persons, whether incorporated or not, for the production or publication of one or more newspapers or for conducting any news agency or syndicate.

(d) *Non-Journalist Newspaper Employee* : "Non-Journalist Newspaper Employee" means a person employed to do work in, or in relation to, any newspaper establishment, but does not include any such person who—(i) is a working jouranlist, or (ii) is employed mainly in a managerial or administrative capacity, or (iii) being employed in supervisory capacity, performs, either by the nature of the duties attached to his office or by reason of the power vested in him, functions mainly of a managerial nature.

(e) *Prescribed* : "Prescribed" means prescribed by rules made under this Act.

(f) *Tribunal* : "Tribunal" means (i) in relation to working journalists, the tribunal constituted under Section 13AA; and (ii) in relation to non- journalist newspaper employees, the tribunal constituted under Section 13 DD.

(g) *Working Journalist* : "Working Journalist" means a person whose principal avocation is that of a journalist and who is employed as such, either whole-time or part-time, in, or in relation to, one or more newspaper establishments, and includes an editor, a leader-writer, news editor, sub editor, feature writer, copy-tester, reporter, correspondent, cartoonist, news photographer, and proof-reader, but does not include any such person who —(i) is employed mainly in a managerial or administrative capacity, or (ii) being employed in supervisory capacity, performs, either by the nature of the duties attached to his officer or by reason of the powers vested in him functions mainly of a managerial nature.

Application of Industrial Disputes Act, 1947 : Section 3 of the Act provides that the provisions of the Industrial Disputes Act, 1947 (Act 14 of 1947) shall apply to Working Journalists, Section 25F of the aforesaid Act, in its application to working journalists shall be construed as if in Clause (a) thereof, for the period of notice referred to therein in relation to the retrenchment of a workman, the following periods of notice in relation to retrenchment of a working journalist had been substituted, namely:

(a) Six months, in case of an editor; and

(b) Three months, in the case of any other working journalist.

Compensation on Retrenchment : Section 4 of the Working Journalist Act, 1955, provides special provisions in respect of certain cases of retrenchment. Under it working journalists are entitled to wages and compensation. Where at any time between the 14th day of July, 1954, and the 12th day of March, 1955, any working journalist had been retrenched, he shall be entitled to receive from the employer :

(a) Wages for one month at the rate to which he was entitled immediately before his retr nchment, unless he had been given one month's notice in writing before such retrenchment; and

(b) Compensation which shall be equivalent to fifteen days' average pay for every completed year of service under that employer or any part thereof in excess of six months.

Gratuity : Section 5 provides payment of gratuity to any working journalist who has put in the prescribed period of continuous service. A working journalist is eligible for gratuity on his retirement or in the case of his death. In case of death his nominee or nominees or if there is no nomination at the time of the death his family members are eligible. The payment of gratuity is without prejudice to any benefits or rights accruing under the Industrial Disputes Act, 1947, and should be paid on retirement, termination, resignation or death. The employer of the establishment should pay an amount equivalent to 15 days' average pay for every completed year of service or any part in excess of six months.

The following are the conditions governing the payment of gratuity : where,

(a) Any working journalist who has been in continuous service for not less than three years in any newspaper establishment, and—

  (i) his services are terminated by the employer for any reason otherwise than as punishment inflicted by way of disciplinary action; or

  (ii) he retires from service on reaching the age of superannuation; or

(b) Any working journalist who has been in continuous service for not less than 10 years, and he voluntarily resigns on or after 1st July, 1961, on any ground other than the ground of conscience; or

(c) Any working journalist who has been in continuous service for not less than three years, and he voluntarily resigns on or after 1st July, 1961, on the ground of conscience; or

(d) Any working journalist who dies while he is in service.

In case of Clause (b) the total amount of gratuity payable shall not exceed 12½ months' average pay.

Where a working journalist is employed in any newspaper establishment wherein not more than six working journalists were employed on any day of the 12 months immediately preceding the commencement of this Act, the gratuity payable to a journalist for any period of service before the commencement of the Act, shall not be equivalent to 15 days' average pay for every completed year of service or any part in excess of six months. But it shall be equivalent to :

(a) Three days' average pay for every completed year of service or any part there of in excess of six months, if the period of such past service does not exceed five years,

(b) Five days' average pay for every completed year of service or any part there of in excess of six months, if period of such past service exceeds five years but does not exceed ten years; and

(c) Seven days' average pay for every completed year of service or any part thereof in excess of six months, if the period of such past sen ice exceeds ten years.

For the purpose of this sub-section and sub-section

(1) of Section 17 "family" means :

(i) In the case of a male working journalist, his widow, children, whether married or unmarried, and his dependent parents and the widow and the children of his deceased son:

Provided that a widow shall not be deemed to be a member of the family of the working journalist if at the time of his death she was not legally entitled to be maintained by him:

(ii) In case of a female working journalist, her husband, children, whether married or unmarried, and the dependent parents of the working journalist or of her husband, and the widow and children of her deceased son; (1) Provided that if the working journalist has expressed her desire to exclude her husband from the family, the husband and his dependent parents shall not be deemed to be a part of the working journalist's family, and in either of the above two cases, if the child of working journalist or of a deceased son of a working journalist has been adopted by another person and if under the personal law of the adopter, adoption is legally recognised, such a child shall not be considered as a member of the family of the working journalist.

(2) Any dispute whether a working journalist has voluntarily resigned from service in any newspaper establishment on the ground of conscience shall be deemed to be an industrial dispute within the meaning of the Industrial Dispute Act, 1947, or any corresponding law relating to investigation and settlement of industrial disputes in force in any state.

(3) Where a nominee is a minor and the gratuity under sub-section (1) has become payable during his minority, it shall be paid to a person appointed under sub-section (1) of Section 5A;

Provided that where there is no such person, payment shall be made to any guardian of the property of the minor appointed, to either parent of the minor, or where neither parent is alive, to any other guardian of the minor:

Provided further that where gratuity is payable to two or more nominees, and either or any of them dies, the gratuity shall be paid to the surviving nominee or nominees.

Nomination : Under Section 5 A the nominee of the working journalist is entitled to the gratuity. Where nomination is made in the prescribed manner in any disposition, testamentary or otherwise, the nominee has the right to receive the payment of the gratuity due to the working journalist. The nominee shall, on the death of the working journalist, become entitled to the gratuity. The amount of gratuity to be paid to the exclusion of all other persons, unless the nomination is varied or cancelled in the prescribed manner. The nomination may become void if the nominee predeceases or where there are two or more nominees all the nominee predecease the working journalist making the nomination. In case the nominee is a minor, it shall be lawful for the working journalist to appoint any person to receive the gratuity in the event of his death during the minority of the nominee.

Hours of Work : Section 6 provides for the hours of work. Under this section no working journalist shall be required or allowed to work in any newspaper establishment for more than one hundred and forty-four hours during any period of four consecutive weeks. This is exclusive of the time for meals. However, this provision of Section 6 (1) is subject to any rules that may be made by the Government under this Act. Every working journalist shall be allowed during seven consecutive days' rest for a period of not less than 44 consecutive hours. The period between 10 P.M. and 6 P.M. being included therein.

Explanation : For the purpose of this section 'week' means a period of seven days beginning at midnight on Saturday.

Leave : Every working journalist shall be entitled to leave of the following categories :

(a) Earned Leave on full wages for not less than one-eleventh of the period spent on duty;

(b) Leave on medical certificates on one-half of the wages for not less than one eighteenth of the period of service.

In addition to them every working journalist is entitled to a casual leave or other kinds of leave as may be prescribed (Section 7).

Fixation or Revision of Wages : Section 8 of the Act provides for fixation or revision of rates of wages. The Central Government may :

(a) Fix rates of wages in respect of working journalist;

(b) Revise from time to time such intervals the rates of wages fixed under this section or specified in the order made under Section 6 of the Working Journalists (Fixation of Rates of Wages) Act, 1958.

The Central Government may fix rates of wages or revise in respect of working journalist for time work and piece work.

Wage Board (Section 9) : "Board" means in relation to working journalists the wage board constituted under this section. In case of non-journalist newspaper employees, the Wage Board is constituted under Section 13C of the Act. Section 9 of the Act prescribes the procedure for the fixing and revising rates of wages. The Central Government for the purpose of fixing or revising rates of wages for the working journalist may constitute a Wage Board as and when necessary.

Composition of Wage Board : The Wage Board consists of:

(a) Two persons representing employers in relation to newspaper establishment;

(b) Two persons representing working journalists; and

(c) Three independent persons one of whom shall be a person who is, or has been, a judge of a High Court or the Supreme Court and who shall be appointed by the Central Government as the Chairman.

Procedure and Recommendations (Sections 10 & 11)

Own Procedure : The Board has the power to regulate its own procedure.

Representation : The Board shall call upon newspaper establishments and working journalists and other persons interested in the fixation or revision of grades of wages to make representation The Board for this purpose may invite representation by notice published in such a manner as it thinks fit.

Time : Every representation shall be made within such period as the Board may specify in the notice.

In writing : Every representation shall be in writing only.

Subject of Representation : The representation shall state the rates of wages which in his opinion would be reasonable. He must consider the capacity of the employer to pay the same or to any other circumstance, whichever may seem relevant to the person making the representation.

Recommendations of the Board: The Board shall take into account the representations. After examining the materials placed before it make such recommendation to the Central Government for the fixation or revision of rates of wages. The recommendation may also specify whether prospectively or retrospectively, the date from which the rates should take effect.

In making any recommendations the Board shall have regard to the cost of living, the prevalent rates of wages for comparable employment, the circumstances relating to the newspaper industry in different regions of the country and to any other circumstances which the Board may seem relevant.

Inspection of Representation : Any representation made to the Board and any document furnished to it by way of evidence shall be open to inspection on payment of prescribed fee. Any person who is interested in the matter can inspect.

Vacancy : Any vacancy occurs in the office of the Chairman or any other member of the Board, the Central Government may fill the vacancy by appointing another person.

Powers of the Board

1. The Board has power to regulate its own procedure; and
2. The Board may exercise all or any of the powers which an Industrial Tribunal exercises powers under the Industrial Dispute Act, 1947, for adjudication of an industrial dispute.

Recommendations

Section 12 of the Act empowers the Central Government to enforce the recommendations of the Wage Board. After the receipt of the recommendations of the Wage Board, the Central Government shall make an order in terms of the recommendations or subject to such modifications, if any, being modifications which do not effect important alterations in the character of the recommendations.

The Central Government may if it thinks fit

(a) Make such modifications in the recommendations; and

(b) Refer the recommendations or any part thereof to the Board.

(c) The Central Government shall consider its further recommendations and make an order either in terms of the recommendations or with such modifications.

The Central Government before making any such modifications shall cause notice to be given to all persons likely to be affected. It shall take into account any representations which they may make in writing. Every order made by the Central Government shall be published in Official Gazette together with the recommendations of the Board. The order shall come into operation on the date of publication or on such date, whether prospectively or retrospectively as may be specified in the order.

Interim Rates : Section 13 A of the Act empowers the Central Government to fix interim rates of wages. The Central Government is of the opinion that it is necessary, it may after consultation with the Board, fix interim rates of wages in respect of working journalists. The interim rates of wages so fixed shall be binding on all employers of newspaper establishments. Every working journalist shall be entitled to wages at a rate which shall not be less than interim rates of wages. Any interim rates of wages fixed shall remain in force until the order of the Central Government under Section 12 comes into operation.

The Section provides for the constitution of Tribunal for fixing or revising rates of wages in respect of working journalists. The tribunal is constituted if the Central Government is of opinion that the Wage Board constituted for the purpose of fixing or revising rates of wages has not been able to function effectively. The Government by notification in the Official Gazette constitute a Tribunal. The Tribunal consists of a person who is or has been a judge of a High Court or the Supreme Court. The function of the Tribunal is to fix or revise rates of wages in respect of working journalists.

The provisions of Sections 10 to 13 A shall apply to the Tribunal, the Central Government and working journalist subject to the following modifications:

(a) The references to the Board therein, wherever they occur, shall be construed as references to the Tribunal;

(b) In Sub-section (3) of Section 11, (i) the reference to the office of Chairman or any other member of the Board shall be construed as a reference to the office of the person constituting the Tribunal; and (ii) the reference to Section 9 shall be construed as a reference to sub-section (1) of this Section; and

(c) The reference in Section 13 and Section 13 A to Section 12 shall be construed as references to Section 12 read with this section.

The Tribunal in discharging its function may act on the evidence recorded by the Wage Board or partly recorded by the Wage Board and partly recorded by itself.

If the Tribunal feels necessary in the interest of the justice it can take up further examination of any of the witnesses whose evidence has already been recorded. For this purpose it may re-summon any such witness for further examination and re-examination.

On the constitution of the Tribunal the Board shall cease to exist and the members of the Board shall be deemed to have vacated their offices.

Non-journalist Newspaper Employees : A separate chapter has been provided in the Working Journalists and other Newspaper Employees (Conditions of Service) and Miscellaneous Provisions Act, 1955, in respect of Non-Journalist Employees. The chapter covers matters relating to fixation or revision of rates of wages, Wage Board, application of certain provisions and constitution of Tribunals, etc. The provisions governing Non-journalist Newspaper Employees are discussed under the following paragraphs :

Section 13 B deals with fixation or revision of rates of wages of non-journalist newspaper employees.

(a) Fix rates of wages in respect of Non-journalist Newspaper Employees; and

(b) Revise from time to time the rates of wages fixed.

The rates of wages may be fixed or revised by the Central Government for time work and for piece work.

Section 13C provides for Wage Board for fixing or revising rates of wages in respect of non-journalist newspaper employees. The Central Government for the purpose of fixing or revising rates of wages may constitute a Wage Board. The Board consists of:

(a) Two persons representing employers in relation to newspaper establishments;

(b) Two persons representing Non-journalist Newspaper Employees; and

(c) Three independent persons, one of whom shall be a person who is, or has been, a Judge of a High Court or the Supreme Court and who shall be appointed by that Government as the Chairman thereof.

Section 13 D specifically provides for the application of certian provisions of this Act to the Non-journalist Newspaper Employees as they are applicable to the working journalists.

The provisions of Sections 10 to 13 A, as discussed above, shall apply to, and in relation to, the Board constituted under Section 13C, the Central Government and Non-journalist Employees, subject to the modifications that:

(a) The references to the Board and working journalists therein, wherever they occur, shall be construed, respectively, as references to the Board constituted under Section 13C and to Non-journalist Newspaper Employees;

(b) The references in Sub-section (3) of Section 11 to Section 9 shall be construed as a reference to Section 13C; and

(c) The references in Section 13 and Section 13A to Section 12 shall be construed as references to Section 12 read with this section.

Section 13DD deals with the constitution of Tribunal for fixing or revising rates of wages in respect of Non-journalist Newspaper Employees. Where the Central Government is of opinion that the

Board constituted for the purpose of fixing or revising rates of wages has not been able to function effectively it may constitute a tribunal. The Tribunal consists of a person who is or has been a Judge of a High Court or the Supreme Court.

The provisions of Sections 10 to 13 A as discussed above are applicable to the Tribunal. This is subject to the modifications that:

(a) The references to the Board and working journalists therein wherever they occur, shall be construed, respectively, as references to the Tribunal and to Non-journalist Newspaper Employees;

(b) In Sub-section (3) of Section 11, — (i) the reference to the office of Chairman or any other member of the Board shall be construed as a reference to the office of the person constituting the tribunal; and (ii) the reference to Section 9 shall be construed as a reference to sub-section (1) of this Section; and

(c) The reference in Section 13 and Section 13 A to Section 12 shall be construed as references to Section 12 read with this section.

The Tribunal in discharging its functions may act on the evidence recorded by the Wage Board or partly recorded by the Wage Board and partly recorded by itself.

The Tribunal is empowered to further examination of any of the witnesses whose evidence has already been recorded. The tribunal may do so in the interest of justice. It may re-summon any such witness for further examination, cross-examination and re-examination.

On the constitution of a Tribunal the Wage Board constituted under Section 13C shall cease to exist and the members constituting the Wage Borad shall be deemed to have vacated their offices.

Certain Acts

The provisions of the Industrial Employment (Standing Orders) Act, 1946 (Act 20 of 1946) shall apply to every newspaper establishment. It is applicable where 20 or more newspaper employees are employed or were employed on any day of the preceding twelve months. (Section 14). The Employees' Provident Funds Act, 1952 (Act 19 of 1952) shall apply to every newspaper establishment in which 20 or more persons are employed on any day.

Law and Agreement

Section 16 of the Act provided for the effect of laws and agreements inconsistent with the Working Journalist and other Newspaper Employees etc., Act, 1955. The provisions of the Act, 1955, shall have effect than anything inconsistent contained in any other law or in the terms of any award, agreements or contract of service.

Where under any such award, agreement, contract of service, a newspaper employee is entitled to benefits in respect of any matter which are more favourable to him than those to which he would be entitled under this Act. The newspaper employee shall continue to be entitled to the more favourable benefits. Any newspaper employee is entitled to enter into an agreement with an employer to obtain rights or privileges which are more favourable to him.

Recovery of Money : Section 17 provides for the recovery of money due from newspaper employer. If an amount is due to newspaper employee from an employer he can make an application to the State Government for the recovery of the amount due to him. The employee himself or any person authorised by him in writing or in the case of the death of the employee, any member of his family can make an application. The provision in this section is without prejudice to any other mode of recovery. If the State Government or such authority is satisfied that any amount is due it shall issue a certificate for the amount to the Collector. The Collector shall proceed to recover the amount in the same manner as an arrear of land revenue.

If any question arises as to the amount due the State Government may on its own motion or upon application made to it refer the question to any labourt court constituted under the Industrial Disputes Act, 1947, or under any corresponding law relating to investigation and settlement of industrial disputes.

Registers, Records etc. : There is a provision for the maintenance of registers, records and muster rolls. According to Section 17A, every employer shall prepare and maintain such registers, records and muster rolls in such a manner as may be prescribed.

Inspectors : The State Government by notification in the Official Gazette may appoint such persons as inspectors. The Government also for the purpose of this Act may define the local limits within which they have to exercise their functions.

Powers and Functions of the Inspectors : Inspectors for the purpose of ascertaining whether provisions of this Act or the Working Journalists (Fixation of Rates of Wages) Act, 1955, have been complied may :

(a) Require an employer to furnish such information as he may consider necessary ;

(b) Enter any newspaper establishment or any premises connected with it.

(c) He may require any one found incharge to produce before him for examination of any accounts, books, registers and other documents relating to the employment of persons or the payment of wages;

(d) Examine with respect to any matter relevant to any of the purposes mentioned above ;

(e) He may examine the employer, his agent or servant or any other person found incharge of the newspaper establishment or any premises ;

(f) He is empowered to examine any person whom the Inspector has reasonable cause to believe to be or to have been an employee in the establishment;

(g) Make copies of or take extracts from any book, register, or other document maintained in relation to the newspaper establishment;

(h) Exercise such other powers as may be prescribed (Section 17 B).

Every inspector shall be deemed to be a public servant within the meaning of the Indian Penal Code.

Any person required to produce any document or thing or to give information by an Inspector shall be legally bound to do so.

Penalties : Section 18 provides for penalties for the violation of provisions of this Act. The provisions are :

1. If any employer contravenes any of the provisions of this Act shall be punishable with fine which may extend to two hundred rupees.
2. Whoever having been convicted by an offence, is again convicted of an offence for the contravention of the same provision shall be punishable with fine which may extend to five hundred rupees.
3. Where an offence has been committed by a company every person who was incharge of and was responsible to the company for the conduct of the business for the company and the company both shall be deemed to be guilty of the offence. They shall be liable to be proceeded against and punished accordingly.
4. Where an offence has been committed by a company and is proved that the offence has been committed with the consent or connivance of or that the commission of the offence is attributable to any gross negligence on the part of any director, manager, secretary or other officer of the company, they shall be deemed to be guilty of such offence and shall be liable to be proceeded against and punished accordingly.

Only a Presidency Magistrate or the Magistrate of the First Class is empowered to try an offence punishable under Section 18. Similarly, no Court shall take cognizance of an offence unless the complaint is made within six months of the date on which the offence is alleged to have been committed.

Indemnity for Acts : Under Section 19, no suit, prosecution or other legal proceeding shall lie against the Chairman or other members of the Wage Board or the persons constituting the Tribunal or an Inspector for anything which is in good faith done or intended to be done.

Any defect in the appointments does not invalidate acts. No act or proceedings of the Board shall be questioned on the ground of the existence of any vacancy or defect in the constitution of the Wage Board.

Government's Power : Section 20 of the Act empowers the Central Government to make rules. To carry out the purposes of this Act, the Central Government may make rules by notification in the Official Gazette. In particular and without prejudice to the generality of the foregoing power, such rules may provide for all or any of the following matters, namely :

(a) Payment of gratuity to working journalists;

(b) Hours of work of working journalists;

(c) Holidays, earned leave, leave on medical certificate, casual leave or any other kind of leave admissible to working journalists ;

(d) The procedure to be followed by the Board, or as the case may be, the Tribunal in the discharge of its functions under this Act;

(e) The form of nominations and the manner in which nominations may be made;

(f) The manner in which any person may be appointed for the purposes of sub-section (3) of Section 5 A;

(g) The variation or cancellation of nominations;

(h) The manner of giving notice under Clause (a) of Sub-section (2) of Section 12;

(i) The registers, records, and muster rolls to be prepared and maintained by newspaper establishments, the forms in which they should be prepared and maintained and the particulars to be entered therein,

(j) The powers that may be exercised by an Inspector; and

(k) Any other matter which has to be, or may be, prescribed.

Working Journalists (Fixation of Rates of Wages) Act, 1958 (Act No. 29 of 1958)

This Act has been passed in India to provide for the fixation of rates of wages in respect of Working Journalists and for matters connected therewith.

The Committee : Section 3 of the Act, 1958, provides for Constitution of Committee. Statement of objects and reasons to the Act, 1958, state on the Committee as follows: "A Wage Board for fixing the wages in respect of working journalists was constituted by the Central Government under Section 8 of the Working Journalists (Conditions of Service) and Miscellaneous Provisions Act, 1955 (45 of 1955) and its decision was published in May, 1957. This decision was challenged by certain newspaper establishments in petitions filed before the Supreme Court, and that Court set aside the decision on 19th March, 1958, on the ground that it did not take into account the capacity of the industry to pay.

To consider the situation arising out of the Supreme Court decision and to frame an agreed scheme in respect of the wages of Working Journalists, several meetings were held with the representatives of newspaper employers and working journalists, but it was not found to come to an agreement. Consequently an ordinance entitled the Working Journalists (Fixation of Rates of Wages) Ordinance, 1958 (3 of 1958) was promulgated on the 14th June, 1958. This Ordinance provided for the establishment of a special committee for the purpose of making recommendations to the Central Government in regard to the rates of wages to be fixed for Working Journalists. It is now proposed to replace the ordinance by an Act of Parliament."

In the light of the judgement of the Supreme Court in 1958 relating to the Wage Board decision and in the light of the other circumstance the Central Government may constitute a Committee. The committee is meant for the purpose of enabling the Central Government to fix rates of wages in respect of working Journalists.

Composition : The Committee consists of the following persons, namely :

(i) an officer of the Ministry of Law not below the rank of Joint Secretary, nominated by the Central Government, who shall be the Chairman of the Committee;

(ii) three persons nominated by the Central Government from among the officers of each of the Ministries of Home Affairs, Labour and Employment and Information and Broadcasting; and

(iii) a chartered accountant nominated by the Central Government.

The Central Government may appoint any vacancy occurs in the vacancy of the Chairman or any other member of the Committee. The enquiry may be continued from the stage which had been reached when the vacancy arose.

The Central Government may also appoint a Secretary to the Committee and provide with such other staff as may be necessary. The secretary may perform such functions of a ministerial or other nature as the Committee or the Chairman may assign or delegate to him.

The Functions : Section 4 of the Act provides for the functions of the Committee.

1. The Committee may call upon newspaper establishments, Working Journalists and other persons interested in the Wage Board decision to make representations. The Committee may do so by notice published in such a manner as it thinks fit. The representations made by them as they may think fit as respect the Wage Board decision and the rates of wages in respect of Working Journalists.
2. Every representation should be in writing and should be made within the period not exceeding thirty days as the

5. Where an offence has been committed by a company and it is proved that the offence has been committed with the consent or connivance of, or that the commission of the offence is attributable, to any gross negligence on the part of any director, manager, secretary or other officer of the company, they shall be deemed to be guilty of an offence. They shall be liable to be proceeded against and punished accordingly.

Powers of the Central Government : Section 13 of the Act empowers the Central Government to make rules to carry out the purposes of the Act. The rules may provide for :

(a) the manner in which notices under this Act may be published,

(b) the procedure to be followed by the Committee in the exercise of its powers under this Act;

(c) the powers and functions of the Committee which may be delegated to any of its members; and

(d) the fees to be paid for inspection of documents furnished to the Committee.

Bibliography

Altschull, J.H.: *Agents of Power: the Role of the News Media in Human Affairs*, Longman, New York, 1984.

Asch, S.: *Social Psychology*, Prentice Hall, New York, 1952.

Baker, R.K., and Ball, SJ.: *Mass Media and Violence, Report to the National Commission on the Causes and Prevention of Violence*, 1969.

Bell, D.V.J.: *Power, Influence and Authority*, Oxford University Press, London, 1975.

Berelson, B.: *Content Analysis in Communication Research*, Free Press, Glencoe, Illinois, 1952.

Berelson, B., Lazarsfeld, P. F. and McPhee, W. N.: *Voting*, University of Chicago Press, Chicago, 1954.

Bhattacharya, Bhabani: *Gandhi the Writer*, National Book Trust, New Delhi, 1969.

Blumer, J.G.: 'The Political Effect of Television' in Halloran, J.D., *The Effect of Mass Communication*, Leicester University Press, Leicester, 1970.

Carey, James W.: *Communication as Culture: Essays on Media and Society*, Routledge, New York, 1992.

Chaney, D.: *Processes of Mass Communication*, Macmillan, London, 1972.

Chopra, Pran: *The Sage in Revolt*, Gandhi Peace Foundation, New Delhi, 1972.

Cohen, S. and Young, J. : *The Manufacture of News*, Constable, London, 1973.

Czitrom, Daniel J.: *Media and the American Mind: From Morse to McLuhan,* University of North Corolina Press, Chapel Hill.

Davis, Dennis K. and Baran, Stanley J.: *Mass Communication and Every Day Life—A Perspective on Theory and Effects,* Woodworth, California, 1981.

Davison, W. Phillips : *Mass Communication Research: Major Issues and Future Directions,* Praeger, New York, 1974.

Davison, W.P.: *Mass Communication and Conflict Resolution,* Praeger, New York, 1974.

Deutsch, K.V.: *Nationalism and Social Communication,* MIT Press, Cambridge, 1966.

Dexter, L. A. and White, D.M. : *People, Society and Mass Communication,* Free Press, New York, 1964.

Dube, S.C.: *Communication, Innovation and Planned Change in India,* International Development Institute, East-West Center Press, Honolulu, 1964.

Eisenstein, E.: *The Printing Press as an Agent of Change,* Cambridge University Press, New York, 1978.

Fiske, J.: *Introduction to Communication Studies,* Methuen, London, 1982.

Giner, S.: *Mass Society,* Martin Robertson, London, 1976.

Hall, S., Clarke, J., Critcher, C.Jefferson, T. and Roberts, B.: *Policing the Crisis,* Macmillan, London, 1978.

Iyengar, A.S.: *All Through the Gandhian Era,* Hind Kitabs Ltd., Bombay, 1950.

Kelley, H. H.: *Prime Time—The Life of Edward R. Murrow,* Little Brown, Boston, 1958.

Klapper, J.T: *The Effects of Mass Communication,* Free Press, Glencoe, Illinois, 1960.a

Kreiling, A.L.: *The Making of Racial Identities in the Black Press,* Ph.D. Dissertation, University of Illinois, 1973.

Lakshmana Rao, Y.V.: *Communication and Development: A Study of Two Indian Villages,* University of Minnesota Press, Minneapolis, 1966.

McLuhan, M.: *Understanding Media,* Routledge and Kegan Paul, London, 1964.

McQuail, D.: *Mass Communication Theory,* Sage, London, 1987.

Natarajan J.: *History of Indian Journalism,* Part II of the Report of the Press Commission, New Delhi, 1955.

Price J.L.: *Organizational Effectiveness,* R.D. Irwin, Homewood, Illinois, 1968.

Schramm, W: *Mass Media and National Development,* Stanford University Press, Stanford, 1964.

Snow, R.P.: *Media Power,* Sage Publications, Beverly Hills and London, 1984.

Szalai, A. et al.: *The United Nations and the News Media,* UNITAR, New York, 1972.

Verma, M.M.: *Gandhi's Technique of Mass Mobilization,* R.K. Gupta and Company, New Delhi, 1990.